9/02

F
Klein   Klein, Rachel

          The moth diaries

THE MOTH DIARIES

THE
MOTH
DIARIES

a novel

RACHEL KLEIN

COUNTERPOINT
WASHINGTON, D.C.

Library of Congress Cataloging-in-Publication Data
Klein, Rachel, 1953–
The moth diaries : a novel / Rachel Klein.
p. cm.
ISBN 1-58243-205-8 (alk. paper)
1. Teenage girls—Fiction. 2. Boarding schools—Fiction.
3. Diaries—Authorship—Fiction. I. Title.
PS3611.L45 M68 2002
813'.6—dc21
2001007226

Book design and composition by Mark McGarry, Texas Type & Book Works
Set in Dante

COUNTERPOINT
P.O. Box 65793
Washington, D.C. 20035–5793

Counterpoint is a member of the Perseus Books Group

FIRST PRINTING
10 9 8 7 6 5 4 3 2 1

for Lyle

PREFACE

When Dr. Karl Wolff first suggested publishing the journal that I kept during my junior year in boarding school, I thought I hadn't heard him correctly. He's been interested in me—or maybe I should say my case—since I was under his psychiatric care, and we talk on the phone every year or so. But I hadn't seen the journal since I handed it over to him in the hospital thirty years ago, and we discussed it on only one occasion, when he made it clear I needed to put that period of my life behind me. Giving up writing in the journal was a first step.

My instinctive response to publication was to say no. I didn't write the journal with the intention of having anyone else read it. And Dr. Wolff kept it only because of a promise he made to my mother before I left the hospital. I wrote it to preserve my sixteen-year-old self. Or at least that's what I thought at the time. Besides, I have a daughter who is the same age I was when I kept this journal, and I want to protect her. I don't feel that she needs to know everything about me.

Dr. Wolff reassured me. All the names would be changed. It would be impossible to recognize me in the person of the narrator. It would even be difficult to recognize the school. Above all, he felt the journal would be an invaluable addition to the literature on female adolescence at a time when risk-taking behavior has reached epidemic proportions. He happened to reread it while packing up his office before retirement and was struck by how convincing my writing was.

I'm not sure I agree with him. But I have always been intrigued by the journals that girls keep. They are like dollhouses. Once you look inside them, the rest of the world seems very far away, even unbelievable. If only we had the power to leap outside ourselves at such moments, we would spare ourselves so much pain and fear. I'm not talking about truth or falsehood but about surviving.

I agreed to Dr. Wolff's suggestion with reservations. If, after reading my journal, I felt he was right, I would allow him to arrange for its publication. Dr. Wolff also asked me to write an afterword, as a kind of closure on the experience. He felt it was relatively rare for someone suffering from borderline personality disorder complicated by depression and psychosis to recover and never have another "episode," as he so kindly put it. He was sure my reactions to the journal would be illuminating.

I can't begin to judge that. When I opened this notebook, I found the razor blade I had hidden among the pages so long ago. Dr. Wolff had kept it as part of the "clinical picture," as he explained. It looked utterly incongruous. It was just a razor blade. And the words on the page were just that—words in a familiar handwriting.

To anyone who wonders whether it's possible to survive adolescence, that's as much as I can offer of reassurance.

THE MOTH DIARIES

SEPTEMBER

September 10

My mother dropped me off at two. Practically everyone is back. Except for Lucy. I can't wait for her to come so that we can unpack together. I'm going to write in my journal until she's here.

After my mother left, I felt an emptiness in my stomach that spread up through my throat to the back of my eyes. I didn't cry, even though I probably would have felt better afterward. I needed to hold on to that feeling, that pain. If Lucy had been here, she would have distracted me. I had a moment of panic when I said good-bye to my mother. I almost begged her not to leave me here. It's so strange. I've been looking forward to school for the past month. I was even excited when I got my new uniforms in the mail. The light blue spring skirt was as stiff as cardboard. I had to wash it before I could wear it. I'm glad I'm not a day student, worried about how I look on the train ride home. They sneak into the bathroom at the station and put on makeup and change from their saddle shoes into loafers, in

case they run into boys they know on the train. I've seen them waiting for the train with their skirts hiked above their knees, and it's
hard to tell that they are wearing a uniform. We boarders couldn't
care less if we look like nurses.

Now that I'm here, I want to run away.

I'm always afraid to leave my mother. I'm afraid that I'll never see
her again. I want to run after her like a little girl, grab onto her skirt,
grope for her hand, sniffle. Instead I stand very stiff and don't say a
word. "Can't you at least say good-bye?" she says. After a few days, I
get caught up in school. Then I'm glad to be away from her, even
though she's all I have left. I like to get letters from her, but I hate it
when she calls. I never call her. Her voice is so heavy. It pulls me
down. I'm always scared when I'm called to the phone. It's incredibly
hard for me to put the receiver to my ear. It wants to swallow me.
I'm struggling to lift it, while the person on the other end is hanging
in space, waiting for my voice.

From my window, I watched my mother speed down the drive. I
lost sight of her car behind the Workshop. When she turned left onto
the avenue, I could see it again, a streak of blue flashing through the
black fence. And then she was gone. My mother always drives too
fast; she doesn't care what happens to her. Lucy's mother would
never drive like that.

I stood at the window for a long time. Then I turned around and
looked at my room, my new room, with my trunk and bags and
boxes piled up in the middle of the floor. It isn't as wonderful as I had
thought it would be all summer long. The walls are dirty. The girl
who lived here last year left smudged black fingerprints in odd places.
There's nothing on the floor. Under the window is a chair with
wooden arms, covered in tan and pink flowered material. It's not
very inviting. I think I'll put some pillows on the sill and turn it into a
window seat. I thought it would be the best room in the Residence.
When I've unpacked and Lucy is next door, it will be different.

I got tired of waiting for Lucy, so I took a walk up to the train station. In the stationery store next to the drugstore, I found an old
French composition book with a mottled crimson cover and a thick

black spine, like a real book, but with blank pages. Somehow it ended up in the back of the store, forgotten. I grabbed it and walked up to the register, hugging it to my chest, afraid someone might snatch it away from me. It's exactly like the journals my father used to keep. It was a sign, and I had to buy it. Now I'm going to fill it with words, the way he filled his notebooks: the pages, the margins, the endpapers all covered with little notes that made no sense to anyone else. I won't tell anyone about it, not even Lucy.

I read the Claudine books over the summer. They were a replacement for school, which I missed so much. I hope the words flow from my pen onto the paper the way they did for Colette: the exact words I need. I've got *Claudine at School* on my desk, for inspiration. She knows what it's like to be shut up in a place like this, where all your emotions are focused on the girls around you, where you dream of a boyfriend but only feel comfortable with your arm around another girl's waist.

Already I've put too many sad thoughts down on these pages. I have to start all over again, very slowly and carefully. Everything has to be perfect. I'm not in a hurry. First, I open the notebook on my desk, flatten the smooth pages ruled with green lines, and uncap my fountain pen, the one my mother gave me for my sixteenth birthday. It's also crimson and feels heavy in my hand. I fill an old glass inkwell that I found on a desk in the study hall with black ink from a bottle. The acrid smell lingers in the air. It is the smell of a writer. I start at the beginning and put a number in the top right corner of each page. There are 155 pages, and I'm going to write on both sides. Three hundred and ten pages, that should be enough.

It took me a long time to get used to school, not to feel that everyone was looking at me and feeling sorry for me all the time. They hated feeling sorry for me. I think I'll be able to be happy this year, sharing a suite with Lucy. That was my dream. Next year I have to think about college. I'll have to start all over again.

I can't believe how lucky we were. I chose a low number in the lottery, and we got our first choice. My room is larger, but Lucy's has a fireplace, and we have our *own* bathroom between the two rooms.

It's so private and spacious. We can go into each other's rooms whenever we want, and Mrs. Halton will never know. We just have to make sure that we are quiet and neat and don't make her think we are the type to cause trouble. No one ever thinks Lucy is the type to cause trouble. She's too sweet. Last year, Mrs. Dunlap was all over us, barging in during quiet hour to make sure we were alone. I hated that. This year we've arranged everything much better.

I don't want this year ever to end.

I'm going to stay in my room until Lucy comes. I don't want to see anyone else, only her.

The door.

It wasn't Lucy. The new girl from across the corridor came over. It's strange to have a new girl in the eleventh grade. And she's managed to get a big room by herself with a bathroom *and* a fireplace. Everyone but Sofia is together on one corridor this year. Sofia wanted a single, and she didn't have a good number. She had to settle for a small room in the front, but at least it's just around the corner from us. Only the rooms on the second and third floors have fireplaces. Usually the new girls get the tiny maids' rooms on the fourth floor. That's all that's left after everyone else chooses. They're stuck up there with the eighth and ninth graders and Mac. Charley came up with that nickname for her. Mrs. McCallum looks like an old bulldog. The new girl is probably rich, and Miss Rood is trying to impress her parents.

I often think about what it was like when the Residence was a hotel. Rich guests came here for a "rest cure," whatever that is. They rode ponies on the playing fields and played croquet and took afternoon tea on the porches and danced in the assembly room after dinner.

In a way nothing has changed since then, except that it's full of girls.

The first time I drove through the tall iron gates of the Brangwyn School with my mother and saw the Residence, I felt as if I had woken up in a dream. No, not a dream. Dreams aren't real. I had entered a different time and place, of curved red roofs and gables, stone arches and tall brick chimneys, all topped with ornaments of greenish copper, like weapons on a battlefield, spears and lances and halberds. This wasn't a school; it was a castle. It was winter, and the playing fields and long, sweeping driveway were covered with snow. The snow made the fields look immense, endless.

Everything about school—the uniforms, the formal meals, the bells, the rules—was like the red roofs and copper spikes: elaborate and confusing. I didn't know how I could get used to it. I thought I would leave before that happened. Then one day, someone said, "I'll meet you on the Landing during break," and even though there were staircases and landings all over the school, I knew exactly which landing she meant, the one behind the library. I didn't have to look at her with a frantic blank stare.

The new girl's name is Ernessa Bloch. She's quite pretty, with long, dark, wavy hair, pale skin, deep red lips, and black eyes. Only her nose is too large and curves down at the end. Pretty is actually too girlish a word for her. Maybe that's because of her manner; she's very polite but not at all shy. She doesn't speak with an accent, but there's something foreign about her. She only stayed for a minute. She wanted to know what time we had to be up in the morning and if breakfast was compulsory. I offered to sign her in tomorrow because she said she was totally exhausted from her long trip. Her answer: "If it suits you."

At last. This must be Lucy!

■

September 11

Sofia came running into my room last night after dinner. "There's a man teaching English," she said. "And he's a poet!"

His name is Mr. Davies. I have him for "Beyond Belief: Writers of the Supernatural." It was my first choice for electives this semester, but I don't care about having a man for a teacher. All the other girls are going nuts. The ones who didn't get into his classes are so jealous of us. I remember once Miss Watson brought a man to school, and nobody talked about anything else all day. Dora is in the "Age of

Abstraction." She's going to read all kinds of heavy things like Dostoyevsky and Gide. I'm glad she's not in my class.

Sofia said, "You're in his class and you don't care? That's supernatural."

He is good-looking, with medium-length brown hair and a moustache. He's in his thirties and married. He wears a wedding ring. After one class, Claire is madly in love with him. There was a pile of poetry books on his desk, and the top one was the collected poems of Dylan Thomas.

Claire whispered to me, "You can tell him that your father was a famous poet, before he killed himself."

She's a stupid cow.

"He wasn't famous," was all I said.

She's jealous of me because her father is just a boring lawyer. She thinks that if her father were a poet, Mr. Davies would fall in love with her. Besides, my father wasn't just a poet; he also worked in a bank. He used to call poetry his hobby.

■

September 12

I have decided to write at least one page in my journal every day, like doing calisthenics. I'll do it first thing during quiet hour. That way I won't forget. I'll write on weekends, too. I want to write about what happens to me during the day—what I have to do for homework, what's for dinner, the score of my hockey game, who's getting on my nerves. No dreaming about boyfriends or anything. I want it to be a record. I'll be able to read it later and know exactly what happened to me when I was sixteen.

I'm going to practice the piano at the same time every day, during my free period right before lunch. I've been working on the same Mozart sonata for almost a year, and I still can't play it the way I want to. I wish I could sit down at the piano and toss off the music without any effort. Instead I have to work so hard. Sometimes I'll play a piece really well, but then it almost feels like it's not me playing. Miss Simpson says I have to work on my concentration. It's true that my mind wanders when I play. I try to concentrate, but after a few minutes, I forget about the music and I'm wondering what's for lunch.

Anyway, the first three days have been perfect.

—

September 15
I broke my resolution, but that doesn't matter. No one is looking over my shoulder. I've been really busy. All my teachers loaded on the homework right from the first class. Lucy is already totally overwhelmed. She's hopeless at chemistry. How is she going to make it through the whole year?

Nothing much happened anyway. I signed up for hockey again, even though Miss Bobbie will never move me up from B squad. It was hard enough to get onto B squad. I'm only there because I'm in eleventh grade. She likes the girls with long, straight, blond hair, the day student types. Not a Jew and a boarder! No matter how hard I practice, I'll never move up. Even though I expected to see my name exactly where it appeared, I was still disappointed when they put up the lists on the Athletic Association bulletin board. And there was Lucy on A squad. She'd be there without doing anything. Of course Miss Bobbie likes Lucy. She's the goddess of field hockey. If she weren't my friend, I would hate her. She came up and put her arm around me and whispered in my ear, "Don't cry. When she sees how good you are, she'll move you up."

What a stupid name, Miss Bobbie. Her real name is Miss Roberts. It's pathetic for an old woman with white hair and sagging skin to have a nickname. She always wears a plaid wool kilt with a matching sweater over a white shirt and navy blue knee socks that fall down in folds around her ankles. It's like a uniform. I'd never wear a uniform if I didn't have to. Sofia likes the uniform, for some strange reason, but then she also loves school.

I'm not going to let that old cow ruin my fall. I love to play hockey, to run up and down the field, out of breath, with my lungs aching and the smell of dry leaves in the air. The light fades, and the players spread out across the field can barely see one another. They sink back into the darkness like ghosts. The white ball, the only thing that connects them, gleams on the grass. There's the sound of the wooden stick smacking against the hard ball, the calls in the empty air, then the jarring, numbing feeling as I whack the ball down the long field and everyone takes off after it and disappears into the dusk. It's beautiful. Even on B squad.

I've got to do some work before I go down to set up. I'm at Mrs. Davenport's table. She lets us finish quickly, have coffee, and then get down to the Playroom for a smoke before study hour. That's because she doesn't eat much. She watches her weight. If you get at a table with Miss Bombay, she never lets you go without eating everything. It takes forever.

After dinner
Poor Lucy is stuck at Miss Bombay's table. And she has to clear. That means we won't have any time together in the Playroom after dinner. I haven't been at Miss Bombay's table since I came to school in ninth grade. It was bad enough that I came in the middle of the year, and then I was put at Miss Bombay's table. I had to go away to school because my mother couldn't have me around. She wanted to wallow in her own pain, alone. At night we sat down to dinner in silence. The only sounds were chewing and swallowing. If we had to speak, to ask for the salt or something, we would whisper and try not to stare at my father's empty place. Every night I would think, I can't stand to have another dinner with her. Then I got to school, and it was even worse. I was terrified of everything: the other boarders, the corridor teachers, the gym teachers, Miss Rood, all the rules and bells. I couldn't even find my way around the school. One night I ran away from the other girls who gathered at the top of the stairs to go down to dinner together and came down the back stairs by the music practice rooms. I had no idea where I was. I stood in the dark hallway

and cried. No one heard me. I could have been dead. At the table, as we stood for grace, I couldn't stop staring at Miss Bombay. Her legs were so big and her ankles so swollen that her calves seemed to go right into her shoes, like thick wooden pegs. Her ankles and calves were wrapped up in ace bandages. She lowered herself slowly into her chair, clutching the edge of the table for support, and sighed with relief when she sat down. I was too petrified to eat. The room was flooded with the sounds of voices and clanking silverware, which got louder as dinner went on. There were conversations all around me. Girls jumped up and delivered the food from a cart, then ran around the table to clear away the plates and threw them back onto the cart. I looked up. My plate was still covered with food, there was a bite of lamb in my mouth, and I found the table had grown silent and everyone was staring at me. I couldn't move my jaw to chew.

"Don't hurry, dear," said Miss Bombay. "Finish your meal."

"Hurry up," whispered the girl sitting next to me. "We want to have a smoke."

I managed to squeak, "Done."

"Go on now, finish up," insisted Miss Bombay.

"No, I'm finished," I said. Only my fear of the other girls made me speak louder.

Miss Bombay sat there without saying a word. I felt that if she made me finish, with everyone staring at me as I choked down each bite, I wouldn't be able to stay at school. When she finally told the girls to clear, I was drenched in sweat, and my legs were trembling under the table. The worst part was that dessert was angel food cake with whipped cream. I wanted a piece so much, and Miss Bombay kept offering me one, but I kept shaking my head. Then I heard Miss Bombay whisper to one of the older girls, "The poor child is still in a state of shock." Nothing could have been worse than those words. I wished I'd taken some dessert and my mouth was stuffed with the soft sweet cake like all the other girls sitting around the table, who seemed to stop chewing at once and stare at me again. This time not with annoyance but with disgusting pity in their eyes.

Now I'm one of those older girls. I hurry through dinner and go down for a smoke afterward. I have lots of friends, and no one stares. I always take a big piece of angel food cake.

—

September 17

There's something strange about the new girl. Or else she's totally out of it. I was coming up the Passageway after gym, and I found her standing there, leaning against the wall and staring out the window. I hurried right past her, but then I remembered how awful it was to be a new girl, so I turned around.

"Are you lost?" I asked.

Ernessa turned away from the window. "No. This is one of my favorite places here."

"The Passageway?" I asked.

The Passageway is just a way of getting from the Schoolhouse to the Science Building to the Residence. There's no reason to hang out there, unless you like a place that's cold and dim and closed-in. The leaded glass windows make it feel more like a cloister than a school. The glass is thick and swirly, and outside the trees on the Middle Field look as if they are melting into the sky. Only pallid light comes through, underwater light. When I get to the Passageway, I almost run.

"I like to look out the windows," said Ernessa. "The world is broken up into little fragments."

"Are you going back to your room?" I asked just to be polite.

"Eventually," she said.

"Then I'll see you later."

She turned eagerly back to the window as if she could actually see something out there. I left.

I have to ask Lucy if she's ever talked to her. I think they're in the same English class. I don't know why Lucy wants to read the romantic poets. Probably because poems are shorter than novels, and she thinks it will be easier. I don't have any classes with Ernessa, and I only have chemistry with Lucy. I hardly have any friends in my classes. I'm mostly stuck with day students. I guess there could be nice, smart day students, but I've never met any.

After dinner
Ernessa is in her English class, and Lucy went on and on about how "brilliant" Ernessa is and how she always has such interesting things to say in class. I'm not sure Lucy would know what brilliant is. I got impatient with her. She couldn't stop talking about Ernessa.

"How can you know how smart someone is after a week of school?" I asked.

"I know she's smarter than me," said Lucy.

"She talks like one of those Magic 8-Balls, you know, 'It is decidedly so,' or 'Signs point to yes.'"

The conversation really annoyed me. Now I can't concentrate on math.

September 19
Lucy's gone home for the weekend, and I don't really have anything to do. I don't feel like doing my homework or playing the piano or even reading a book. Why do I feel so lost with her gone, even though I have lots of other friends? I don't even need to be with her; I just need to know that she's in her room, with only the two doors between us. I can always go in there, flop down on her bed, and say, "Let's do something." Lucy pulls me away from my books and my thoughts and makes me laugh and eat junk food and be silly like the other girls. I hope she doesn't start going home every weekend. She lives only two hours away, and her mother doesn't mind picking her up. My mother doesn't want me home on weekends. She says she misses me when I'm gone, but she's gotten used to being alone.

They're all down the hall in the TV room. Except for Ernessa across the hall, probably. She's kind of like me, but much worse. I don't think she cares about being friends with anyone. She spends all her time in her room with the door closed. It's the only closed door on the corridor. I would never think of going in there without knocking. I've only been in there once, when the door was left open and she was talking to Dora. I figured they were probably discussing Nietzsche or something, which is all Dora wants to talk about. Other than taking drugs, which she apparently does a lot. In her spare time, Dora's writing a novel based on Nietzsche's philosophy. She's already written three hundred pages, she says. She tried to explain it to me. It's a dialogue between Nietzsche and Brahms. Actually, I was trapped in her room while she read passages from *Thus Spoke Zarathustra*. She's only bothering with me because there's no one else who would listen to her without going, "Oh, please . . ." At the same time, I'm supposed to feel flattered because she's enlightening me. Dora's the kind of person you think you like until she manages to insult you by treating you like an idiot. In the end, I don't know if I even like her or if she likes me. I get the best grades, and she thinks she's the smartest. The most intellectual. She always says, "I don't take grades seriously. They can't measure real intelligence, just how well you can regurgitate what the teacher feeds you."

Ernessa seems pretty smart. Maybe she'll be able to understand Nietzsche better than me, all this stuff about the Superman and the myth of the eternal return. Anyway, I stuck my head in, because I wanted to see what her room looked like, not because I wanted to listen to some heavy philosophical discussion. Ernessa gave me a look that said, "What are you doing here?" I wasn't interrupting anything important. They were talking about furniture. Ernessa wanted to move her dresser over by the door. "It's going to block the doorway," I said. She ignored my comment and picked up the dresser and carried it across the room. Dora and I stared at her. Dora asked, "How can you carry that? It's got to be incredibly heavy." Ernessa seemed surprised. "Now if you'll excuse me," she said.

No one talks like that around here.

She stood by the door, waiting for us to leave. I don't like the way Ernessa looks at me. I had thought we might become friends, but I don't think we will.

Her room also smells even though it's perfectly clean and practically empty. A dresser, a desk, a desk chair, a bed, bare floor. That's all. Maybe the smell is coming from the bathroom. It's a kind of mildewy, rotten smell.

Dora gave me Nietzsche to read, and I did look through it. I can't understand how someone could write a novel based on that book. It's an incredibly pretentious thing to do.

This was underlined:

"Woe to all lovers who cannot surmount pity.

"Thus spoke the Devil to me once: 'Even God has his Hell: it is his love for man.'

"And I lately heard him say these words: 'God is dead; God has died of his pity for man.' . . . Thus spoke Zarathustra."

The point being what?

—

September 20

The weekend is crawling by. Lucy probably won't be back until right before supper, another three hours. By ten o'clock this morning, I started to feel anxious. I'm waiting for something to happen, but I have no idea what the something is. I should practice the piano. I should do my homework. I should read a book. After lunch I went and bought a package of cookies from Carol, who sells them for the Service League, got into bed, and read "My Sister Antonia" for English while I ate the cookies. It's still September, but my room is so cold. My hands and feet were like ice. I couldn't warm them up. But I forgot about them because I loved the story so much. I read it over again right away when I finished. I went from the last page back to the first without stopping, sinking deeper and deeper into the twilight language. I want to write a story like that, to set up everything so carefully, detail by detail, that when something totally outlandish happens, it seems perfectly natural, even inevitable. It's a perfect story. I just need something to write about. How do writers come up with really good stories? I'm sure no one else in the class will like it.

They'll say, "What's the point we're supposed to get?" They want everything explained, even though they are taking a class on the supernatural. What do they expect? I admit Mr. Davies has come up with some bizarre stories. A few are so hard to find that he's had to leave his own copies of the books in the library, and we can only sign them out for a few days to read them. He says he doesn't care what order we read them in, or if we read all of them, which means that most of the girls will hardly read any. He doesn't understand that no one reads anything that isn't on a test. He also doesn't notice that when he's talking to us so enthusiastically, the girls are whispering to each other or passing notes or staring out the window. I'm trying to read everything right away.

I'm going to copy out the list to remind myself to make notes about the stories as I go.

"Carmilla" by Sheridan Le Fanu
"The Great God Pan" by Arthur Machen
"My Sister Antonia" by Ramón del Valle-Inclán
"The King in Yellow" by E. K. Chambers
"The Black Spider" by Jeremias Gotthelf
"The Jews' Beech Tree" by Annette von Droste-Hülshoff
"The Man Whom the Trees Loved" by Algernon Blackwood
"Sredni Vashtur" by Saki
"Rappaccini's Daughter" by Nathaniel Hawthorne

A nap until Lucy gets back. She has to be here soon.

I took my nap, and Lucy still isn't back. I don't feel like going out and being sociable. The only thing the others want to do is get stoned. Especially Charley. I always see her slipping into Ernessa's room across the hall. They smoke dope together. That's the only thing they have in common. Ernessa seems to have a good supply. Charley doesn't understand why I don't like to smoke. I lose control of my thoughts.

This is my favorite passage from "My Sister Antonia":

One afternoon my sister, Antonia, took me by the hand to go to the cathedral. Antonia was much older than I; she was tall and pale, with dark eyes and a smile tinged with sadness. She died while I was still a child. But how well I remember her voice, her smile, and the chill of her hand as of afternoons she led me to the cathedral. Above all, I remember her eyes, and their tragic gleam as they followed a student who walked up and down the cathedral portico, enveloped in a blue cape. I was afraid of that student: he was tall and gaunt, and his face was that of a dead man. His eyes were the eyes of a tiger, terrible eyes, beneath a stern, finely molded forehead. To make him seem even more like the dead, the bones of his knees creaked as he walked. . . . He caught up with us at the door of the cathedral and, drawing out his skeleton hand, took some holy water and offered it to my sister, who was trembling. Antonia looked at him beseechingly, and he whispered with the spasm of a smile: "I am beside myself."

When I close my eyes, I can hear the soft creaking of his knees as he paces the corridor outside my room. I wonder what it would be like to be a Catholic, to dip your hand into the cold water and to believe in its holiness.

▬

September 22
Yesterday Lucy wasn't back at quiet hour. Usually we spend part of it together in her room. That's why we have a suite. My first year I felt so alone in my little cell. I didn't realize how much I've come to look forward to spending that time with her until she didn't show up. We talk a little at first. Then I sit in her chair and read while she does her homework at her desk. I don't need to sit at a desk to work. I can study in bed, on the floor, in a chair, standing up. Lucy needs to sit at a desk. She says it helps her to focus. Usually I don't want to be

friends with someone who's not smart, but with Lucy that doesn't matter. She's not stupid. She just doesn't do very well in school. She has a different kind of intelligence from me. She knows how to get along with everyone. Last year, I helped her with her German homework. Even though I'd never taken German, I could do the translations for her.

You have to trust someone before you can have rituals with them. My father and I had our afternoon walks, our bedtime reading, and when I was really little, the ritual of my bedside lamp at night. I could only go to sleep with the light on, and every night my father would come in after I fell asleep and turn off the lamp. If I woke up in the middle of the night, I would turn the lamp back on, but it was never on in the morning. I used to think my father stayed up all night to make sure that my lamp was turned off. Later I found out he stayed up late to write poetry. The lamp had a turquoise base and a little white shade with turquoise dots. When the light bulb was turned on, the dots glowed.

After my father died, I tried to hold on to him by repeating our rituals. When I took walks in the Botanic Garden, I kept expecting him to be there. I peered down the pathways, around trees, through the glass walls of the conservatory, across the water of the pond in the Japanese garden. If he came back, this was where I would find him.

I didn't see Lucy until we had our smoke in the Playroom after dinner. I asked her if she'd had an away hockey game today. "I was in Ernessa's room. She was helping me with my German. She's so incredible. Totally fluent. I didn't want to come back to my room because I was afraid Mrs. Halton would see me."

Mrs. Halton never comes out of her suite during quiet hour. She wouldn't come if you were burning the place down. Besides, it's only across the hall. Lucy seemed annoyed at me. She can do whatever she wants during quiet hour. I don't see how she can spend an entire hour in that room. It has such a smell. It's not just the old socks smell of Charley's room. I gag when I pass by Ernessa's door.

September 23

Being a poet doesn't impress me. I would rather Mr. Davies was just a plain English teacher. He's going to teach a poetry writing course next semester. Everyone will read their poems out loud, and the class will comment on them. How awful! Today after class he asked me to stay for a few minutes. I could see Claire burning up. She is completely mad about him and is always hanging around after class to try to talk to him. She has no idea how ridiculous she is. I guess this is what the word "besotted" means. He doesn't interest me at all. There's something mushy about him. I wonder if his poems are the same way. He asked me if I wanted to take his poetry class. Everyone has to write something to get into it, but he was sure that I would be good.

"You're the only one in the class who understands the stories we're reading," he said. "The other girls are either bored or confused, or both. Besides, you have the sensibility of a poet. That's a good start."

That annoyed me. How does he know what kind of sensibility I have?

He really just wanted to talk about my father, the great poet. He's trying to find out about my father through me, but I won't let him. Why should I talk about my father to anyone? Lucy never asks me about that. That's what I love about her.

Claire was waiting for me out in the hallway. She wanted to hear every word he said to me. I felt like telling her what an ass she's making of herself. She follows him around like a sheepdog with her wide nose and thick lips and the hair falling in ringlets over her dark blue eyes. I expect her to start panting and to let her pink tongue hang out of her mouth.

The other day, Sofia came to my room in tears because Claire had told her that the dark hairs growing around her nipples were disgusting and would turn men off. Sofia was ready to pluck them. I told her not to do that. They'll grow back even thicker and blacker. Then she'll never get rid of them. Claire knows Sofia's obsessed about her body. I think it's an Italian thing, to worry about how you present yourself to men. Sofia's always talking about cutting *una bella figura* in bed, even though she's never been to bed with a man.

"Have you ever seen Claire's tits?" I asked. "They're like sausages."

She unbuttoned her shirt and pulled down her bra. "What do you think?" she asked. "Tell me honestly."

I stared at her tiny breasts, which she pushed up with her hands. Her nipples were a pale pink that melted into the white skin surrounding it. There were three or four long black hairs around each nipple. I'd never seen anything like it.

"Your breasts are beautiful," I said. "Really beautiful. Who cares about a few hairs?"

Sofia laughed. She always laughs about herself the instant she's finished crying. She's always going on bizarre diets, like eating two prunes and a dried fig before every meal. She knows she's silly. But she can't help herself. I know that next week she'll be down at breakfast, eating sticky buns and oatmeal. She can't lose weight. I don't know why she tries.

In a way I like Sofia more than anyone else here, but it bothers me that she's always so quick to believe stupid things that other people say just because they pretend to know what they're talking about, whether it's sex or the meaning of life. Yesterday at breakfast, I heard Sofia at the other end of the table: "So there's no reason to go on living. Life is meaningless. There's really no significance to anything. Why do we live if we're only going to die in the end?"

She sort of has a point there.

The whole time she said this, she held a sugar doughnut in her hand, ready to take a bite of it. It's Dora again. She's been reading Camus and Sartre and has fed Sofia a bunch of crap about existentialism and the meaning of life. Or rather, the lack of meaning of life. Sofia doesn't read the books herself. She just listens to what Dora says and becomes even more depressed about her parents' divorce. That's what's depressing her—not some abstract philosophy. Who cares what Nietzsche says if you feel fine? Everyone at the table burst out laughing when Sofia made her statement. I did too.

I yelled down to her, "Sugar doughnuts are worth living for."

A quote from Nietzsche before I give Dora back her book: "I wish were wise! I wish I were wise from the heart of me, like my serpent!"

I'm sick of Dora.

■

September 24

I got back ten minutes late from hockey practice. As I ran up the stairs, I thought that with my luck this will be the one afternoon Mrs. Halton decides to check on us and I'll get a detention and won't be able to go to dinner in Chinatown this weekend. I turned the corner onto the corridor and saw someone slip into the doorway opposite my room. Of course, it could have been anyone wearing that long blue skirt and white shirt with the tails hanging out, but I knew it was Lucy. The door to Ernessa's room was closed when I reached it. It looked like an enormous blank eye.

I was right. Lucy wasn't in her room. What do the two of them talk about? I wouldn't think they would have anything to say to each other.

■

September 25

Yesterday Sofia did something strange. She went to Miss Rood to talk about her feelings of dread and hopelessness. Miss Rood isn't exactly the kind of person I'd ever confide in. But Sofia really likes Miss Rood, and she talks to her all the time. Miss Rood is nice to Sofia because she comes from a "good" family. It's almost all right that her father is Italian. That kind of foreignness is acceptable. Italy is Rome and the Renaissance and all that. It's different for a Jew from Eastern Europe. Western civilization didn't begin on the border between Poland and Russia. Miss Rood tolerates us. She doesn't make a secret of it.

Dora told me Ernessa is Jewish. That makes three of us, sort of. I'm sure Ernessa's relatives didn't come from some unpronounceable town that no longer exists. They probably came from Prague or

Warsaw or Budapest. Dora likes to think she's Jewish even though her mother comes from a Waspy Boston banking family and she's never set foot in a synagogue. Her Jewish father is a psychiatrist, and she thinks it makes her seem more intellectual to be Jewish. At least I am totally Jewish. Both my parents were born Jews and called themselves Jews.

Miss Rood listened to Sofia for an hour; then she sent her away with a book under her arm. It was Miss Rood's own copy of Walter Pater's *The Renaissance*. I know that because when I opened the faded green cover, I saw her name on the endpaper: Hilda Rood. Miss Rood would never give me a book to read. And, of course, she doesn't realize that Sofia will never read this book.

Now I understand where she got the name for her dog. It's like calling your dog Plato. Practically every afternoon during hockey practice I see Miss Rood in her long tan raincoat and brown oxfords walking Pater around the Upper Field. She could wear any kind of shoes, but she wears oxfords to set a good example for us. We couldn't care less about examples. All we want is to be able to wear loafers to school. Pater's always pulling on the leash, and she's always trying to hold him back. His shrill barks echo in the still fall air, muffled as if his mouth were stuffed with wool.

I sat in the big chair under Sofia's window and read the last few pages of Pater. Then I read parts out loud to Sofia, so she'll know what to say when she talks to Miss Rood again. Like the part where he quotes from Victor Hugo: "We are all under sentence of death but with a sort of indefinite reprieve." I read with a stiff British accent, and we laughed so hard.

Miss Rood: grizzled white hair, with a few traces of reddish-brown like rust stains left over from her youth, pale watery blue eyes behind thick pink-rimmed glasses, mottled skin. Her large pink hands, whose veins stand out like twisted wires, actually turned these pages and underlined passages. What can someone like her, whose life consists only of keeping hundreds of young women under control, know about art and beauty and hard, glittering ideas? Miss Rood burning with the flame of ecstasy? She's old and used up. As I read, I had an image of Miss Rood standing very straight and stiff before her lectern at assembly, leading us in the singing of the daily hymn, lifting her arms as her raspy voice started the first few notes, only to be drowned out by our higher, purer voices.

I couldn't read to Sofia anymore. I pretended I couldn't stop laughing.

September 27

Last night was our dinner in Chinatown. There were supposed to be ten of us, but Ernessa didn't come. Sofia, Carol, Betsy, Kiki, Charley, Lucy, Dora, Claire, and me. At first Lucy wasn't going to come either because she had so much homework, but we made her come, and I promised to help her with her English paper. It's not much of a Chinatown, and it's in a kind of rundown part of the city, but it still feels exotic. I love those red and gold beams curved like the roofs of a pagoda and all the neon and huge black Chinese letters. It's a little island of bright lights surrounded by dark buildings and empty parking lots. We had to drag Charley and Kiki inside the restaurant; they were trying to buy some pot on the street. We headed for the back of the restaurant, where we sat around a big round table with a lazy Susan in the middle. It was lucky that we were off by ourselves because we were noisy, and Charley, Kiki, and Betsy kept making really stupid and rude jokes about the waiters and imitating their accents. Sofia pulled me into the chair next to her. Everyone ordered a different dish, and we shared them. There was so much food, and I kept eating and drinking tea and turning the lazy Susan around and around.

For some reason, during dinner Dora leaned over and said, "Lucy looks so beautiful tonight."

Lucy was seated directly across the table. Her face was flushed, her lips were red, and her eyes were glassy, as if she had a fever. The lights were low, and the flame of the candle in front of her flickered, throwing her face into shadow and then suddenly illuminating it. She did look beautiful tonight; there was something unexpected in her expression. She looked back at me, and I could see that she was unhappy.

I stared at Lucy and blushed as if Dora had paid me a compliment. Tonight Lucy was like a lover, and everyone at the table recognized it. Dora was just saying what the others felt. It made me uncomfortable and pleased at the same time.

I couldn't sleep last night. It must have been all the tea I drank. I'm exhausted today.

Lucy just stuck her head in. I told her I would be there in a minute. She looks exhausted too.

September 29

Lucy hasn't been around at quiet hour for ages. I'm sure she's across the hall with Ernessa. I don't know why Lucy takes German and French, except that her father insists that she has to learn German. She's terrible at it, even worse than at French. It torments her. I'm not going to get upset about her spending time with Ernessa. It'll give me more time to write in my journal. What I don't understand is why Ernessa is so interested in Lucy, who is sweet and wonderful but not her type at all. She never reads books unless they are assigned for a class. And she hardly ever manages to finish them. Dora and I are more her type. But if it helps Lucy with her German and she can stand to spend time in that putrid room. . . . The only other person who sets foot in there is Charley, but the smell of their pot probably smothers everything else. Besides, Charley would do just about anything for a toke. But Lucy is different. She's very straight.

It's such a big room, and Ernessa leaves it as empty as a monk's cell. She's like a monk. I mean a nun. She never eats snacks or drinks soda, and she doesn't seem to miss them. All she does is smoke a lot. Nuns probably don't smoke. She always rushes down to the Playroom to light up after dinner, without bothering with coffee. If I didn't drink coffee after dinner, I'd never get any homework done. I always eat so much, and then up in my room the heat is stifling when it gets cold out, even with the window open. I open a book and start to read, and my eyes close and. . . .

I don't think Ernessa ever opens the window in her room. That must be why it stinks so much. I knocked on her door once when I was looking for Lucy. She didn't just say "come in." She came to the door and opened it herself. She stood there, filling the doorway, waiting to hear what I could possibly want from her. Meanwhile, I thought I was going to retch when the door swung open. I had trouble saying, "I'm looking for Lucy. Do you know where she is?" I'm sure she's quite smart and interesting, but she always makes me feel like a pest. I'm not going to knock on her door again.

September 30

Is there something wrong with me? I don't have urges. The other girls have to eat or smoke or take drugs or talk on the phone or buy clothes or go to parties or listen to music or be with boys. I don't need any of that.

Last night Sofia came to my room after lights out. She was starving. She wanted to raid the kitchen. Nobody has tried that since last year, when a bunch of girls were caught and got into a lot of trouble. Lucy didn't want to go. She really doesn't like to break rules, but I was up for it. We talked Lucy into it, and then Sofia went out along the rain gutter to get Charley from next door.

Charley discovered the gutters years ago, when we were in ninth grade and up on the top floor. One night I woke up, and she was outside, banging on my window like a huge bat. I opened my window, and she fell into my room. She had crawled along the gutter all the way from her room, which was three doors down the hall. At first I thought she was crazy to do that, up on the fourth floor. If you fell, that was it. But the gutters are copper and about a foot wide, so if you crawl on your hands and knees and don't look down, it's not that scary. Before long we were all doing it. That year I only got caught once in Charley's room after lights out, even though we had Mac as our corridor teacher. She'd stand out in the corridor after lights out, waiting to catch us going into each other's rooms. I feel sorry for those poor ninth graders. She's tormenting them the way she tormented me the moment I set foot on the corridor.

Of course, Charley was up for it. "Now that you mention it," she said, "I've got the fucking munchies."

We decided to wait until twelve. That's when Miss Wells at the switchboard in the main lobby goes to bed. We walked right down the front stairs in our pajamas as if it were the middle of the day. In the dark, the dining room felt empty beyond empty. The round tables were all ringed with chairs, and no one was sitting at any of them. We ran through the room, afraid the silence would reach out and grab at us.

We saw the night watchman right away, sitting at the back of the kitchen, reading a newspaper and eating crackers. He lowered his newspaper and smiled. We all wanted to run back upstairs as soon as we saw him, but Charley went on ahead and started talking to him. I can't believe how ballsy she is. The three of us stood back, our arms around each other, and kind of giggled. After a bit, Charley beckoned to us. I had to drag Sofia and Lucy over, they were so scared.

"This is Bob," said Charley. "Don't worry, he's cool. He's not going to report us. He wants to play a game with us. If we can guess what his real job is, we can pig out. He'll let us take as much as we can carry in a pillowcase. Cereal, Pop Tarts, all kinds of goodies. We have three tries. One each night for three nights. Kind of like Rumpelstiltskin. It's a total goof. What's our first guess?"

We stood in a tight little circle. No one would look over at Bob, but Charley wasn't in the least bit fazed. She was hanging out with seniors when she was in ninth grade, kind of like a mascot. She's wiry, boyish looking, and absolutely fearless. She doesn't care if she gets caught doing something wrong. I took the first guess. I was sure I knew the answer. He's a poet, and this is how he supports his writing. My father worked at a bank during the day and wrote poetry at night, sometimes all night long. Even when he was offered teaching jobs, he stayed at the bank. He liked it.

Of course I was wrong.

If I'd thought about it, Bob doesn't look at all like a poet. He has a receding hairline, wisps of brownish hair, and thick glasses. He looks like a dolt. If he'd been a poet, he would have been reading Keats or Shelley instead of the evening newspaper. Everyone was pissed off at me because I had wasted a guess. We ran upstairs. The cooks come very early in the morning to get started on the rolls for breakfast. Sofia was annoyed. She went to bed starving.

OCTOBER

■

October 1

The second guess, shoe salesman, was wrong. It was Charley's stoned idea. I don't think we're going to be able to guess this. Not unless we follow him into the woods like Rumpelstiltskin. But it was all we could talk about all day long. Lucy wants to bring Ernessa along tonight. She thinks she'll have a good idea. I didn't say a word.

■

October 2

Well, we have our pillowcase full of food. I'm not in the mood to eat it.

Ernessa appeared in Lucy's room right after midnight, and we all went down together. When we got to the kitchen, Bob was sitting in his chair, reading the paper, and munching on crackers as usual, as if he hadn't budged from that spot for the last three days. His gray sweater was covered with crumbs.

He always pretends not to notice us until we are standing right in front of him.

Ernessa didn't say a word; she just stood there, scouring him with her eyes.

"I see you've brought a new friend along tonight," said Bob, lowering the sports section so that he could peer over the top. "That's kind of cheating. You think she'll do any better?"

"What's the mystery?" Ernessa said to us. "He's a mortician."

Bob was floored. He dropped his newspaper in a heap on his lap. "She's right. I work in my uncle's funeral parlor during the day. Embalming bodies, putting clothes and makeup and jewelry on dead people, combing their hair. How did you get it?"

"I smelled it when I walked into the kitchen," Ernessa said.

"How do you know what a funeral parlor smells like?" I demanded.

"I was in one when my father died. It's the kind of sensation you never forget."

She was looking at Bob while she talked, and no one else paid any attention. They were already hurrying to fill the pillowcase. I was the only one who heard what she said. I sniffed the air and detected the greasy smell of London broil, which we'd had for dinner. The food, the game, the night watchman munching on his salty crackers, it was all so stupid.

Ernessa didn't want any of the food. Neither did Charley. She's getting really weird about eating because she's stoned all the time. I don't know what the others thought about the end of our adventure. Nobody said anything. Sofia took a box of cereal to bed. Then we stuffed the pillowcase in the back of Lucy's closet and went straight to bed.

She hadn't smelled it at all; she had known it the moment she entered the room.

■

October 4

Sometimes I forget what a strange place the Residence is. I get so used to it that everything starts to seem perfectly normal. Tonight Sofia and I were sitting in the chair next to the reception desk waiting for dinner bells. I was sitting on Sofia's lap, and my legs were dangling over the arm of the chair. Miss Olivo was behind the desk, where she sits all day long, answering the phone and signing girls in and out. That's all she does.

"Girls," she called out to us in her irritating voice, "don't sit like that. It's not proper behavior for young ladies."

I jumped up. Miss Olivo's voice had an edge to it that made me feel I must be doing something wrong, not sitting harmlessly on my friend's lap. When I got up, Miss Olivo turned away quickly. I stared at her. She sat at the desk, with her hands folded neatly on the blue blotter in front of her. Her head wobbled from side to side, the way it does all day long, and she began to hum to herself tonelessly.

Is that proper behavior?

The bells rang, and Sofia pulled me by the arm into the dining room. As soon as we were out of sight, we burst into uncontrollable laughter.

■

October 5

I wish we could talk about books or politics or anything other than sex and food and drugs. That gets so old. Everybody always says the same thing over and over again. Tonight I got my wish, sort of. We were sitting in the Playroom after dinner. Everyone was quiet. No one had anything to say. Lucy and Ernessa were off together, talking by themselves. I don't know what they talk about, but I doubt it's German poetry. I doubt Lucy even knows who Rilke is. Out of the blue, Sofia said, "I've had a few talks with Miss Rood, and I've decided that life isn't meaningless after all. There's so much beauty all around us. It's up to us to discover it and to give purpose to our lives."

"Give purpose to our lives? What kind of line is she feeding you?" asked Dora.

"Walter Pater," I said. I knew that Sofia had already forgotten what I read to her, so I quoted, "'To burn always with this hard, gem-like flame, to maintain this ecstasy, is success in life.'"

"That's it," said Sofia.

"That stuff was dead and buried in the 1890s," said Dora, "along with Miss Rood. Don't be fooled. She's not a real person. She's a fossil."

"Maybe art really can save us," I said. "It shows us that there's something besides our own messy lives."

"What did art ever do for you?" asked Dora.

She's jealous of me for having "artistic" parents. I should have gotten up and left then, but it would have been lost on her. She was too busy lecturing Sofia, who was listening openmouthed.

"Life *is* absurd," said Dora. "You have to learn how to be fearless and to triumph over that absurdity, not to pretend that it isn't true. You have to do what Nietzsche says and seize the thyrsus, be tragic." Sofia looked overwhelmed by the mention of Nietzsche. (She could never figure out how to pronounce his name, much less read his books. But it sounds Germanic and profound.)

"What the fuck is thyrsus?" shouted Kiki from behind us.

"It's the ritual staff of the Greeks," said Dora, "entwined with the grapevine. Bacchus carries it. You know all about that."

"I do?" asked Kiki.

"He represents drunkenness and sex," said Dora. "The thyrsus is a giant dick."

Everyone started to laugh. "Fuck you," said Kiki, matter-of-factly. We all know that Kiki lost her virginity at fifteen, or maybe fourteen, and has already had lots of boyfriends.

While we were laughing at Kiki and I was thinking how much I disliked Dora, Ernessa came over. She stood right behind Sofia and said to Dora, "I think Nietzsche's ideas, if you want to call them that, are rather reductionist, not to say simpleminded."

"Meaning what exactly?" asked Dora. She's not used to being challenged.

"He divides the world in two. The Dionysian and the Apollonian. The rational and the irrational. On-off. Night-day. There is nothing in between."

"Nothing else except boring, hypocritical, everyday life. That's good enough for most people, but it's not really being alive. More like living cocktail party death."

"What does it mean to be really alive?" asked Ernessa.

"Not to have any fear," said Dora.

"Is that all? Then you might start by giving up your precious Nietzsche. Really being alive feels entirely different. It feels like ecstasy without losing your self." Ernessa turned to Kiki and added, "Like having an orgasm with your eyes wide open."

Dora turned away from Ernessa and addressed the rest of us: "She's a false prophet. 'Believe with me in Dionysian life and in the re-birth of tragedy. The time of the Socratic man is past: crown yourselves with ivy, take in your hands the thyrsus, and do not marvel if tigers and panthers lie down fawning at your feet. Dare now to be tragic men, for ye are to be redeemed!'"

"*The Birth of Tragedy*," said Ernessa.

We were all speechless.

They were both in on a secret from which I was excluded. I had to go down to the library later on to find the quote. I couldn't begin to remember it.

No one even laughed.

"Oh, no, not the thyrsus again," said Kiki. "I'd rather have the real thing." And she got up to leave.

I imagined Dora in her room, poring over her Nietzsche, memorizing quotes just so that she could make us plebeians feel stupid. Ernessa gave her the perfect opportunity to show off.

The bells rang for study hour, and everyone put out their cigarettes and hurried upstairs. I was the last person to leave the Playroom. I kept staring at the empty blue plastic sofa, which sticks to the backs of our sweaty legs, hoping that it would reveal something that had eluded me in that conversation. It didn't. I wish I were like Ernessa and could keep up with Dora. But even if I knew what I was talking about, Dora still wouldn't take me seriously. She refuses to.

When Ernessa talks, no one can ignore her. I'm going to ask Miss Norris about this the next time I see her. I'm sure she'll be able to explain it to me.

October 6

I feel incredibly dense. That's the only word for it. Nothing can penetrate my brain.

I brought my journal to my Greek lesson and read to Miss Norris what I had written about the discussion last night (with some editing). When I finished, she said, "You have to understand, dearie, the Greece of the great tragedies was an extraordinary place. The most contradictory things were joined together. There were cults and magic and early science. There was rationality and irrationality. There was beauty and violence. Opposites were twins. Even Plato is filled with the strangest ideas. It sounds to me as if your friend Ernessa thinks of herself as a Dionysian, a soul in permanent revolution, but one who also manages to see clearly and to stay in control."

She paused and smiled at me. "Ancient Greece is so foreign to our way of thinking, my dear. We tend to make of it whatever we please. The way we do our dreams."

I wanted to tell her that Ernessa was definitely not my friend, but instead I said that I didn't really understand what she was saying. What is all this Dionysian and Apollonian stuff?

"Write down what I said in your journal. We can come back to it later."

I'm just not as smart as Dora and Ernessa, and I don't care about reading philosophy.

October 7

Ernessa's stopped asking me to sign her in at breakfast. She must have found someone else to do it. I said to her, "You should get up for breakfast. You're missing the best meal of the day. Mrs. Wing gets there at four to make sticky buns and crumb cake and doughnuts. I can smell the fresh rolls all the way up in my room. It's what gets me out of bed in the morning."

"That kind of food doesn't interest me," she said. "It's too sweet. All that sugar. White death."

What kind of food does interest her? She's never at lunch. She goes straight to her room after class. When she was at the dinner table right behind mine, she was the server, and she spent so much time serving that it was almost time to clear before she sat down at her place. She was always the one to volunteer to get seconds from the kitchen when it was something good. In between she just moved the food around on her plate. I watched until her black eyes met mine across the tables. I had to look away. Of course she turned down desert, even when it was a caramel cornflake ring with coffee ice cream. No one can resist that.

"Ah, Ernessa, dieting?" I overheard Mrs. Davenport say coyly.

She doesn't need to diet. She has a beautiful body, firm and muscled and strong and not too skinny. She smokes like a chimney. She's the first one down in the Playroom after dinner, and she's there a lot on the weekends. She always has a cigarette in her mouth. She inhales so deeply that you think she's going to suck the lighted cigarette down her throat. It's the way a man smokes. I always get smoke in my eyes and have trouble holding the cigarette between my fingers. I don't even like smoking that much. I do it to hang around the Playroom. Maybe I bum one cigarette a day.

▬

October 10

I never thought Lucy would get on my nerves.

She decided to stay at school this weekend, and I just assumed we would do something together. When I went into her room after breakfast, she wasn't there. The bed was made, and all the doors were closed. No one else knew where she was. I ran down and looked at the sign-out sheet. Both Lucy and Ernessa had signed out at the same time: 7:30 A.M. She didn't come back until right before dinner, and I didn't have a chance to talk to her until we were getting ready for bed. She's avoiding me.

At first she wouldn't tell me where she had been. "Just out. I went by myself." Finally I got it out of her by saying I knew she and Ernessa had signed out together. I probably shouldn't have said that. She says they went riding all day out in the country. By the time I got her to tell me where she'd been, she was really angry at me. I was miserable because she made me feel I'd dragged something out of her that she didn't want to tell me. I asked her why she made such a big deal about it. "I thought you'd be annoyed with me for not asking you to come," she said. "But I know you don't like to ride. And the weather was so beautiful I couldn't resist. It was almost like summer."

I went into my room and closed both doors behind me. I didn't slam them. I closed them quietly. To show her that I don't want to have anything to do with her. I don't care how she spends her time. I'm not her keeper.

"You don't like to ride." I've never ridden a horse in my life, and Lucy knows that. I'm afraid of animals.

October 11

I was walking in the Botanic Garden with my father. It was a bright day but windy and cold despite the sun, and I slipped my arm through my father's and drew close to him. It was the beginning of spring. The tiny, perfectly formed leaves were unfolding, and the flower buds on the trees were still green. I thought to myself, How can I wait another week until the flowers open up and show their colors? I knew exactly where I was standing in the Garden and which trees I was looking at: the magnolias on the terrace with their dark, twisted branches and fat, fuzzy buds like a baby's fist about to unclasp itself and reveal . . . nothing.

But if I was standing next to my father, resting my head on his shoulder, why was I also standing off to the side, watching from a distance the two people in front of the sea of creamy magnolia blossoms, which had suddenly materialized in the few seconds I had turned my head away? My father's outstretched hand pointed to something in the distance. He was talking as he pointed, but I couldn't hear what he was saying because he was so far away. My father was wearing his overcoat and the brown wool cap he always wore, but I wasn't wearing any of my own clothes. I had on a black coat and a black beret. It slowly dawned on me that this was my father, but it wasn't me. I could tell by the offhand way she walked that she was a girl and not a woman. Another girl was walking with him in the Garden.

They walked away. Neither one turned to look at me. I couldn't follow behind them. I couldn't move from where I stood.

I hate dreams like that. I wake up in the morning still angry and frustrated that I couldn't do in my dream what I needed to do.

October 12

This morning at breakfast, Claire made a snotty comment about how much time I spend with Mr. Davies: "It's obvious you're in love with him." She's absurd. She's the one who pesters him all the time and wants to visit him at home on the weekend so that she can meet his wife. Who cares about his wife? It's gotten so bad that I even feel embarrassed for her. I like to talk to Mr. Davies about books. I get excited when I read something that I really like, and there's no one else to talk to. I have nothing to do with Ernessa, and Dora always lectures me. What I read can't possibly be of significance. She is still lecturing Sofia about philosophy. Being in love with Mr. Davies would be like being in love with my father. I'm much more in love with someone like Lucy—not sexually but emotionally.

October 13

Charley is out of control. She's trying to get thrown out of school, and I think she's going to succeed. Last night, she and Carol threw an easy chair out the window of Carol's room into the courtyard. It made an incredible noise, as if it were being sucked down to the ground and then exploded when it hit. Mrs. Halton's rooms face the courtyard, and she heard it. She came running down the corridor, calling out, "Girls, girls, what happened?"

Everyone was standing by the doorway to Carol's room. Mrs. Halton went in, and Charley shrieked, "We didn't get a chance to stop her. Kiki just went over to the window, opened it, and jumped. She was screaming something about—"

Mrs. Halton fainted before she reached the window. She crumpled to the floor. I've always wanted to see someone do that. I thought it only happened in books. They both got two weeks' detention. Charley was pissed off. You get a comment for shouting out a window; what does she expect for throwing a chair out a window? Now everyone will be watching everything Charley does. She'll get thrown out if she looks cross-eyed. And she's always going into Ernessa's room for a joint. She gets stoned practically every day. I don't know how she can function.

She's also not eating much, probably copying Ernessa. Why is everyone so fascinated with Ernessa? Lucy trails after her like a puppy. Everyone tries not to eat like Ernessa. Charley goes up to her room and has a diet Coke for lunch. This will last for two days at most. I don't understand it because she's not interested in boys and she doesn't really care how she looks. On the other hand, Lucy and I were just talking about how creepy it is to watch Charley's body change. She was always so thin, and now she's filling out, getting big. I can't get used to seeing her like this. Every time I look at her, something seems wrong. She doesn't have breasts or hips; she's just becoming wider. I remember the first time I saw her. She had just come back to school after vacation, and she was leading her mother down the corridor. Her mother is large, with broad red cheeks and tightly curled gray hair. I couldn't believe that she was the mother of the wiry girl at her side. But maybe Charley's going to look like her mother in the end. All of a sudden one day, she'll be large too. Her parents have planted a bomb inside her, and there's no way to stop it from going off.

I never want to look older than I do today. I don't plan to let it happen. When I'm waiting for dinner in the lobby downstairs after setting up, I leaf through *The Brangwyn Echoes*. There are pages and pages of photos of class reunions, of women with children and grandchildren. Fat matrons with black pumps (small, conservative heels) and matching handbags. Were they once like us? Their legs are thick, their hair is short and permed, they have no waists, and their dresses are like sacks. They all have the obligatory string of pearls around their necks. They are another species. And it happens so soon, after a few years. My mother doesn't look like an old woman. She's still as beautiful and thin as she was when she got married.

One day last fall I noticed that my body was no longer flat. I panicked. I went on a diet for a few weeks, and all I could think about was food. As soon as I thought about not eating, I had to eat. At the end of two weeks, I said to Lucy, "I can't stand this anymore. I hate being on a diet."

"Thank God," she said. "That was all you could talk about. I got so sick of listening to you. Now we can have honey buns again on the weekend. I had to eat them in secret while you were on your diet."

Lucy and I like to buy frozen honey buns at the supermarket and heat them up in the kitchen on Saturday afternoon and eat them with tea. It's something I look forward to all week, just sitting together in the kitchen and concentrating on our honey buns. We hardly say a word. She really doesn't have to worry about being fat. She has no fat on her, except for a strange little pot belly.

Her belly reminds me of the paintings my mother likes. For a while, the only books she had in her studio were about Flemish painters—Memling, David, Petrus Christus, Van Eyck. All their virgins have rounded bellies, like Lucy, just noticeable beneath their blue dresses. They have wan faces and lank blond hair and bulging foreheads. Their skin is untouched by the sun. They've only seen beyond their rooms through a window. The world is far away but crowded with tiny trees and bushes and rocky mountains and castles and wide fields with animals and peasants and stalks of wheat and beyond that water and sky and clouds. You can't see anything like that from the

Residence, only bushes and trees and iron fences. Then it just stops. The faces of the virgins aren't even pretty. The only word I can think of is pure. You can't imagine them speaking a word or eating food.

I was so surprised when Lucy said that about my going on about dieting. I couldn't remember even saying one word. Actually, I was annoyed at her for a few days. I felt so stupid. It's stupid to be obsessed about what you put in your mouth.

"Rappaccini's Daughter": "'My father,' said Beatrice, feebly—and still as she spoke, she kept her hand upon her heart—'wherefore didst thou inflict this miserable doom upon thy child?'"

The father slowly poisoned his daughter, until even her breath was deadly and a bouquet of fresh flowers withered in her grasp. But was her soul tainted?

October 14

Today Lucy and I spent the entire quiet hour looking for the gold cross that she wears around her neck. She has no idea what happened to it. She only takes it off when she swims, and she hasn't been swimming all fall. She's afraid her father will go nuts because he gave it to her as a present when she was confirmed. We turned everything inside out looking for it.

Even though crosses make me feel uncomfortable, Lucy looks naked without her cross. I'm so used to seeing it around her neck, lying in the pink hollow of her collarbone. I noticed right away that it was missing. A part of her is gone.

We decided that if she can't find it, she'll buy another one. I'll lend her the money if she needs it. I have no idea how much a gold cross costs.

I wasted a whole hour helping Lucy, and I have a huge math test tomorrow, but I don't care. I haven't done anything with her for so long. It was fun.

October 15

I have my suite with Lucy and I have Mr. Davies for English and I have Greek with Miss Norris and I have my piano lessons with Miss Simpson and I have Sofia and plenty of friends. . . .

October 16

I used to love the fall. But the fall doesn't know if it wants to live or to die, to be reborn or shrivel up.

I used to want so much to be happy and normal and carefree like Lucy. That was all I wanted. I thought that by living near her, I could be like her. It's a way of letting things happen to you without thinking about them, of being exactly what you are and nothing more. Things flow over you the way a wave breaks over your head, and you are lost underwater, weightless, unsure if you will ever surface and not caring if you do. You just have to be born that way.

Some days I wonder how I'll get through a whole lifetime of thinking. A life that's just words, words, words, shuffling around in my head. Was I born that way?

October 17

I feel much better today (Saturday). Lucy decided to stay at school again, and we took the train into town for the day. I think she wanted Ernessa to come along with us, but I didn't give her a chance to ask. I said, "Let's go alone. Then we can do whatever we want."

We wandered around for hours. When we got tired, we sat in a park and looked at the people walking by and made up outrageous stories about them. They all had terrible secrets to hide: murder, incest, adultery, alcoholism. Actually, I made up the stories, and Lucy laughed at them. We had a nice lunch and ate huge fudge sundaes. It was perfect. On the way back to the train station, Lucy dragged me into a record store. She's been dying to buy Cat Stevens's *Tea for the Tillerman* ever since Carol played it for her.

As we walked down the wide sidewalk, Lucy sang to herself and swung the paper bag with the record back and forth. I wasn't really listening to the words. Longer boats were mixed up with keys and doors and distant shores.

"I don't really get the words," she said. "Do you?"

"I've never heard the song," I said.

She must have listened to Carol's record a lot because she kept on singing and she knew all the words to the song.

"It doesn't make any sense to me," I said, annoyed. "How can boats win you?"

Lucy looked over at me and smiled. "Sorry. I just can't stop singing it."

Lucy knows I don't like that music. I try to listen to it, but it bores me. She thinks I'm much too snobby. Sometimes I can't understand why we're such good friends.

On the train ride home, we were both tired, that nice kind of drowsy feeling when it's growing dark outside and you're speeding along effortlessly. Everyone out there is exposed, but you are protected, safe inside. The world looks greenish and far away through the tinted train windows, like an old painting with yellowing varnish. I read a book, and Lucy put her head on my shoulder and slept. I can still be happy.

▬

October 18

Sunday and quiet. Lucy went to church this morning, and I'm alone. I'm trying not to think about being alone. Lucy will be back in two hours. Nothing has happened since yesterday so I'm going to write about Miss Norris.

This is my second year taking Greek with Miss Norris. She has an apartment on the fourth floor that she used to share with her mother, but now she lives by herself. She's old, probably in her seventies.

I think she's spent most of her life at the school. She must have gone off to college (Brangwyn College across the street?) and then come back here to live with her mother (what happened to her father?), who also taught Greek and Latin. With anyone else, that would seem twisted, but with her it's perfectly natural. She's at school but not exactly part of it. I never see her with the other teachers. She doesn't seem to need anything more than her books and her birds and her plants. I wish I could be like that. I always feel better at the end of my lesson, even if I have to struggle with the translation. Maybe it's the sunlight that streams into the rooms at that end of the Residence. My first year I used to dream about being an older girl and going into her apartment. That's why I took Greek. I imagined if I entered her realm, I would become part of it: the light and the singing birds and the mysterious symbols of that language, like marks left by birds in the sand. Her hair is white. Her skin is white. All the color is fading from her. She places her hand on the table, and I can follow the course of her blood through the bluish veins under the paper-thin skin. I can see the blood moving. Everything about her is fragile and old. But when she smiles and raises her white eyebrows, she looks like a little girl. She can do whatever she wants. She lets her birds fly around the apartment, flitting in and out of the plants in front of the windows, and she speaks to them as if they were children. They stop to listen to her voice.

"The Great God Pan": "'You see me standing here beside you, and hear my voice; but I tell you that all these things—yes from that star that has just shone out in the sky to the solid ground beneath our feet —I say that all these are but dreams and shadows: the shadows that hide the real world from our eyes. . . . it may be strange, but it is true, and the ancients know what lifting the veil means. They call it seeing the god Pan.'"

What happens to someone who lifts that veil? Is there another veil right behind it?

October 19

Mr. Davies has had it with Claire. I can tell. He almost never calls on her, and he gets a pained look every time she plants herself in front of his desk after class. She thinks up all kinds of excuses to stay after class and talk to him. I used to think it was funny, but now I feel sorry for him. He doesn't know what to do with her. He's not the kind of person who can be blunt. Today he told her that they needed to have a talk. He set up a meeting for tomorrow. She ran up the Passageway to tell me. I guess she forgot that she was annoyed with me.

"I think he likes me," she said breathlessly. "I can tell from the way he looks at me. When he left the room, he came so close to me that he brushed against my shoulder and I could smell his body. It really turned me on."

She was probably blocking the doorway.

I don't know why I ever liked her. When she finds out what he has to say, she'll be angry at me again.

October 20

It was just as I predicted. Right before quiet hour, Claire burst into my room, already in tears, and screamed at me: "What did you tell Mr. Davies about me?"

Her face was bright red, and damp hair hung over her wet eyes. I told her that her name has never once come up in any conversation I've had with him, but of course she didn't believe me.

"Then why does he think I'm too interested in his personal life, as he put it?"

"Come on," I said. "It's not like it isn't obvious."

"But you spend all your free time sitting by his desk mooning at him, and he doesn't accuse you of anything," she yelled. "You look like you want to climb all over him, sitting on the edge of your chair and leaning—"

"That's nothing. And he knows it. We talk about books."

"I can talk to him about books too," she said.

"Really?"

"I don't believe a word you say," she screamed. "You're turning Mr. Davies against me. You don't want anyone else to talk to him. Admit that you want him all to yourself."

"I won't admit a thing," I said.

"You're so possessive. It's the same way you are with Lucy. You can't stand it if she has other friends. Everyone knows. You're always peering around corners looking for her."

I really lost it then. I told her to get out of my room or I'd call Mrs. Halton. I was afraid I would hit her. She slammed the door so hard that Mrs. Halton came anyway. I could hear her voice all the way down the corridor. "Girls, girls, stop this at once." I'm never going to speak to Claire again. I have no idea what she meant about Lucy. I wish Lucy would come so I can tell her what happened. Then I'll be able to laugh at Claire. I think Lucy has a hockey game this afternoon. I'll have to wait till after dinner.

After dinner

Lucy's response surprised me. Actually, she didn't really want to hear about Claire at all. We were in the Playroom, and I pulled her aside to tell her what happened this afternoon. I could tell that she was only listening to me because she was being polite.

"I can see why Claire was so upset," said Lucy when I finished.

"But she didn't have to blame it on me," I said. "I didn't have anything to do with it."

"Mr. Davies hurt her feelings."

"She deserved to have her feelings hurt. She acts like an idiot. I feel sorry for Mr. Davies."

I just walked away I was so annoyed. There was no point in continuing that conversation and getting into a fight with Lucy, too. She went right over to Ernessa, who was sitting off by herself, apparently waiting for Lucy. I watched Ernessa pull a cigarette out of a pack, hand it to Lucy, and light it for her, the way a man would. Lucy sat forward, on the edge of her chair, smoking her cigarette and listening to Ernessa. That was why she was so impatient with me. She's never been like this before. I could always count on her to be on my side.

■

October 21

The sight of my blood is the beginning of the end.

Today I was waiting for Mrs. Halton in the sitting room of her suite just before quiet hour so that I could get her to sign a permission slip for this weekend. I had just come in from hockey, and my legs were sweaty under my gym tunic. Her sofa is a dark crimson velvet, and it looks as if no one has ever sat on it. I didn't dare touch it. I wandered around the room, looking at all the knickknacks she has set out on a round, glass-topped table: a porcelain shepherdess, a black lacquer Chinese box, a music box covered with red brocade, a photograph of her dead husband in a silver frame. A whole life, gathered up in a few objects and a lifeless photograph. Was he ever alive and real or just a piece of paper? I could barely stand these sad things in this sad room that she is so proud of. It reminds you that a life no longer exists. How do we know that our life really happened and that we are not simply accumulating details, making it all up as we go along?

Before I knew what I was doing, my hand reached out and lifted the porcelain shepherdess. I wanted to touch its smooth, cold surface. As I lifted it, I felt something drip from my nose. A drop of red blood, so dark it was almost black, fell onto the glass in a perfect circle. I put my hand to my nose to stop the bleeding and looked around the room for a tissue to wipe up the blood. Ernessa was standing right behind me, peering over my shoulder at the table. She must have slipped into the room while I was lost in my stupid thoughts. I tried to wipe the blood off the table but only left a sticky smear where my finger touched the glass.

"When I was a little girl, the farmers said that a nosebleed was a sign of good luck," she said.

I refused to acknowledge her. I stared at the glass-topped table, the smear of blood, the objects.

"Don't worry, I won't tell Mrs. Halton that you played with her precious shepherdess."

I carefully put the figure back on the table.

"You shouldn't be sad about these cheap, sentimental things," she said. "I feel like sweeping them all into a pile on the floor."

I don't care much for Mrs. Halton, but what harm are her illusions? Let her keep them. Ernessa's words were so cruel.

"She needs these things," I said. "To go on living."

Ernessa's face was so close to mine. "I don't need things to remember my father," she whispered in my ear, "things that I can hold in my hands. Pieces of paper that capture images of the wrong moments. Time slips around them without a ripple."

I turned to look at her. The fierce expression in her dark eyes surprised and frightened me. It had nothing to do with the sound of her words, which rose and fell softly.

"I don't need them either," I whispered.

I ran down the corridor to my room, clutching my nose with my hand. I didn't know if I left a trail of blood behind me. When I reached my room, I slammed the door and went and locked myself in the bathroom. The blood was running down my hand, in rivulets between my fingers and over my wrist. I saw my reflection in the mirror, and it looked as if I'd been hit in the nose. I've never had such a bad nosebleed. When I tilted my head back, I could feel the thick blood in the back of my throat. The metallic taste made me gag. I rinsed off my hands and face, watching the running water in the sink turn the deep red to pink. I sat on the toilet for a long time, with my head between my knees, pinching my nose to stop the bleeding. I'm still shaking.

After dinner

I had to learn how to be with other people and how to have fun. Ernessa's not like the rest of us. She'll never be like us.

I found Ernessa all the way across the dining room and stared at her until she turned her head. I wanted to see whether she would acknowledge our meeting. She looked in my direction for a long time, but she seemed not to be looking at me. When I turned around, I saw Lucy at the table behind me, her eyes returning Ernessa's gaze. Ernessa no longer had that fierce look; she was almost dreamy. Her eyes were large and soft, her lips were parted. Her pale skin was without a blemish. For a moment I almost understood why Lucy liked her. Lucy didn't even see me turn to look at her. I didn't think those pale blue eyes could be so intense.

I went to my room right after dinner and pulled out a pile of photographs from the back of my desk. I unfolded a strip of photographs of Lucy and me. We took them in a little booth in the train station downtown. They are already turning brown and fading, and it's only been a year. We were trying hard not to laugh, to look serious. By the last frame, we had broken down. I'm certain I was happy then, so happy that I wasn't even aware of being happy. I looked at an old black and white photograph of my father. It's creased, with a corner torn off. He's probably not handsome to anyone but my mother and me, with his round face and thinning hair and brown eyes set deep in his face. I think he's happy. He's not smiling, so I can't be certain that he's happy, but he's sitting at the kitchen table at the beach house, and my mother is behind him, by the sink, slightly out of focus, but nearby. I can't make out the expression on her face. He used to like to know that she was near him. He'd reach his arm out for her without being aware of what he was doing. It was like a nervous tic. And sometimes she wouldn't be there, and he'd look around, puzzled. That night she was there. A bottle of wine and two half-filled glasses were on the table. I don't remember the evening, and I have no idea who took the picture. Someone else must have been there. I was probably already in bed, falling asleep to the murmur of voices coming from the kitchen. In fairy tales, there's always a time when everyone experiences happiness, even if it has to be lost forever the next moment. Ernessa is totally wrong: they're not images of the wrong moments.

■

October 22

This morning at breakfast I said, "Has anyone actually seen Ernessa eat food?"

Only Kiki was interested, probably because she eats whatever she wants and is still like a rail. The others all think it's cool not to eat. They admire Ernessa for being able to resist food.

"Maybe she's one of those secret eaters," Kiki said. "She pretends to diet and then binges on junk food after lights out. She probably has a stash of goodies in her closet. You should know, Lucy. You've been spending a lot of time in her room. Do you two pig out together?"

"I don't feel like talking about Ernessa," said Lucy. She was talking to Kiki, but she looked at me while she spoke.

Even Kiki's remarking on how much time Lucy spends with Ernessa.

"There's a disease that people get," said Betsy, "where they starve themselves to death. They stop eating and their body begins to feed on itself."

"Remember Annie Patterson last year?" asked Carol. "All of a sudden she looked like a concentration camp survivor. You could see all the bones in her face. It looked like a skull. And she still wouldn't eat. That's why she had to leave school."

"I don't think that will ever be my problem," said Sofia with a sigh.

"When you lose too much weight," said Betsy, "your body can't stay warm and you begin to grow fuzz on your arms. It's not hair, it's more like down. Kind of like an animal."

Everyone was grossed out and told her to be quiet.

"Look, I read this in a book," said Betsy. "I'm not making it up."

"I don't think Ernessa is starving herself," said Kiki. "Take a look at her. She has the perfect bod. But if you think she has this disease, feel her arms for fuzz."

"This is really fucking stupid," said Lucy, and she pushed back her chair and left without finishing her breakfast.

I've never heard Lucy curse before.

I'm just as annoyed at Lucy as she is at me. I only brought up the subject of Ernessa not eating to see if anyone else has noticed. I'm not making it up. She doesn't eat. I'm glad I'm going to Wilmington with Sofia for the weekend. I want to have a whole weekend without thinking about Ernessa and Lucy once. After breakfast, it crossed my mind to feel Ernessa's arms, to see if they are covered with fuzz. She's not the kind of person you touch, though, and she always wears long sleeves and tights, even when it's warm out. Somehow I don't think she's going to join us for strip poker.

A few days ago she came into Lucy's room while Sofia was on the toilet, taking a pee. All of a sudden, Ernessa shouted, "Shut the door!" We all stopped talking. The only sound was the stream of piss hitting the toilet bowl.

"I can't," shouted Sofia. "I'm on the toilet."

"I don't want to hear you on the toilet," said Ernessa.

Lucy hurried over to the bathroom and pulled the door shut. She was embarrassed.

Going to the bathroom in front of each other means that we have no secrets.

I guess Lucy doesn't pee in front of Ernessa, since she finds it so disgusting.

October 23

Today I did something that I've never done before. I was in Mrs. Halton's sitting room again, finally getting her to sign my permission slip, and I said to her, "I have to complain about Ernessa's room. It smells so bad. I can't stand to walk by it."

The words came out by themselves.

"No one else has complained," said Mrs. Halton as she signed the form. She wasn't really paying attention to what I said. It's true that no one else is bothered the way I am. But I'm very sensitive to smells.

In the summer, at the beach, I can't stand it when the bathroom gets all mildewy because the towels and bath mat are always wet.

I could have dropped the subject, but I didn't want to. "The smell is nauseating. I can't stand it. My room is just across the corridor."

Mrs. Halton looked up at me from under her half glasses. "I thought you would be more sympathetic to the poor girl. Since you're both in the same situation."

"What do you mean?" I demanded. I wanted to know if she was politely referring to the fact that we were the only Jews around. But she meant something different.

"About her father," said Mrs. Halton, now flustered. She straightened the papers in a brass letter holder on her desk as she spoke, so that she wouldn't have to look at me. "The unfortunate situation . . . that is, he took his own life."

"I didn't know," I said. "But it doesn't make any difference. I don't have anything against her. It's just that her room stinks, and it's bothering me."

"I'll talk to Ernessa. But she's very particular. She won't allow anyone in there to clean. She promised to take care of it herself. Her room is always neat when I inspect it. Maybe she only needs to air it out."

Why is Ernessa always allowed to keep her door closed when the rest of us have to leave our doors open so our rooms can be inspected after breakfast?

She shouldn't be allowed to get around the rules. Last year I pushed my dresser into the closet so that I could have more room, and Mrs. Dunlap made me move it back. She told me: "The school bulletin says that each room will be furnished with a desk, chair, bed, dresser, and lamp. What if a visitor comes to inspect your room and doesn't see a dresser? That won't do at all."

I'm not trying to get Ernessa into trouble. I've never "told" on another girl like that. But I can't stand the smell.

I never tried to get sympathy from anyone. I never used my father as an excuse for anything.

October 25

After dinner

Lucy was so cold to me. I didn't see her all weekend, and she didn't seem at all pleased to see me. She's never been like that before. Did I just imagine that we were best friends and shared a suite?

When we signed in, I tried to look back over the sign-up sheets to see what Lucy did over the weekend, but Miss Olivo was getting annoyed. It was almost time for dinner, and there was a long line of girls waiting to sign in.

"I just want to make sure I remembered to sign out when I left on Friday," I muttered.

I asked Dora what Lucy did over the weekend. I was afraid to ask Lucy. She'd never tell me if she did something with Ernessa. I'm sure she did. I tried hard to be casual. Dora didn't know anyway. For once I was glad that she didn't really pay attention to what I was saying.

I wanted to get back to school, but now I'm sorry that I'm back. This has ruined the whole weekend.

October 26

It was so nice to be away with Sofia, just the two of us all weekend. I didn't think about school once.

Sofia understands something important that the other girls can't, that nothing is quite the way it seems. They are all so literal-minded. We can also talk about our families for hours without getting bored.

We had Sunday lunch at her grandparents' house. Estate, I mean. Their house used to be a little stone cottage, about two hundred years ago. Over the centuries, various wings have been added on to it. There's even an elevator and secret passages between the upstairs bedrooms. (I don't know why. I doubt her ancestors were having clandestine love affairs or political intrigues.) Sofia took me down to the basement. It's a warren of dark little rooms. In one there are shelves with ancient cans of food, all rusty and dirty. You'd probably die if you ate it. There's also a little gas stove and a machine her grandfather rigged up with an old bicycle to generate electricity. If there were a nuclear holocaust, who would want to survive? You'd never be able to come out of your shelter. You'd be trapped underground until you ran out of food and water. Pretty soon the air raid shelter would start to feel like your tomb.

Her grandparents are always very nice to me, especially her grandfather, even though I've never said more than ten words to him. It must be because of my father. He used to say that rich people love to rub shoulders with poets and artists. Sofia's grandfather spends his time working on scientific inventions and raking the leaves on the grounds because he's so rich that he never has to work. Sofia thinks it's very sad. Up on the hill behind the house is a little studio that her grandmother had built so that she could paint. She doesn't paint anymore because she's almost blind, but she painted until she was almost eighty. Her paintings are everywhere in the house. The strange thing is that all the paintings look as if they were done by a young woman. They don't change; they have an charming innocence. I'm already much more self-conscious.

After lunch we went up to the attic. It's an enormous room, filled with bookcases and rugs and furniture. It's like a house itself. From a drawer in a desk, Sofia took out the journals her grandmother and her great-grandmother kept when they were younger. She found them up there, but she's never told anyone because she's not sure if she's allowed to read them. We read from them out loud. Her grandmother was very matter-of-fact. She listed all the things she did each day—where she went, what she ate, the weather, that sort of thing. Nothing moved her; even her tour of Europe hardly made an impression: "Reached Zurich at nightfall. Could barely stay awake during dinner. Today weather the same. We had a delightful cruise on the lake and stopped to dine at a little town with a medieval castle." Her great-grandmother was the exact opposite. She went on and on in syrupy prose: "The hand of One far greater than us had taken up His brush and drawn it across the sky in huge swathes of purple and red. From the deck of the boat, I could see His handiwork illuminate the entire sky, clear to the horizon. It was a canvas as vast as Michelangelo could dream up. The majestic beauty clutched at my heart and made me giddy. I reached out and grasped the hand of my beloved."

Her great-grandmother ran away with her sister's fiancé when she was sixteen years old. She was madly in love with him. Sofia's grandmother could never forgive her mother for disgracing the family. That's why she's so emotionally repressed. Maybe she can only let go and express beauty in her paintings. I love to hear stories like that. I could listen to them all day.

In the end, it doesn't matter if the words are true or a lie. They serve the same purpose.

"The King in Yellow": A book whose words are beautiful, true, and simple yet destroy the reader by driving him mad. Would I be able to resist looking at it? Is there any book I could resist?

■
October 27

Night

For the first time, I'm embarrassed to write something in my journal.

After lights out, Charley came into my room along the gutter. She didn't need to. We don't have Mac breathing down our necks anymore. Mrs. Halton is so lazy that nothing would drag her out of her room. I still go along the gutter sometimes, just to do it. The roof slopes down under you, and you can't see the ground below. It doesn't feel so high. Charley has always been the bravest of us. Once on the fourth floor, she stood up and walked a few feet as if she were on solid ground, holding out her arms and balancing herself. I nearly had a heart attack when I saw her do it.

Charley came to tell me something she's found out about Willow. When I heard there was a girl in the class named Willow, I imagined someone so tall and thin that she swayed in the breeze, with wavy blond hair that fell to her waist. Willow is perfectly nice, but she's chubby and has dark, wispy hair. Her huge brown eyes never blink, like the eyes of a cow. She's from San Francisco, the only girl from so far away besides Ernessa. About a month ago, she met a man on the train going into town. He started talking to her, and she probably just giggled. He's a businessman, in his forties, married and with kids, and now she's having an affair with him. He picks her up after school in his car, on the corner outside the front gate, and takes her to a hotel downtown where they "get it on big time," as Charley puts it. Charley caught her getting into his car a few days ago, and she made Willow tell her everything. What a mistake. Everyone knows that Charley can't keep her mouth shut.

If I had to pick one girl in the class who is the most unlikely girl to do something like this, it would be Willow. She looks like an overgrown baby. And she's always laughing. She sounds like she's hiccupping when she laughs, and her chin shakes. She told Charley that she loves having sex. It's an addiction, like eating chocolate. She can't help herself.

My first year at school, we sat at the back of the assembly room, right in front of the row of teachers, and I used to spend the whole assembly staring at the seniors sitting on the stage behind Miss Rood. There was one senior, in the front row on the left, who fascinated me. I don't know why. When I saw her in the hallway of the School-house with her friends, I used to follow her. I liked to watch her walk, to look at her black hair. It touched her shoulders without a ripple. Her name was Ellen Mardsen. I thought she was so beautiful and so grown up. She was perfect, even though she wasn't particularly smart or nice or interesting. Each morning, I stared at her over the top of the red hymnbook. I forgot about how much I hated singing hymns. Then one day, she wasn't in assembly. Her seat wasn't empty. All the seniors had moved over one seat to fill the space she had left. She had never existed. I must have imagined that glossy sheet of black hair fitting her head like a helmet. After assembly, there was a buzz. All the teachers tried to stop it, but they couldn't control us once we reached the Passageway. Ellen had left school because she was pregnant. She couldn't hide it any longer, and her corridor teacher had discovered it over the weekend. They made her leave right away. Her mother picked her up the same day. They couldn't have someone like her around for a instant longer. She was a bad example for the rest of us. She was a disease you could catch.

I never noticed anything different about her.

I can't imagine what it would be like to have sex with a man. To be so intimate with another person. Not to hide anything. I don't know if I could do that. It would have to be a boy anyway, not a grown man, someone as scared as me.

After Charley left, I tried to go to sleep, but all I could think about was Willow in bed with the married man. He was on top of her, moving up and down. I saw his hairy arms and back, his balding head, his sagging stomach. The thought of them together made me ill.

Last year so many seniors snuck out at night and met their boyfriends over at Brangwyn College. There was an epidemic of sex.

For now, girls are all I need.

■

October 28

After hockey I was starved, so I went to buy a chocolate turtle from Sofia. She's selling candy for the Service League. I opened the door and saw Sofia sitting on the floor with a huge glass jar of honey between her legs. She was reaching into the jar with a spoon, but when she heard me, she was so startled she dropped the spoon into the jar. It drifted down through the thick golden-brown honey and came to rest against the glass as if it were stuck in amber.

"Sorry," I said. "I didn't mean to scare you. What's that?"

"A new diet," she said sheepishly.

"Honey's a diet?"

"Well, it's a variation on a diet. It's the one Lion's on, where she eats a grapefruit before each meal and then she's not so hungry."

"Yes."

"I'm eating citrus, lemons, and grapefruits, with honey, because they are so sour. And sometimes just honey."

"I was looking for you at lunch, but I couldn't find you," I said.

"I don't want to be tempted."

"Then I'll buy some of those chocolate turtles, so you won't be tempted to eat those."

"I don't have any more. That's why I'm on my diet."

I stared at her.

"Not all of them. Just most of them. I kept putting fifty cents in the box and eating a turtle and putting fifty cents in the box and eating a turtle and putting fifty cents in the box."

I started laughing. I haven't laughed so hard in ages. I had to stop; my stomach was hurting. I love Sofia. No one else can make me laugh like that.

"You can have some honey," said Sofia. "If I can get this damn spoon out."

"No, thanks," I said. "Why is Lion on a diet? She doesn't even have an ass. It's totally flat."

Lion is called that because she has a mane like a lion. Her light brown hair is incredibly thick, and it sticks straight out. She has such a strange-looking body. Nothing matches; the parts seem to come from different people: no ass, sagging breasts, rolls of fat around her stomach, slender calves, and bony ankles.

"That's because she had to spend a year in bed lying on her back because she had such a bad reaction to penicillin. She doesn't like her boobs, they're droopy. And her stomach's too fat."

"No diet is going to change her boobs. That's they way they came."

Sofia doesn't believe me. She thinks a diet can transform someone. But in two days she'll be back at lunch, so it doesn't matter anyway.

———

October 29

When I first came to school, all the girls were nice to me, but I knew they talked about me behind my back. I would have, too. No one comes to school in the middle of the year unless something has happened to her.

I wanted to be like the girl in the room across the corridor, and they wouldn't let me. Her room was painted light blue, and there was tan carpeting on the floor. During the day, the door was left wide open. The light streamed into the room. I could see the white rays gathering in a pool on the floor. They were like the thin arrows of light that came through the Virgin Mary's window to announce the arrival of the archangel Gabriel.

When I sat at my desk, I could look across at an enormous pile of stuffed animals under the window. I hadn't brought anything like that to school. I had no idea what I might want. I didn't expect to stay for long. My room was bare and dark. The wooden floor was stained and gouged. The sun came in on the other side of the building. My window was just a bright square lighting nothing. The light blue room was full of things: photographs of a family, bottles of perfume and boxes of powder, jewelry, writing paper and pens and stamps, records, pillows, and more stuffed animals on the neatly made bed. And every surface was dusted with powder. I dreamed about being friends with the girl with long blond hair and a pretty face who lived in that room, the girl who wore a gold cross around her neck. I dreamed about being invited home with her for the weekend, to a nice house filled with the same kinds of things that filled her room.

I became friends with Lucy, the girl in the blue room, and it still was a dream. But after a while, it began to feel inevitable.

The first time Lucy asked me to come sit with her while she took a bath in one of the enormous claw-foot tubs in the bathroom down the hall, I was so scared. But I didn't know how to say no. What if I did something wrong? What if I got nervous and laughed when she was getting undressed or stretching out, naked, in the tub? What if I were too serious and could never laugh? What if she decided that she didn't like me after all? What if she only felt sorry for me? I wasn't used to being with other people like that.

After one week, we had our baths together, we went down to breakfast together, we came up from lunch together, we spent weekends together. Everyone linked our names together; they belonged together, like rhymed words.

I've got to go. It's time for dinner. The second bell just rang, and I haven't changed yet. I've got to find something clean in my closet. I'll write more after dinner.

After dinner
It happened to another person, to a pitiful girl who tried to disappear into the dark corners of her room.

October 30
I was in Lucy's room, waiting for her to get out of the bath. The door to the bathroom was open, and I was lying on her bed, reading "Carmilla" for my English class. It's about a woman named Carmilla who arrives under mysterious circumstances at a castle in Styria (wherever that is, was, if it ever existed). A young English girl, who lives in the castle with her father, falls under the spell of Carmilla. Actually, she falls in love with her and abhors her at the same time, but she can't resist her. At first I thought the story was too contrived, but that's just the style. Before long, I was pulled into it and couldn't stop reading. Once I realized that Carmilla was a vampire, everything that followed made perfect sense. There was no other possible explanation.

Lucy got out of the bath and came into the room with a towel half wrapped around her. I looked up from my book. Her skin was so pink and clean. But there was surprise in those blue eyes. Ernessa stood just inside the doorway of the steamy room, with the sweet smell of powder already hanging in the air, and she seemed for a moment more like an animal. Frozen still.

Lucy wasn't exactly embarrassed, even though she was naked and the towel didn't quite cover her. There's not much to see anyway. She still looks like a little girl. She barely has any tits or behind. She didn't know what to do, and Ernessa didn't move.

I remember how lucky I felt to be friends with the girl in the light blue room. But Ernessa just walked into the room, without bothering to knock, and Lucy didn't object. This is something we have always done together, every night, when all the other girls are in their rooms getting ready for bed. I don't want to give it up. Ernessa had no reason to be in the room. She leaned over to see what I was reading, shrugged her shoulders, and, without a comment, sat down on the chair and began to quiz Lucy about her German.

Then Ernessa interrupted herself and said, "Your skin is still burning red from the bath. How can you stand such hot water on your skin?"

"It's relaxing," I said from the bed. "We always take a hot bath before bed."

Ernessa ignored my comment and went back to the German.

Lucy looked at me the whole time. It was I, not Ernessa, who made her uncomfortable. The whole time Ernessa acted as if she were keeping an eye on Lucy, and Lucy didn't object at all. I knew she wanted me to leave them alone, but I wouldn't leave.

Why is this happening to me?

■

October 31

All I wanted was to be not too smart, not too sensitive, not too beautiful, not too anything. Ordinary. But here no one is ordinary, not even Lucy. There is always some problem, some secret, even for the girls who are here because all the girls in their family have gone to this school for the past fifty years. Why else would you be here, locked away in a castle with dormer windows and sloped roofs and tall red chimneys and copper ornaments? It always comes out. Everyone has something that embarrasses them. Secret love affairs, liquor bottles in the closet, stepparents who hate them. Death. Charley's mother is an alcoholic. Sofia's parents are divorced and hate each other. Her father lives in Italy. Dora's parents are on sabbatical in Paris, but she doesn't get along with her father, so she decided to board at school for the year. Claire fights with her stepfather and calls him a racist bastard. There is a girl in the class below us, Alison, whose parents died in a car crash. A flaming wreck. And so on. *Und so weiter.* I'm probably the only girl at school who loves her mother, except for Lucy. My mother and I are like pieces of driftwood, rising and falling on the ocean's swells. I'm always afraid I'll float away and lose her. My father was a poet; my mother is an artist. Nothing was ever normal in my house. A suicide is not normal.

Ernessa would scoff at this. She doesn't care about anything ordinary.

NOVEMBER

■
November 1

Dreams bore me. Other people's dreams really bore me. I can't stand to listen to people reciting their boring dreams in great detail. I'm only writing down the dream I had last night because I'm not sure if it was a dream. Everything looked exactly as it does when I am awake. Usually when I'm dreaming, I know it's a dream. But this felt more real than my life. I was asleep, and my upper lip started to swell, and my mouth suddenly felt so dry. My tongue was thick in my mouth. It no longer belonged there. I stood up, amd my legs were stiff as wood. In just a few minutes, I would be unable to move. I recognized the feeling. I was beginning to die. I went into Lucy's room and asked her to help me. She was sitting in her chair, facing the window, and she turned around to look at me when she heard my voice. She smiled sweetly, but she didn't say anything. There was an immobility in her expression that betrayed a sternness underneath. She would smile that blank blue smile while I died. I woke up and found myself back in my room, sitting on the edge of my bed. At first I felt all right, and I was relieved that it was only a dream, but then a heaviness in my feet started to spread like heat up my legs. I bent over to take off my shoes. Underneath, my socks were soaked through with sweat, and I had to peel them off. My feet were thick and swollen and covered with blue marks. I thought, they look like blueberry pancakes, where the berries have erupted in the batter.

I struggled hard to wake myself from my dream; it didn't want to let me go. Each time I awoke, I found myself in another dream. I staggered out of bed and into the bathroom. My mouth was as parched and swollen as it was in the dream. The water caught in my throat.

Afterward I was afraid to go back to sleep. I won't be able to look at Lucy in the same way after this dream. I now know how hard and unfeeling she can be behind that insipid smile. She's always been that way.

After dinner

It's late Sunday night, and I need to polish my shoes. I always put it off to the last minute. Lucy has the polish. I've been avoiding her.

It's been weeks since I've polished my shoes. That's why Lucy and I decided to get brown oxfords this year—you don't have to polish them every week. Oxfords are like orthopedic shoes, but saddle shoes are like nurses' shoes. (The bottle of liquid white shoe polish even has a picture of a nurse on it.) I'd rather look like a cripple than a nurse. Besides, saddle shoes get so dirty. I got so many comments last year for dirty shoes. I had to stay for study hall after school practically every Friday. Miss Bobbie stands by the assembly room doors on Monday morning, her hands on her hips, staring down at the floor, and she checks every shoe that goes through the doorway. Our plan worked. This year I haven't gotten a single comment. Our oxfords are like wing-tip shoes with a flap of leather over the laces. They look like golf shoes. They are so clunky that I almost like them. It's just that they are heavy and hard to break in.

I can't believe it. I just went into Lucy's room to get the shoe polish from her. She was sitting at her desk, spreading white shoe polish over a pair of saddle shoes.

"What are you doing?" I asked.

She was totally flustered, but what could she do? The shoes were covered with wet polish. She couldn't exactly hide them.

"I'm polishing shoes," she mumbled.

"Whose shoes are they?"

"Ernessa's. She doesn't know how to polish shoes. I said I'd do it for her. She's gotten so many comments."

"It's not really a skill, polishing shoes. I'm sure she could pick it up."

"She's never done anything like that before."

I wanted to scream at Lucy, but I just went back to my room and closed the door on her. I didn't bother to ask for the polish. I don't care if Miss Bobbie gives me a comment tomorrow.

I'm going to keep the door closed. Lucy is always playing her Cat Stevens records, over and over again. I keep hearing the words of that stupid song about being followed by a moon shadow. I'm being followed by that song. The needle gets stuck on those words, and now they're stuck in my head. I can't concentrate on my homework with that music playing.

Lucy doesn't seem like Lucy anymore.

—

November 2

Study hour

I was lying on my bed, reading, and my eyes were just about to shut. I couldn't keep them open another second. Suddenly there was a piercing scream out in the corridor. I jumped out of bed and ran to the door. Everyone else was standing by their open doors. Only Ernessa's door stayed closed. And in the middle of the corridor stood Beth, screaming and clutching her wrist. At first no one could figure out what was the matter. Beth wouldn't answer our questions. Then she raised her arm, and a sickly little dribble of blood ran down to her elbow.

"I'm going to die!" she shrieked. "I'm going to die!"

We all stood at our doors, staring at her. No one went to help her. Mrs. Halton finally emerged from her room, took Beth by the arm, and dragged her up to the infirmary. I could tell that she was annoyed. Beth had probably interrupted her television show.

"I don't know why she was screaming," cracked Kiki. "If you cut yourself with a razor, you have to expect some blood."

Usually Beth is such a little mouse. No one notices that she's around. I don't know how she ended up on our corridor. She isn't friends with any of us. But she got a great number, and she wanted a single room, so she picked the room next to Charley. Sofia tried to trade rooms with her, but she refused.

There are other, less painful ways of getting attention. This isn't going to make any of us feel sorry for her or want to be her friend.

Girls are always saying things like, "I'm so unhappy that I'm going to overdose on aspirin," but they'd be awfully surprised if they succeeded. They have no intention of dying. At the first sight of blood, they panic.

She disturbed me for no reason. I love that moment, when you stop struggling to stay awake and your eyelids sink down and you slip effortlessly into another realm that's beckoning to you. Now I'm wide awake.

▬
November 3
Who is Carmilla? Dark, depressed, death-drawn.

"Her name was Carmilla."

"Her family was very ancient and noble."

"Her home lay in the direction of the west."

Who is Ernessa?

November 4

My mother's parents were orthodox. My mother always hated not being able to drive a car or turn on a light on the Sabbath. She didn't care if she ate pork or mixed meat and dairy. She says she no longer feels like a Jew, even though she can recite every single prayer. Sometimes I wish I knew all those prayers.

At my first assembly, I reached out for the red hymnbook, tucked into the little rack in the chair in front of me, along with the other girls, and opened to the correct page, just as Miss Rood instructed us. But when the music started and everyone rose to sing the hymn, I became so flustered I could barely get out of my chair. Was I supposed to sing a Christian hymn? Would I be punished if I refused to sing? Would I be punished if I did sing? Why had my mother sent me here? I looked around, and everyone held their hymnbooks open and sang along, even the girls who thought they were so cool. I moved my lips around the words and did not utter a sound. That night I called my mother and asked her what to do. She laughed at me and told me I should do whatever made me feel comfortable. But I need to know. It is important to me. Sometimes I mumble the words, sometimes I sing, sometimes I move my lips, sometimes I do nothing. I haven't figured out what to do.

Ernessa understands this. Today in assembly, when we started to sing, her face got red. She grabbed the chair in front of her so tightly that her knuckles were about to pop out. Her dark hair fell over her face, and she stared straight down at her feet. She didn't even bother to take out the hymnbook and pretend to sing. I held the hymnbook open, but I kept looking over at Ernessa, two rows in front of me and off to the right. Then she turned slightly, just enough to let me see that she wasn't suffering; she was smirking. Had she read "Carmilla" over my shoulder?

Of course, Lucy sits next to Ernessa, the luck of the alphabet: Blake, Bloch. A convenient coincidence.

After assembly, I ran to catch up with Dora in the Passageway. I pulled her aside and asked her if she had seen Ernessa when we sang hymns this morning.

"What are you talking about?" said Dora. "No one cares that you're Jewish. This is turning into a full-blown persecution complex."

Ernessa can't do this every morning. One of the teachers would notice.

After dinner

I found the passage I was looking for in "Carmilla":

> She sat down. Her face underwent a change that alarmed and even terrified me for a moment. It darkened, and became horribly livid; her teeth and hands were clenched, and she frowned and compressed her lips, while she stared down upon the ground at her feet and trembled all over with a continued shudder as irrepressible as ague. All her energies seemed strained to suppress a fit, with which she was then breathlessly tugging; and at length a low convulsive cry of suffering broke from her, and gradually the hysteria subsided. "There! That comes of strangling people with hymns!" she said at last. "Hold me, hold me still. It is passing away."

Ernessa = Carmilla?

Maybe a vampire is just someone who wants to take over someone else, to see their reflection not in a mirror but in another person's face.

Lights out

The most horrible thing has happened. It's taken me an hour to calm down enough to write about it. My hand was shaking so much that I couldn't hold my pen. I came into my room after my bath this evening, and Charley was sitting at my desk with my open journal in front of her. She was reading it.

"This is some weird shit that you're writing about," she said.

I grabbed the journal away from her.

"Don't get all bent out of shape," she said. "I just came in your room and sat down at your desk to wait for you, and the notebook was lying open. I couldn't help reading it."

"It's private," I said. "You shouldn't read someone else's private writings."

"Then you shouldn't leave it sitting around for everybody to read. I don't think Ernessa would appreciate some of the things you write about her. What are you making such a big deal about? I didn't find out any deep, dark secrets about you. Like you're a dope fiend or something."

She's right. I should never have been so careless.

"No," I said, trying to appear calm, "there's nothing interesting like that. It's notes I've been making for my English paper on vampires. Creatures who come back from the dead and suck the life out of young girls."

Charley started to laugh, and I realized that I'd managed to turn the whole thing into a joke. When I finally got her out of my room, I closed the door and sat on the edge of the bed, hugging my journal. I didn't feel safe until she was gone. I'm going to hide this from now on. All the time. It would be much worse if anyone else saw it.

I've spent so much time on this journal, composing each entry carefully to get it just right. I have to keep reminding myself that it's not ruined because Charley read a few lines. She had no idea what she was reading.

November 9

His last day on Earth.

November 10

I haven't written much. Whom am I confessing this to? I already know I've broken my resolution to write every day, and I don't care. I haven't done much of anything. I've felt almost too sad to exist. I can barely get out of bed in the morning, and then all day I think of nothing but crawling back into bed and pulling the covers over me. Yesterday Sofia came to my room in the evening, and we lit candles and sat in the dark, without speaking. I don't know what I would have done without her. When I started to cry, she came over, put her arm around me, and cried too. I was glad she cried.

My mother didn't call. I didn't expect her to. What could she say that would make either of us feel less abandoned?

I can't get the words out. They stick in my throat like fish bones. Once, last year, I was in the drugstore eating French fries after school with a bunch of girls. We were all joking around, not really talking about anything, the way we always are when we stuff ourselves with fries. Suddenly, Sarah Fisher said, "I miss my mother so much. Right now. I used to come home after school and lie on the kitchen counter and stare up at the ceiling and talk to my mother and eat snacks while my mother made dinner."

No one said anything. We thought about her dead mother, and we were embarrassed. I was the most embarrassed of all. I wanted to cry, but Sarah didn't cry.

I can't say a word.

Every year I think it will be easier, because I have grown away from the living person he was. I'm not panicked the way I used to be, when I held on to thoughts of him so tightly that I couldn't draw the air into my lungs. Now I want to know him only as a dead person. I'm beginning to feel that he was always dead.

Lucy didn't notice anything. Sweet Lucy the betrayer. This was her test, and she failed dismally. I knew she would. She acts as if nothing has changed, but all our private rituals are over—quiet hour, going down to meals, getting ready for bed. I always used to know where she was, as if there were an invisible cord binding us together. She's drawn lines around herself and pushed me outside them.

November 12

I've survived another year without him.

Lucy apologized to me for not thinking about my feelings. Sofia must have talked to her. I don't care. I'm much happier.

I practiced the piano for the first time in weeks. I haven't played, even though I hate to disappoint Miss Simpson with a terrible lesson. I am playing Chopin's Nocturne no. 11, Bach's Prelude no. 4, and a new Mozart sonata, no. 7 in C. The Mozart is so long—twenty pages. But it's not too hard. I love to play. I can't understand why I didn't touch the piano for two weeks.

Maybe it's because I hate the practice rooms on the bottom floor of the Residence, and the only other place to play is in the lobby by the front desk. I like to be alone when I play, but the rooms are dank and cold. My fingers get stiff, and the piano keys stick. You have to pull them up with your pinky as you're playing. Also, the smell down there bothers me. It's gotten much worse. Sometimes I want to retch. I found the janitor and asked him if there was water in the basement or something because it smelled so bad, and he said no, but some of the girls must have gotten in there and made a big mess. There was dirt all over the place. There were also dead rats and a dead squirrel. That was causing the wretched smell. Anyway, he's cleaned the whole basement out.

"You girls ain't allowed down there, 'specially with it overrun with vermin like it is. I put down traps and poison. You go tell your friends to stay out."

I can't get his speech right. I always feel embarrassed when I talk to him because I can't understand half of what he's saying. I keep having to ask him, "What? What?" He used to be the only man in school before Mr. Davies came. (Except for Bob, and no one ever sees him, except when they sneak into the kitchen at night.) I'm probably the only girl who has ever talked to him. The other girls don't think he's a person; he's a janitor. They're a little afraid of him, not because he is a man but because he's black with frizzled gray hair.

I wouldn't set foot down there.

November 13 (Friday)

Today we had an interesting discussion in English class, for a change. Because it's Friday the thirteenth? Actually, it turned into a conversation between Mr. Davies and me since everyone else was too bored to pay attention. They were perfectly happy to whisper or pass notes. Claire just stared at Mr. Davies. After class, Claire was waiting for me in the hallway. She started up again, "You're always monopolizing Mr. Davies's attention. No one else has a chance to get a word in."

I just walked away without bothering to answer her. What an idiot she is. Nobody's stopping her from talking in class. If she'd done the reading instead of spending her time smoking dope with Ernessa and Charley and fantasizing about having sex with Mr. Davies, she might have something to say.

Mr. Davies started by asking the class if we found the character Carmilla to be convincing. "Does she fill you with dread and fascination?"

All the girls laughed out loud. Mr. Davies got very red in the face. Why ask them? They only know clothes and boys and makeup. They'd love to talk about that. Besides, they probably haven't read the story. Someone had to say something. I said that I started to believe in the character when the writer realized what she was.

Mr. Davies looked puzzled.

"When the character he had created became real to him, the rest of the story did too," I explained.

"In other words, you agree with Coleridge about the poet's 'willing suspension of disbelief.'"

"I don't mean suspending anything. I mean creating something that exists, just the way everything in this room exists. Bringing it to life."

"It's a symbolic story," said Mr. Davies. "That's the point. Not whether things are real, but what they mean."

I realized what he was trying to do. He wanted to convince me that the supernatural doesn't exist. The whole point of the course is that it's just a figment of the writer's imagination, an expression of his subconscious. Like a dream. Or memories. My father would have understood me. He would have agreed that, fundamentally, Mr. Davies has no imagination. I had to answer him.

"I'm not interested in symbols," I said. "I'm interested in what's real, even if it doesn't look real. I want to know what it's like to be Carmilla. Does she ever suffer? Is it boring to live forever? What is it like to remember your own death? Things like that. Don't you want answers? Doesn't anyone else want answers?"

I looked around the room, and all those girls were looking back at me and smirking. They had the smug look of girls who don't care about anything.

They follow the second hand as it sweeps around the clock, waiting for the loud clang of the bell to release them. They jump up from their chairs and run out of the room and never give any of this another thought, except maybe to comment, "She's really weird, isn't she?"

■
November 16

I'm sick of writing about them in my journal. They take up space that doesn't belong to them. I don't like Ernessa. I don't even know if I like Lucy anymore.

We were in the Playroom after dinner having a smoke. Sofia was lying on the sofa with her head on my lap because she felt so awful. She's practically hemorrhaging from cramps. She gets up at night and has diarrhea and then has to vomit. The other night she woke me up in the middle of the night, and I stayed with her for hours while she sat on the toilet. The nurse says she'll have to have tests if it doesn't get better. Sofia's scared of all the blood, but she's even more scared of going to the hospital. Lucy came over to give her a hug, and of course Ernessa was with her.

"This really is a curse," moaned Sofia. "Do I have to go through this for another thirty years just so I can have sex?"

"You can have sex anytime," said Ernessa. "This is so you can make babies."

Everyone groaned.

When Ernessa came near Sofia, I thought Ernessa was going to retch. She hurried back to the other side of the room and sat by herself with her cigarette until the bells rang. Lucy kept looking over at her. To see if she was all right? She wasn't the one paralyzed by cramps. Ernessa turned herself into a column of smoke. The rest of us went up together, and she waited until we left the room before she came up.

I won't say anything to Lucy and get her more annoyed at me. She'll tell me to stop obsessing about Ernessa, the way I obsessed about my diet last year. Every time I bring up Ernessa, no matter what I say, Lucy gets all huffy and says she doesn't want to talk about her. She acts as if I never talked about anything else.

I bet Ernessa hasn't had her period yet and the whole thing grosses her out, like eating and "becoming a woman," as they say in health class. She barely has any tits anyway. She's even more flat-chested than Lucy, who basically has little bumps with swollen nipples. Even Charley is more developed than Ernessa, and I know she has her period.

I got my period for the first time a few months after I came here. I had just turned fourteen. I didn't tell my mother until I came home for spring break.

"I was afraid you weren't going to get your period because you were so traumatized by everything that's happened in the last year," said my mother. "How do you feel?"

I didn't answer her.

"Grown up?" she asked.

"Daddy only knew me as a girl," I said. "He wouldn't recognize me."

"Don't talk like that," said my mother.

"Are you the only one who can talk like that?" I asked.

She went into her studio, closed the door, and wouldn't talk to me for the rest of the day. I don't know why I had to hurt her. I've always been so careful not to talk about Daddy.

I actually don't mind that I have breasts and pubic hair and my period. It doesn't mean that I'm a woman. It means I'm just like the other girls. I understand Sofia. Sometimes when I have my period, I bleed so much that I can't believe there's any blood left to circulate through my body. It's violent. My body is still revolting against this.

November 17
She's insinuated herself into this journal the way she's insinuated herself into Lucy's life. I can't stop it. It's not supposed to be about her. It's supposed to be about school, my friends, my teachers, my books.

She was waiting for me. I had come through the doorway on the ground floor of the Residence this morning, when I heard the sound of someone playing the piano. I looked down the long hallway, and the doors to all the practice rooms were shut. The music was coming from the room I always use. That's the best piano, and I'm used to it. It's mine. Then I realized that the person was playing my Mozart sonata, in F, the one I worked on last year. I struggled so much with the allegro. I've only been happy with the way I've played it a few times, and I played it for almost a year. It's partly the piano. I always play better at home. But the piano wasn't causing any trouble this time. She was playing the allegro so precisely that it sounded like a military march. She never faltered; each note was perfect. I waited until she finished playing the first movement.

When I pushed open the door to the room, she barely acknowledged my presence. There was no music on the stand. I thought I was going to cry. It was a huge joke on me.

"I didn't know you played the piano," I said. I forced myself not to run away, to pretend that what was happening was perfectly normal.

"I hardly ever play anymore," she said.

"But you play incredibly well."

"My father was a musician," she said. "I inherited everything from him. Just as you did from your father."

"I didn't inherit anything from my father," I said.

I had the feeling that Ernessa didn't want me to go. She wanted to talk to me some more. About our fathers. She wanted me to stay. I closed the door on her and ran away. She started to play the adagio as soon as I left the room. I didn't want to hear her play it. The music followed me down the hallway. She was playing lightly, clearly, exactly the way Miss Simpson tells me to. The allegro has too much momentum. Once I start, it carries me breathlessly to the end. I don't understand anything about it except its motion. I don't know where it's going. The adagio is different. I place my hands on the keys, and the music rises out of them and guides my fingers. It's beckoning me on to a hidden place. I'm walking through the woods, and in the distance I can see an open meadow where the sun pours down on the tall grasses. I move toward it, pause, turn around to see where I've come from, continue down the path, start to skip along. The light draws me on.

It's impossible for that crummy old piano to sound like that. Maybe I continued to play the sonata in my head as I walked away. I'll never be able to play Mozart like that if I practice until I die.

Why does she want to take everything away from me?

November 18

What's really real about people? Is there a kernel of "realness" that remains no matter what? Someone like Claire is totally fake. She pretends to be liberated and smokes pot all the time, but she's going to become just like her mother—with a husband, kids, two cars, a nice suburban house, TV and stereo, etc., etc. She can't escape it. She's the kind of person who will laugh at the pictures of herself as a schoolgirl because she won't recognize the person staring back at her. (An image of the wrong moment?) But you can be fake on a deeper level than that, where everything about you can change from one minute to the next. Like an onion, you peel away layer after layer until nothing is left. Maybe it's not even your fault.

When Annie Patterson stopped eating, she became a totally new person. There was a just enough left of her old self that each time you looked at her, you noticed how different she was. It wasn't just her looks. She herself changed. She became frightened. She was hunched over. She looked smaller, like an injured bird. There's nothing more pathetic than a bird lying on the ground, flapping its wings, without any hope of lifting itself into the air. By the time she left school, she could barely hold her arms up. She spoke in a whisper. Before she had always seemed so big and happy, but there was an incredibly sad person inside. Which one was real? Even when I feel sad, I never feel as if the sadness has taken over everything. There is always a tiny part of me that's untouched, that I can return to.

My father loved to read me fairy tales about people turning into trees and lions and birds and caterpillars, about people coming back from the dead. People never grew old when they were under a spell, so if the prince was happy being a tree, he could live that way forever. When I was little, I didn't like to hear these stories, even though the prince always turned back into a prince, found his princess, became a king, and lived happily ever after. I would yell at my father to stop reading and pull the covers over my head. He always laughed at me and kept right on reading.

■

November 20

I have been really good about not talking about Ernessa and trying to ignore her, but I can't escape her.

This morning after practicing the piano, I went to lunch the back way by Miss Rood's apartment. I didn't notice Ernessa until she was right next to me. I'm sure she should have been in class. She's never in school at the right time, and no one but me seems to notice. I don't understand how she gets away with it, day after day. She always has an excuse.

Pater ran up to the glass door of the apartment and began hurling himself against it and barking like mad. Sometimes he does that when I walk by, but today he was totally crazed. We both looked through the glass doors, hung with long velvet curtains tied back with thick cords, down the dim hallway at the heavy, dark furniture and the crimson-patterned rug. Then we looked at each other and began to laugh. Neither of us could help it.

"That dog is nuts," I said, surprised to find myself laughing with Ernessa. "He's going to smash through the glass."

"I hate that yapping," she said. "The sound drives me crazy. I really can't bear it." She wasn't exactly talking to me.

There was a light behind us, and our faces were reflected in the glass, floating above the yapping dog, whose brown fur reminds me of Miss Rood's hair. For the first time, I realized, with a shock, how much we resemble each other. I guess that's not so surprising. We're both Eastern European Jews, the only two real Jews in the class. (Dora doesn't count.) We have curly black hair, large noses, dark dark eyes. I've never really thought about whether or not I'm pretty because the boys at the tea dances are never interested in me. I always have to be "fixed up" with a date. They think Lucy is pretty. But you can't forget Ernessa's face. The other girls look washed out when they are around her. Even Lucy.

Now I understand why Betsy thought that Ernessa and I would hit it off together. She made that comment the first week of school. We were the same type. I thought she said that because Ernessa is smart. She meant Jewish, as in you're the same type of creature from another planet. That's the kind of thing a day student would say, which is why I have nothing to do with any of them. Actually, the day students are much worse than the boarders. They like to make jokes about Jews. Why do Jews have such big noses? The air's free. Why did the Jews wander in the desert for forty years? Someone dropped a quarter. Then they pretend to be embarrassed when they see me staring at them. I'm not afraid to stare at them. They're too stupid to know what they're saying; they're just copying their parents. They nudge each other and giggle together. They try to be cute. I hate that word. Cute. It's so insipid. In the end, they get annoyed when I won't stop staring at them. I have no right to stare. "Take a picture. It'll last longer."

I never heard an anti-Semitic remark until I came to this school. In almost two years, Miss Rood has never spoken a word to me. I've never sat at her table for dinner, but I've been at every other table. I'm the smartest girl in my class, but she never asks me what college I want to go to. She tolerates me. I suppose my mother would have sent me to another school if I'd asked her to. But after I became friends with Lucy, I stayed.

It's been my fault all along with Ernessa because I was jealous of her and Lucy. Maybe we could have gotten along from the beginning. Maybe we are the same "type."

November 21

My father was sitting on my bed. He was reading me a story. I was lying on my side, following the words on the page. The book was thick, with the title in gold and black letters on a silky turquoise cover. The pages were so thin that the type came through on the other side. It was my father's book from when he was a little boy.

"Once upon a time a poor Servant Girl was traveling with her boxes through a wood, and just as she got to the middle of it she found herself in the power of a murdering band of robbers. . . ."

"Why did they rob a poor servant girl?" I asked my father. "She probably had nothing to give them."

My father didn't answer. He kept on reading. "'What shall I do now, a poor servant girl like me; I can't find my way out of the wood; nobody lives here, and I must perish with hunger.'"

"How did she get lost? She knew where she was going before the robbers came. Don't read anymore if it's going to be like this. I don't want to hear this story."

My father was not reading the words in the book. Or I could see through the page and couldn't tell which side he was reading. The story went on. The servant girl, in despair, placed herself in God's hands. At that very moment, a white pigeon flew by and saved her. With a magic key, he gave her food, clothes, a place to sleep. The little servant girl lived happily in the forest. Then one day the white pigeon asked her for a favor. Would she go to a little cottage and steal a gold ring away from an old woman? "With all my heart," she answered. The girl went straight away to the cottage, but before she had a chance to steal the gold ring, the old woman ran out the door with a birdcage in her hand. The girl ran after the old woman. You could see the gold ring in the beak of a green bird. The bird was holding on to it, very tightly. You ran for a long time after the old woman. You couldn't catch her even though you were young and strong and the woman was old and bent. No matter how hard you pushed yourself, the old woman always managed to remain a few steps ahead of you, taunting you with the caged bird. You moved your legs up and down, but you didn't go forward. Finally, you caught up to the old woman, you reached out your hand and touched the bars of the cage, but the old woman ran around a bend in the path and disappeared from sight.

"That's not the way the story ends," I shouted at my father. "I know how it's supposed to go. The servant girl gets the gold ring. She saves the prince, who had been turned into a tree by an evil witch. Every day he became a white pigeon for a few hours. As long as the witch had the ring, he couldn't turn back into a man. All his servants and horses had also been turned into trees. The servant girl freed the whole forest. And she married the prince and became a princess. It always ends that way."

My father kept on reading the story, while I shouted at him. "And in the end," he read, "you were lost in the forest. You sank back against the trunk of a tree, placing yourself in God's hands, determined to remain there whatever happened."

■
November 23

My journal is being ruined by lies. I should go back and cross out everything I wrote about Ernessa last Friday.

After school, Dora, Charley, and I went over to the coffee shop at Brangwyn College. I love to go there. We drink coffee, smoke cigarettes, and sit around pretending to be college students. Only we're wearing uniforms. Charley always wears her gym tunic, which makes her look like she's about twelve years old. Dora rolls up the top of her gray skirt, which she wears practically all year round, and pulls on black tights underneath and a black sweater on top. She changes from her saddle shoes into little black boots. She puts gold hoops in her ears and a little pink lipstick on her mouth. When she comes out of the bathroom, she looks like she belongs there. The uniform is completely hidden. If someone from school found us, she'd get into trouble for being out of uniform, for wearing makeup, for her gold hoops. It wouldn't really matter, because we'd all get into so much more trouble for smoking outside of school. They let us smoke in the Playroom but not outside school. It's totally hypocritical. They realize they can't stop the boarders from smoking if we have our parents' permission, but they want us to appear to be proper young ladies when we leave the school grounds. Proper young ladies who think about nothing except sex, drugs, and cigarettes.

For some reason, no one has figured out that we come here.

Dora discovered it, of course. She likes to sit with her coffee and a cigarette and read philosophy. She's so fake. When Dora first got her wire-rimmed glasses, I was convinced she was only wearing them to look like an intellectual. I was surprised to find out that they have real lenses in them. Sofia has a pair of glasses that basically have plain glass in them, and she's always forgetting to wear them. She never remembers her glasses and her copy of *The Stranger* at the same time, but that's all right because she isn't really reading it. I have to admit that Dora is beautiful. She has long, thick, brownish-red hair like the mane of a horse and dark green eyes. But when she puts on her glasses, she looks forty years old. It's all a pose. Like being crazy. Her father's a shrink, so he assumes everyone is crazy. He encourages her fakeness. She's been seeing a shrink since she was ten years old. She wouldn't like it so much if she were really crazy.

Dora wants to be friends with me because my father was so crazy that he killed himself. I should tell her that he was perfectly sane when he decided on the razor. She once told me that all great artists went mad or killed themselves, or both, in the end.

"It's nothing to be ashamed of," she said. "Shelley swam the Hellespont and drowned. Keats basically committed suicide by nursing his brother who was sick with TB. Kleist, Trakl, Walser, Hölderlin . . . Ever heard of them?"

I covered my ears.

Before we left school, I told Dora and Charley that we should ask Lucy and Ernessa to come with us. (It feels wrong, putting those two names together, but everyone does it now. It makes no difference that we picked a suite together with my number. I could have gotten one of the best single rooms, like Ernessa's. I've allowed this to happen. I never even tried to stop it. Just as I never tried to stop my father.) We couldn't find them, and of course after we'd been there for half an hour, they came in together. Ernessa didn't even look in our direction. Lucy smiled at us, feebly. She was too afraid to come near us, her so-called friends. She followed Ernessa like a sheep to a table on the other side of the room. She walked with her shoulders hunched over. Her skirt hung like a sack. Her hair was matted and uncombed. It always used to be perfect. All of a sudden, she doesn't care how she looks. She looked like a stranger. And she always used to seem so familiar.

They sat down together. I heard Lucy order a coffee, and they both lit up. When the coffee came, Lucy wrapped her hands around the mug as if she were trying to get warm. It's not that cold outside. Their cigarettes rested in the black plastic ashtray in the middle of the table. They leaned together as if they were in the middle of an intense conversation, and the smoke rising from the ashtray wreathed their heads. This is exactly the way I imagine the college students who come here in the evenings with their boyfriends. I felt sick, but I couldn't look away from the two of them.

Ernessa was changed too. All her features were exaggerated and crude. How could I have ever imagined that she and I look alike? Her eyebrows were so thick that they almost met in the center of her forehead. Her upper lip was pulled forward. It couldn't quite reach over her teeth, which were much larger than I remembered. They were smoker's teeth, crooked and yellow.

I started to talk, to fill the silence, without thinking about what I was saying.

"Look at Ernessa. I can't believe I thought she was so beautiful. She looks like an animal. There's something wrong with her."

"Maybe she has hair on her palms," said Charley. "I'll go check."

"Shut up," I said. Charley is perfectly capable of doing that. Then Lucy would never speak to me again. "Don't you think her interest in Lucy is . . . sort of not normal?"

"I can dig that," said Charley. "Maybe she's a dyke. It wouldn't exactly be a first for the school. Look at all those fucking gym teachers with their plaid kilts and their short hair. Like can you visualize Miss Bobbie getting it on with—"

"I don't think Lucy goes in for that kind of thing," said Dora. "She's too much of a daddy's girl. She likes boys."

"Not Lucy, you idiot, Ernessa," I said. "She's pursuing her, the way a boy would. She's so nice to her, and she's such a bitch to everyone else."

This gave Dora a chance to play professor. "I admit she does have an inordinate fascination with Lucy who is, well, we all know, very sweet and pretty, but not terribly compelling. Let's face it. Lucy is . . . an airhead, and really, when you look at her carefully, she's predictably pretty. All that straight blond hair that Daddy won't let her cut. Please. I thought Ernessa was more interested in discussing philosophy, but I doubt she's doing much of that with Lucy. So it must be the sweet and pretty that appeals to her. Lucy is her image of what Kant calls the 'sublime.' We all have one." She looked at me.

I knew in that moment that they had been talking about Lucy and me behind my back. They couldn't possibly understand.

"I adored my father," I said.

I don't know why those words came out. I had never admitted that to anyone before, and now everyone would know.

I ran out of the coffee shop without bothering to put my jacket on. I didn't want anyone to see me crying. Especially Lucy and Ernessa. The others thought I was upset about my father. But he wasn't in my mind at all. I was furious at Dora for insulting Lucy.

■

November 24
I know the others don't like it when I bring up Lucy, but I can't help it. It doesn't bother them that the names Ernessa and Lucy have become one word in their minds when they don't even belong together. The only thing that bothers them is that I'm always trying to pry these names apart.

Just saying her name makes me feel better. It brings her closer to me. I have her, if only for the few seconds while the sounds are on my tongue. I can see that everyone is getting annoyed at me, but I keep on talking. They look away and stop listening to what I'm saying. Suddenly they take great interest in the bowl of oatmeal on the table in front of them. They go to get some more coffee. When they turn away, I lose her. Of course she isn't at breakfast anymore. Someone always signs her in. She never asks me to.

I know exactly how ordinary she really is. But if I had the chance, I would talk about her endlessly.

■

November 25
I am home. My mother came to get me for Thanksgiving vacation. I couldn't stand to be there any longer, with the doors to the bathroom always closed now and us hardly speaking to one another. Each avoids the other.

I was downstairs, sitting in the window seat, watching each car that passed. Of course, my mother was late, and Lucy was the first to be picked up. At least she came over and said good-bye to me. I was afraid she was going to leave without a word, and I was going to have to spend the entire Thanksgiving vacation thinking about that. Pretty soon everyone else had left, and I was all alone. I had a book open on my lap. I kept reading the same words over and over again, even though they made no sense to me: "to him that anguish came through Love, to which it is in a sense predestined, by which it must be equipped and adapted."

Ernessa was reading the words on the page over my shoulder. I sensed her there, but I didn't turn my head. I recognized her breathing before she spoke.

"That's one of my favorite books too," she said. "Proust. I read him a long time ago. In French. But I've never forgotten it. I envy you starting it. Starting is so much better than remembering."

How long ago could she have read it? She's only sixteen, seventeen at the most. I hate it when we share anything. And of course she read it in French. My mother drove up then. I grabbed my bag and ran outside to the car.

Ernessa followed me out the door. She was wearing a black coat with a velvet collar and a beret on her head. I don't think I could wear such sophisticated clothes. I'd feel too awkward. Somehow Ernessa manages to look like a very chic woman and a little girl at the same time. Her coat was beautiful. I wish I had one like it. I'm wearing my mother's old ski jacket instead. She says we don't have any money to buy clothes right now because she hasn't had a show in ages.

As we drove off, I turned around and saw Ernessa getting into a green car with a man, a handsome man with dark hair. He was about my mother's age. Her father is dead, so who is this man?

Once I answered the phone on the corridor, and a man with a heavy accent asked to speak to Miss Ernessa Bloch. I knocked on her door and called her. She rushed past me to get to the phone, almost knocking me over. I passed by her again on my way to Sofia's room, and she was speaking very excitedly in a language that I didn't recognize. Some words sounded a bit like French, but I couldn't understand a word.

Another time, I heard her speaking on the phone in English. I just caught the end of the conversation before she hung up the phone. She was saying, "I think that will be quite convenient. . . . Good day to you." She sounded like a character in a novel.

■
November 27

Late at night

I know the smell that seeps under her door like dirty water and runs into the corridor. It's the smell that came from Milou when he was dying: a rotten smell that mingled with the overly sweet perfume of the blue hyacinths that my mother was growing in the kitchen. The two smells became inseparable.

My mother said that his body was already beginning to decay, even though he hadn't died yet. His eyes were rheumy, and the lids stuck together. Dried blood and brown mucous dribbled from his mouth and clung to his whiskers. My mother wiped his face with a damp cloth and held him like a baby. She kissed his putrid face and whispered in his ear and cried. I gagged whenever I came near him.

Milou finally died in my mother's arms. We wrapped him in a white sheet and buried him on a warm winter day when the ground was soft. He was underground, but his smell saturated the room. Whenever I came into the kitchen, I looked over at the corner where he had died, expecting to see him. The hyacinth flowers dried up. Their perfume faded, but his smell was still there, hovering like a spirit above the spot. He wasn't completely dead while his smell remained.

■
November 28

At night I wake up with a start and can't get back to sleep. I lie very still while the emptiness absorbs me. My mother sleeps and sleeps. I don't dare disturb her. She sleeps all day and all night. As I sleep less, she sleeps more. She's stealing my sleep from me.

After my father died, I came to Brangwyn.

The first night at school, my eyes opened in the middle of the night. I was lying on a narrow white metal bed, in a cage. My mother wasn't asleep in the room next to mine. If I pressed my ear to the wall, I could hear the regular breathing of a stranger. My loneliness was complete. But when I raised my head off the pillow, I saw a sliver of yellow light under the door. Out in the hallway, the long expanse of speckled black linoleum was as cold as ice. At one end was the bathroom with its tall white stalls. That was permitted. At the other end, Mrs. McCallum stood guard. Her wrinkled head with its doglike face would pop out of her doorway if I rustled my sheets. Like a troll, she barred my escape down the stairs. I didn't know the password. She would never let me by.

Inside my room, with the door closed tight, I was safe. The line of light under my door comforted me. I closed my eyes and fell asleep at once.

■

November 29

I'm the first person back. I asked my mother to bring me early. I said I had a paper due tomorrow and needed to use some books at school. Four days with her were more than I could take. Something has happened to her since I left for school. Now I know why she never calls me. She's started spending all her time in the studio. She even sleeps on a cot in there. But she won't let me in the room. I used to sit with her while she worked. I made her tea, cleaned her brushes, helped her stretch canvases. We would chat about nothing for hours while she painted. I spent most of this weekend sitting on the sofa reading Proust. The only time my mother left her studio, which she locked behind her, was to go to Thanksgiving dinner at my aunt's house. She says that she's finally able to express her grief at what my father did, and she doesn't want anyone to see it yet. It's still too raw. Maybe she'll never show it to anyone. She's very protective of that grief.

When I decided to stay at school, I had my mother pack up all my books and ship them to me. She didn't want to, but I made her. Even the children's books that I had read to death and were falling apart and covered with crayon marks. My room at home feels so empty and cold without the books. It's not my room anymore. I hate being there.

All weekend, she kept playing the same music, over and over again. The record would finish, and she would just lift up the needle and put it back at the beginning. It drove me crazy. I anticipated where it would skip and she would have to go over and adjust it. I had to leave the house and go for a walk. Finally at breakfast on Saturday I got fed up, and I asked her why she kept playing the same record.

She told me it was Mahler's Fifth, and my father played it incessantly before everything happened.

"I'm trying to understand exactly how he felt," she said. "This music fed what ate him up, made it hungrier. I hate this music. But I think it also gave him strength to write, so I have to listen."

I try not to get upset around her, but I started to cry.

"Don't be sad," she said. "I'm not sad anymore. That would be self-ish. He was utterly unhappy alive. Every morning he opened his eyes so slowly, and he gazed around the room reluctantly. He was shocked to discover that he was still breathing. I used to think that it was because of me that he left. I blamed myself for it, and for the pain that it caused you. But now I understand that he was just taking the first step away. That's what Mahler has taught me. He had to break with us first, the two people who bound him to this Earth. He had to go off with another woman. It didn't matter who. Anyone would do. And she knew it. He was trying to make us hate him. He was betraying us in a little way so that we could accept the ultimate betrayal. After he left, he kept listening to Mahler's Fifth; that's what she told me. Incessantly was the word she used. It drove her crazy. She gave me back his record afterward. And now I finally understand everything. I understand how stupid I was not to understand what was happening right in front of me. That was because I was only thinking about myself. I wasn't thinking about him. About his suffering."

That's *her* theory.

I have *my* theory. He was so unhappy that he couldn't feel anything. He hated life. He couldn't remember what love was. It was all the same to him.

I remember once going to talk to my father in his study. He was sitting at his desk. There wasn't even an open notebook or a book in front of him. He was looking at his books — the shelves with books stuck in sideways and the piles all over the floor. He spoke in his deep poetry-reading voice: "I used to say, 'Books, my food.' But now all my food has been poisoned." I laughed at his joke. But it wasn't a joke.

Last summer at the beach, I thought my mother was getting better, but now I realize how wrong I was. She wants to nurture her grief, until it can live by itself. That's her child now. I'm just in the way.

School, books, Lucy. I'm going to see if anyone else is back.

No one. They all want to stay away until the last possible moment. It's so quiet here, quieter than it is in the middle of the night. Then I imagine everyone in bed, breathing, dreaming, turning over. Even Mrs. Halton is gone. Time has been put to sleep.

Do ghosts have to be frightening? Maybe they are comforting, like the touch of a familiar hand.

The last time I saw my father alive, we went for a walk together in the Botanic Garden. We loved to walk there, our arms linked, wrapped in silence. The air was misty, and I was shivering. All the leaves had fallen from the trees. The trunks were dark with the wet. "At one time I liked to come here in the spring," said my father, "when it was all colors and perfumes. Impressions. But now I like this time of year best. Between fall and winter, when everything appears without a show. As it is. It's harder to identify trees from their bark and buds and shape, but it's essential."

I need to ask him: Are people like trees? Is there a season when we can see them as they really are?

"The Man Whom the Trees Loved": He understood the trees, their need to be protected, especially in the winter when no one else cared about them. The trees loved him in return with a love that was so strong that it consumed him.

November 30

Pater is dead!

By the middle of the morning, everyone in school knew about it. He was found on the Upper Field on Sunday morning with his throat cut open. That's a pretty horrible way to get rid of a dog. Actually it was worse. Betsy said his head was almost completely off and he had been opened up like a fish.

I knew exactly what he looked like when they found him. His grizzled rusty hair was matted with hard clumps of dark blood. The little legs stuck out behind him, so stiff they didn't touch the ground. Black flies clung to his eyes and his mouth, feeding at the moist openings.

Miss Rood didn't mention it during assembly, but under her thick pink glasses, her nose was red. It was obvious something was wrong. She's never like that. She's never even sick. At least she has feelings. (I once heard a rumor that she was engaged to someone who died during the war. World War I?) I felt sorry for her.

All the students were away from school last weekend. Local kids are always sneaking onto the grounds, trying to trash the "snob school." No one suspects any of us.

Pater never runs free.

I know it was Ernessa. All of me knows it. I remember how our reflections floated on the glass, how the dog disappeared behind them, except for the crazy barking. She's the one who couldn't bear the sound of it, just as she couldn't bear the smell of the funeral parlor where her father lay in a coffin. Or so she claims. Pater was just an annoying little dog, but she hated him as if that yapping was meant for her ears alone, a special torture just for her. I can't understand hatred like that. At lunch, I told Dora and Charley what Ernessa said to me that day in front of Miss Rood's apartment and how she's always suddenly appearing where she shouldn't be. They were both seriously creeped out.

I said, "My father would say: 'Ernessa's not following you. Perhaps you're following her but at a great distance.'"

They were pondering that when Lucy walked up with her tray.

Lunch is the only time she spends with us now. She skips breakfast. Sometimes she'll rush in at the last minute while they're clearing away the food and drink a cup of black coffee by herself. She claims she wants to lose some weight, even though she's already skinny. "My pot belly," she said when we all objected. I remember how annoyed she got when I went on my diet last year. But that was when we had tea together in the afternoon on weekends. Now I hardly ever see her on the weekends. Even when she's just doing homework in her room, she keeps all the doors closed.

We all stopped talking at once. She sat down a little ways away. After a bit she said, "What's the matter? Am I interrupting some private discussion or something?" She sounded sad.

"Oh, no, not at all," I answered. But she was interrupting something. We turned to our food, which had gotten cold, and ate pretty much in silence. Now finally I'm not alone with my suspicions of Ernessa. We don't know yet what she is.

Lucy's across the hall with Ernessa most of the time. But she might as well be on the other side of the world.

DECEMBER

December 1

Today they put up sign-up sheets for tryouts for the basketball teams.
I almost didn't sign up. I don't have the energy to try out again, just
to end up on D squad again with all the klutzes who don't even care
about playing. And Miss Bobbie always coaches D squad. It never
makes any difference how well I play. Even though I score most of
the baskets, I always stay at the bottom. I didn't see Lucy's name on
the list when I signed up. Last year she was on B squad, even though
she isn't any better than I am, and she has a good chance of making
JV this year. It's harder to make A squad in basketball because the
teams have fewer players. I'm going to ask her after dinner.

After dinner

Lucy said she's not trying out this year. It takes too much time, with
all the practices and games. She's tired as it is. And she's behind in all

her classes. I asked her what she's taking instead. Calisthenics. That's for the girls who don't want to do anything but have to pretend that they are taking gym. I don't believe a thing she says. She's always behind. Lucy loves to play sports. I'm sure she's just doing calisthenics to be with Ernessa. They've become inseparable. Lucy doesn't care about any of the things she used to care about. Ernessa's taken her over. She's consuming her.

December 2

I'm thinking of changing my mind about basketball tryouts. Not calisthenics. I'd never do that—jumping jacks and lying on your back with your feet in the air. They may offer modern dance with Mrs. Harlan if they get enough girls. She's the only gym teacher who's not a mannish-looking jock, even though she wears a kilt like the rest of them. She's married. And she's very nice to me. When I got caught by Miss Bobbie for not wearing a shirt under my sweater, Mrs. Harlan stopped me in the hall and said, "If you don't want to get into trouble and end up in study hall every Friday afternoon, you should just follow the rules. It's not that hard to wear the regulation shirt."

I hate being around Miss Bobbie. This year I hate her more than ever. And she hates me because I'm a Jew. That's all. At least I have a reason to hate her. I can't stand to look at the dimpled brown knees and puckered thighs beneath her kilt, the sagging skin under the short white hair.

Today in basketball tryouts (what a joke) she came up to me and asked where my friend Lucy was. "She had a good shot at JV this year," she said.

"She doesn't have time for the team," I answered. "She's not doing well enough in school."

"I'll have to have a talk with her."

I'm definitely going to take modern dance if they offer it. I think I can get Dora and Charley to do it with me. Certainly Dora.

*

"The Jews' Beech Tree": "The Hebrew characters on the tree read: 'If you approach this place, you will suffer what you inflicted on me.'"

December 3

It's early for snow. When I looked out the window this morning, everything was white. It didn't snow much, just enough to cover everything. It's cold out, and the snow isn't melting.

I guess it's time to pull out the winter skirt. I can't put it off any longer. Is there anything duller than gray wool?

December 4

Last night Charley, Dora, and I snuck out after lights out. I haven't done that since my first year, when I used to go out at night with Autumn and drink from little bottles of airline liquor that she stole from her mother. That year I didn't care what happened to me. I went out with Autumn, and I was never scared. I don't have anything to do with her now. I haven't spoken to her in over a year. I've done very well in school, and I don't want to mess everything up by being kicked out. I don't want to be the way I used to be. It was too sad.

About twelve o'clock, Charley came into my room to tell me that Ernessa was not in her room. "I've knocked on her door, and unless she's sleeping the sleep of the dead, she's not in there. I tried to open the door, but it was locked. I don't know where she got a key. Let's check for Lucy."

I was already over by the bathroom, turning the doorknob. I pushed open the door to her room silently, then looked in. That empty bed with the covers thrown back would make me so unhappy. But she was sound asleep in her bed and didn't wake up.

"Somehow I don't think Ernessa's over at Brangwyn College meeting a boy," said Charley. "She's not the type. And besides it's too cold out."

"Let's get Dora," I said.

"Let's go out and look for Ernessa," said Charley. "I'm in the mood to get high."

We went out in our nightgowns, with coats over them. I don't know what we were expecting to find. It's easy to rig the alarm with a piece of wood and to jam the wood between the doors to keep them from locking. Not much of an alarm system. Everyone knows where the piece of wood is hidden.

We walked along the drive, up to the tall iron gates. The gates are always left wide open, even in the middle of the night. Dora and Charley kept turning around, as if they heard footsteps following us. When we reached the gates, I looked back at the Residence. During the day, the drive is always lined with the day students' cars, mostly yellow and green VWs. It was practically empty. The snow made everything so still.

I knew at once why Ernessa was out here, walking by herself in the night. She wanted to see the Residence and the Upper Field and the drive as they were before they became a school for young ladies, when guests took tea on the wide porches and rode in pony carts. It's what I always think about. Not what it is, but what it was. Somewhere out there, she was looking at the porches and imagining.

I didn't say anything to Dora and Charley. I followed them through the iron gates even though I wanted to turn back. They wouldn't have understood why I wanted to stay inside those gates. When I'm at school, I forget that the world exists. I don't have to believe it's real. Everything outside the gates is shrouded in mist. I can see the outlines, but there's nothing of substance there.

The night was clear. There were only a few ragged clouds that shone silver in the moon's light. The moon was high in the sky and so bright it was almost pure white. All the craters and mountains on its surface were so sharp that they seemed drawn by hand. Just on the other side of the iron fence was the Residence with its spires reaching toward that moon, a night cathedral. Do I really live there and go to school there? Is it just a dream?

We didn't get far. We stood right outside the front gate. It was very cold, and we had to stamp our feet to keep them from becoming numb. The frozen grass coated with snow crunched with each foot-step. We weren't out there for more than ten minutes, standing by the corner on the wide avenue. Occasional headlights rushed by. I wonder what the drivers thought of us: three girls out in the middle of a winter night, wearing coats over their white nightgowns. Maybe we looked like spirits to them.

We decided to go back. As we went down the drive, I looked over the shimmering field toward the edge where there are masses of bushes, where Pater died. That's where it would be—a long black animal, huge wings that push against the air, a dark streak on the frozen ground. It would show up so clearly in the moonlight against the snow, if I waited. The others ran to the door. They called out to me to hurry up. Yet each time I turned to go inside, I thought I saw something. I needed to study the dark, until it took shape and revealed itself. Finally the moonlight was clouded with ashes, a spot of gray in my vision. It was nothing. That only happens in books.

Charley held the door open for me. "Jesus, what took you so long?" she shouted. "I'm freezing my fucking butt off, and it smells like dead fish here."

"Shut up," I answered.

There was the horrible smell, worse than ever. Tomorrow I'm going to ask the janitor first thing to do something about the base-ment. I'll never be able to practice. The smell clings to everything.

We raced up the stairs, and on the first landing I thought I heard a thumping sound below us.

When we got to our corridor, Dora and I went straight to our rooms, but Charley stopped at Ernessa's door and started banging on it and yelling so loudly that I thought she would wake up everyone. "Hey, Ernessa, where the fuck are you? It's the middle of the night."

"Stop it!" I hissed at her. "You're crazy!"

But she kept on banging. "You out copping a lid somewhere? You'll have to share."

There was no response.

"You asshole," I said to Charley. "You're going to get us all caught."

"You ballin' at Brangwyn College?"

I grabbed Charley's arm and pulled her toward her room.

"See," said Charley. "I told you she's not in there."

I heard noise from Lucy's room, and the door to her room opened, but by then I had closed the door to my room, and I was leaning against it. My heart was pounding so hard. I hope Charley keeps her mouth shut about our nighttime adventure.

December 6

Charley has become extremely spooked out by Ernessa, but she doesn't understand why. She's not ready to hear it. She doesn't understand that the truth is what you can't see but are certain of anyway. We've decided not to tell anyone else that she was gone from her room in the middle of the night. I do feel better having someone to talk to about this who doesn't look at me as if I'm a raving lunatic. At the same time, I'm nervous that Charley will open her big mouth and say something stupid by mistake. She'll end up turning Lucy totally against me.

December 7

I'd had an idea in my head all day, but I wasn't sure if I was going to do it until I did it. I couldn't tell Charley. I don't trust her.

Just a little after lights out, I ran across the corridor to Dora's room. I wanted to go along the gutter from Dora's room and look in Ernessa's window. The idea of spying on her frightened me. I didn't know what I would do if she were in her room and saw me. I could pretend that I was going down to Carol's room, which is next to hers, but I knew she would know better.

Dora watched the hallway while I pushed open the window and climbed out onto the gutter. I was wearing a nightgown, and it kept riding up past my knees as I crawled toward her window. The copper gutter was cold and slick. My hands were so stiff that I couldn't hold on to the edge. It was only a few feet, but I moved inch by inch, and Dora kept calling, "Hurry up," from her window. I was too scared to turn around and tell her to shut up. I could feel the moon behind me. Her room was visible through the gauzy curtains. The empty bed was made. It was as bare as in the beginning of the fall, when Dora and I watched her move her dresser across the room by herself, when she was being sort of friendly with us. The dresser was still there, practically blocking the doorway.

I crouched down on the gutter and pressed my head against the glass, to keep my balance. The moonlight streamed into the room in a thick beam. My shadow fell across the floor, and all around the shadow, inside the beam, millions of particles of dust were floating in the air. A breeze blew into the room, even though the window was closed tight. Now I could see that everything in the room—the desk, the dresser, the floor, even the bed—was covered with a thick layer of dust. The breeze swept the dust up into the moon's light. Suddenly, there was so much dust swirling through the room that it was hard to tell where the edges of solid things ended and where the air began. I heard Dora's voice calling me from her window, "Quick, come back. Someone's out in the corridor."

I couldn't turn away. My forehead was stuck to the frozen glass; it soothed my burning face. The gutter felt much too narrow. If I tried to turn around and crawl along it, I would lose my balance and fall back into nothingness. Inside the room, millions of particles of dust were gathering, forming themselves. A swarm of small brown moths flew toward the window, toward the light of the huge moon. They banged against the glass in front of my face, thumping their little bodies, trying to reach the light. The noise they made was deafening. I could feel the beating of their wings through the glass, like breath from a thousand mouths. If I turned around to look at the moon, I would feel that same longing for the light. I would fly toward it. I could hear the moon whisper from far away, calling every creature with wings.

"You've got to come *now*," called Dora.

This time her voice was in my ear, and she was tugging on my nightgown. She was out on the gutter, too, and I thought I might take her with me. I pushed my nightgown up around my waist. The burning cold of the metal against my skin no longer mattered. Somehow we managed to make it back. When I reached Dora's window, I followed her in headfirst. We hid together under the covers, listening to the shuffling footsteps outside her door.

I had to tell her what I'd seen. That Ernessa was not in her room, again, that the bed was never slept in, that the room was empty and covered with dust like thick gray soot. I didn't tell her about the moths and the wings and the moon.

I opened the door cautiously and ran across the corridor to my room. I was so relieved to be back in my own bed. I lay there, listening to my pounding heart. It was so loud I was sure the sound was echoing along the empty corridors and down the stairs. I finally calmed down and fell asleep. I dreamed I was playing basketball on B squad. In the dream, everything was exactly as it is in real life but exaggerated, like a very bright and loud movie. I woke up with the feeling that I had played basketball all night.

I keep looking around to assure myself that this time I really am awake.

■
December 8

If I ask Dora, she'll tell me that I went out on the gutter last night, that the moonlight fell on my back while my forehead was glued to Ernessa's window. But what I saw wasn't real. And I know it wasn't a dream.

Dull brown dust moths swirling in the beam of light and thumping against the glass. They're swarming around my brain, fluttering wings, crowding out everything else, banging against the inside of my head.

I need to write and distract myself.

During the summer, my father and I used to sit outside at night, with flashlights on our laps, and search for moths. Some had dark bands across their wings and deep blue eyes in yellow circles. In spite of their shyness, they would show themselves in our narrow beams of light. One night, in a tangle of wild honeysuckle that grew over the fence and buried us in its scent, we saw a pale green moth with two long tails that fluttered like ribbons in a little girl's hair. The luna moth was as large as a bird. The yellow eyes on its wings gleamed in the light. We were excited for hours after the moth had flown away, and we kept turning our flashlights back to the spot where it had been. While we waited for it to return, we played a game: describing the color of the moth. A poet's game. My favorite was the color of sea foam on a gray day, seen from underwater. The color of wet rock lichen. The color of white dogwood flowers, just as they are unfolding from the buds. The color of the moon as you approach it in a spaceship. The color of a comet's tail.

Finally, we went to bed, but I couldn't sleep. I listened to the whirring wings and insect bodies banging against the screen. Every sound outside was the green luna, trying to get into my room to show itself to me one more time.

Why wasn't that enough for my father? He only had to remember the delicate creature, flitting through the white honeysuckle on wings of sea foam. That would have helped him. It was the most beautiful thing I've ever seen. More beautiful than poetry. How could he have forgotten it?

December 9

I asked Dora if it were possible to hallucinate without taking drugs. She must know. She's supposedly the expert on psychedelic drugs. "Sure," she said. "That's called being psychotic." Maybe the light of the moon can make you hallucinate. If not, I'm losing my mind.

December 10

"Il arriva chez nous un dimanche de Novembre 189 . . . " That's how far I've
gotten in *Le Grand Meaulnes* by Alain-Fournier. Tomorrow I have a
big French test on the first five chapters. It doesn't look that hard. I
won't have to look up too many words. No more hanging out at
night with Dora and Charley. If I have to stay up late tonight, I'll be
able to sleep over the weekend. I hate to stay up and force myself to
work when I can barely keep my eyes open. Even though Dora is
supposedly such an intellectual, she doesn't work very hard in school.
Charley doesn't give a flying fuck. Her words. I'm glad I have something to do. I'm going to make myself read now.

December 11

This morning Sofia put a note under my door: "I never see you anymore. You're spending all your time with Charley and Dora. I'm sad."

I felt terrible, but I can't help it. I can talk to them about Ernessa.
Sometimes she's all I want to talk about, all I want to think about. I
haven't spent any time with Mr. Davies either. I bet Claire is happy
about that.

I don't want Sofia to be involved.

At lunch I came up behind her and gave her a big hug and kiss.
We've decided to spend Saturday together in town. We're going to
the museum and out to lunch. I should look forward to it. She's one
of my closest friends. My dearest friend. But I have to force myself to
pay attention to her.

My French test went pretty well. I managed to do at least two
weeks of reading in a single night, so it was fresh in my mind. The
book is like a beautiful confusing dream. Childhood—even a sad
childhood—eventually becomes a place we think we've dreamed or
stumbled across and want to find again but never can. I should write
about that, not the stuff Mr. Davies has assigned. Maybe later, when I

have more time and can think clearly. I'm going to try to finish the book over Christmas vacation.

"Sredni Vashtur": The child shared a desolate childhood with phantoms and wild animals, and a god answered his cruel prayers.

■
December 12

On the train into town, I laughed for the first time in ages. Sofia told me how she managed to visit her boyfriend in town last year without lying about what she was doing. She would sign out for the day, and when she got back, Miss Olivo would always look up, her head shaking precariously on her neck, and ask her where she had been. Sofia would say, "I saw the museum." The train passes by the museum, which rises above the river like a Greek temple, and she would make sure that she looked out the window and saw the museum each time. "That way I wasn't lying," said Sofia. "Miss Olivo must have thought that I was really interested in art, because I saw that museum practically every weekend."

Sofia's the kind of person who meets boys in train stations, restaurants, everywhere. Her boyfriend was a sophomore in college. I secretly envied her when she talked about him. Their relationship seemed so sophisticated. She spent most of her time with him sitting on his lap while he tried to talk her into sleeping with him and she tried not to get talked into it. In the end she was too scared to do it, and he got sick of trying to talk her into it.

After Sofia and I had been in the museum for about an hour, I felt much calmer than I have in weeks. All of a sudden, I wasn't thinking about anything. The quiet in my head made me realize how accustomed I've become to the din.

Just before we left the museum, I went to the first floor, where my mother's painting is hanging by the cloakroom. I've been so angry at her since Thanksgiving. But when I saw her painting, I let go of the anger. If only she can find that part of her again. The painting is so beautiful. It's sort of abstract, but with the same two images that keep reappearing in her paintings: an owl in a silvery yellow sky and a boat on a bright red river. I'm not sure what they mean. Sometimes the owl is a bird, and sometimes there's an owl head on a human figure whose body dissolves into the sky, like the angels without feet in old Italian paintings. Sometimes the boat is empty. Sometimes a person is paddling it with her hands. I know what my father always loved in her, even at the very end when he had practically forgotten about love. She was like the luna moth for him, and at times he couldn't stand it. She can't forgive herself for not saving him. But he didn't want to be saved. I'm the one who needs her.

On the train back to school, that anxious feeling returned, like a wave that you don't see until it crashes over you and knocks you down. I was in such a hurry to be back in my room, to get to my journal, and to keep an eye on everything. Nothing happened while I was gone.

December 14

I knew all along that something like this was going to happen. I just didn't think it would be this bad. Yesterday Charley went out with Kiki and Betsy and Carol. She'll hang out with anyone who wants to smoke pot. They were coming back from town and somehow they ended up at the wrong train station and they had to get back to school and no trains were coming because it was Sunday, so they all decided to take a cab back to school. The driver got out of the cab for a minute to make a phone call, and while he was gone, they drove off. They stole the cab! I have no idea why they would do something so stupid, and nobody can tell me. Who was driving? Whose idea was it? I think it was just a joke, but once they started driving, they kept on going.

They were arrested by the police and brought back to school late last night, and none of them came to breakfast this morning.

After dinner

I got a disconnected story from Claire: They were all stoned out of their minds, and they were afraid the driver had gone to call the police because they were yelling so much. So they stole a cab? Basically, nobody knows what happened. Or they're not saying.

After midnight

I went into Dora's room after lights out, and Charley was there. We had to be extremely careful not to get caught because we would have been in serious trouble. Charley's convinced she's going to get tossed out of school for this and the other girls will just be suspended because they have connections. They're all rich, blond Waspy types. Also, Charley's grades are not so hot, and she's gotten so many comments and detentions already this year. She doesn't seem to care. She says she's sick of boarding school.

"I'm ready to get out of this pit," she said. "You guys should too."

I talked to her for half an hour, and I still can't figure out what happened.

Ernessa went with them into town.

In the middle of the afternoon, she gave Charley a tab of acid. She said she only had enough for the two of them. It was the first time Charley dropped acid. By the time they got to the train station, she was completely flipped out.

Charley said, "I looked up at the front of the building, and it was moving, sort of pulsing in and out. There were tongues of fire coming out of the roof, and the columns were writhing and twisting. It was cool, you know, but really scary. They must have carried me into the station and onto the train. I sure didn't want to go in there."

"What about Ernessa?" I asked.

"I think she got off the train with us. For sure, it was her idea to take a cab back to school so we wouldn't be late. She told us she had enough money to pay for it. She even found the cab for us. But I don't remember her ever being in it. Of course, I can't remember everything. I just know that when the police tried to stop us, I kept on driving. I was laughing, and it was like my hands were melted onto the steering wheel."

Basically, Charley is screwed.

December 15

Betsy, Carol, Kiki, and Charley are home. It's just an extra week of vacation. They know that their parents will get them out of this. No one feels sorry for Charley. They all blame her, the pothead. When they were stopped by the police, after a very short chase, Charley was driving the cab. Now they say it was her idea in the first place. It was lucky that no one had any dope on them, because they were searched at the police station. They had smoked it all in the park downtown.

No one wonders where Ernessa disappeared to.

Ernessa even managed to be back at school on time. Dora checked the sign-out sheet for the weekend. She signed in at five forty-five on Sunday. Miss Olivo always checks the time when you sign in.

December 16

Last night Dora asked me to come to her room after lights out. She had tried to call Charley earlier that afternoon, but Charley's mother wouldn't let her come to the phone.

"Her mother acted like it was my fault," said Dora, "but I wasn't even with them in the cab. I tried to stop her from smoking dope all the time. If she had stayed with us, this wouldn't have happened."

"I want to ask Charley about Ernessa," I said.

"She's the one who's to blame for all this," Dora said. "She thinks she's so smart and she can do anything and no one will touch her. Maybe it's time for her to be caught. If they knew she was dealing, they'd bounce her in a second."

"I don't know how she manages to get away with everything," I said.

"You know," said Dora, "I asked her if she wanted to read my manuscript, and she said she wasn't interested. She said fiction bored her. All the dreary details. 'I only read poetry,' she said. She's so full of herself. And her ideas about Nietzsche are just ignorant."

I feel so tired. I've had enough of this game, or whatever it is. Christmas vacation starts in two days. Then I'll have to deal with my mother for three weeks. I didn't say anything to Dora. I was hoping she would drop the subject.

"I'm going to find out what she's up to at night," said Dora.

"I don't want to," I said.

"But I do," said Dora.

She went over to the window and opened it. We both stuck our heads out. It was cold and windy outside. The moon was completely hidden behind clouds, and in the faint greenish light from below, I could barely make out the gutter.

"It's too dark," I said. "You can't see a thing."

"I could feel my way along," said Dora.

"Don't," I said. "I almost fell last time. I'm never going to do it again. It's too scary. If her room is empty, you still won't—"

"Look," said Dora, nudging me with her elbow.

The gutter was nothing more than a thick green line. The wind whipped my hair across my eyes. At the far end of the building, by Claire's window, I saw something. I whispered, "Is that Claire?"

The person stood up and started to walk toward us along the gutter. She walked as if she were on the ground, without hesitation, without a single misstep, the way she played the piano. When she reached her window, she turned and stepped into the glass.

Dora slammed the window shut.

"Do you think she saw us?"

"I don't know," I said.

This morning at breakfast, I asked Dora if it had really happened last night.

"I think so," she said. "But maybe it wasn't what we thought it was. Maybe she left her window wide open."

What did we think it was?

There's one thing I can't understand. Why does Ernessa want me to see that she isn't like the rest of us?

I'm going to nap until dinner.

After dinner

I almost missed dinner tonight!

I lay down on my bed during quiet hour, and right away I fell into an incredibly deep sleep. Even asleep, I could sense how heavy it was, as if a huge hand were pushing me down into the mattress. I was with my father. At first we were just lying together on my bed at school, flat on our backs with our hands folded carefully on our chests and our eyes closed. I was lying there, but I was also standing by the side of the bed, looking down at the two bodies. "Are we both dead?" I asked them. No one answered. All of a sudden, I felt someone tugging at my arm and pulling me. I turned around and saw the back of the person pulling me. "What are you doing, Daddy?" I asked. He wouldn't answer me. He just kept pulling, harder and harder. I had to grab onto the metal rail at the head of the bed and plant my feet firmly on the floor to stop him from pulling me under. I kept looking around my room to see if there was anything I could use to hit my father, to make him let go of me. At the same time, I was feeling how unbearable this was and how I needed to wake up and end this dream. I was back on my bed, this time by myself. My father was gone. I could see myself lying flat on the bed, straining to lift up my head, to sit up, to get out of bed. I managed to lift my head up with an immense effort, just a few inches, and then it fell back onto the pillow, and I had to begin again. And again. I was so weary of it. My eyelids were so heavy, they pressed against my eyes. I didn't think I could ever wake up. I leaned over the bed, to get a better look at my sleeping self. Suddenly the eyes opened wide, and my two selves stared at each other in astonishment. I was wide awake. My eyes were open. But I was paralyzed as if in a dream.

I didn't get up until the last bells. Dinner was already starting. I could hear the clatter of dishes as the servers brought out the carts piled high with platters of food. I wasn't even dressed. I was still wearing my sweaty gym tunic. I pulled on some stockings with huge runs and threw on a dress. When I opened the door, Ernessa was standing there. She had been waiting all this time for me.

"You overslept too?" she asked with fake concern. "We better hurry if we don't want to get a comment."

I ran down the hall.

After dinner, Dora and I sat in the corner of the playroom, where Lucy usually hides with Ernessa. I asked her if she believed in the supernatural, "the physical manifestation of the unconscious in our waking life," as Mr. Davies always puts it. So that we know that it's real and unreal at the same time.

"The spirit world," I said. "What we saw going into Ernessa's room last night."

"That's for children," said Dora. "I don't think there are spirits, or the undead, or anything like that. Fairy tales. They scare you, but you want to hear them. Nietzsche says people would rather have the void as a purpose than be void of purpose. It's just another kind of religion."

"I used to be like that," I said. "But I've changed."

"In the end there is a rational explanation for everything."

"But you were scared last night, weren't you? When we looked out the window?"

"Late at night everything takes on a spurious significance," said Dora. "During the day, it would have seemed perfectly normal. Ernessa is a weird, unpleasant person with bizarre sleeping habits who thinks she knows everything. Maybe she sleepwalks all night."

"Not along the gutter," I said.

Now we were the ones who were whispering.

Ernessa walked into the Playroom, and I tried not to look at her. She sat down with the others and immediately brought a match to her cigarette, waving the smoke around her into a cloud. Her head was leaning in our direction. She seemed to be listening to us. She even nodded her head when Dora spoke.

"I'm going to prove it to you," said Dora. "Come to my room after lights out."

"No, I've had enough. I told you last time. Please don't go," I said.

"Don't be so melodramatic," said Dora. "It doesn't suit you. I'm going to find out about her."

"Now you're being stupid."

I got up abruptly and left the room. I could feel Ernessa's eyes on my back, burning through the cloud of smoke and into my skin. I'm not going to leave my room at night.

December 17

Five A.M.

Dora never was my friend, really. She looked down on me. I always knew that. She pretended to be my friend, because she resented Ernessa, too. We shared that dislike.

It's still dark outside. I'm waiting for the sky to lighten so this night can be over. The ambulance is gone. The police cars are gone. Dora is gone. From my window, I watched them carry out the stretcher. Her face was covered with a white sheet.

Suddenly everyone was up. The Residence was shaken awake. All the lights went on. I sat up in bed, as if a hand had yanked me upright, and my entire body was vibrating. There were sirens; an ambulance and police cars raced down the drive. Flashing red lights swept through my room. And outside the door, girls were shrieking and crying. I couldn't stand that noise. Voices of men boomed down the corridor, along with heavy, hurrying footsteps. I was terrified. Then the sounds came together and formed words. "This is her room here." "She didn't go out this window." "It's got to be the next room."

I could hear them banging on Ernessa's door. She would come to the doorway in a long white nightgown that completely covered her arms and legs and came up to her chin. She would open the door slowly, pretending she had only just woken up. Her room would be empty of dust and the sound of wings like breath.

"You're certain you didn't hear a thing? One of your classmates had an accident directly below your window. A fall."

"I'm a very deep sleeper," she would say. "Nothing ever disturbs me once I've fallen asleep. I sleep like a dead person. Why don't you ask some of the other girls?" Her voice would be flat. She would ask the policemen to leave her alone. It would sound like a command.

I opened my door and saw the nurse taking Lucy and Sofia away. They were crying. Their shoulders shook as they walked down the corridor. I stood by, watching them. Everything is worse in the middle of the night, especially when you've been snatched out of a deep sleep. You don't know where you are or where your dreams end and the world begins.

Dora fell from the roof gutter outside Ernessa's window. No one heard her fall, but the cook saw her body in the courtyard at four when she came to start breakfast. She was lying on the pavement, her arms flung wide, her head twisted behind her shoulder. The wind ruffled her nightgown, which was bunched up around her middle. Her white legs were still. She looked dead.

I could have stopped her from doing such a stupid thing. I could have told her what she would see so that she wouldn't need to see it for herself. I could have told her that not believing in something doesn't protect you from it. I could have told her about the moths swarming out of the dust and moonlight and how they flit around in my head.

I stayed in my room.

She never was my friend.

Vacation starts tomorrow.

I'm going to lie down on my bed and try to rest. It's painful to keep my eyes open, but where will I be when I close them?

Ten A.M.

At assembly, Miss Rood told us that Dora was dead. That made it official. The day students knew that something was wrong because all the boarders were sitting there with red eyes. Everybody started to cry again when Miss Rood spoke. I knew she was dead, but when

Miss Rood said the words, my face got really hot, and I began to shake all over, inside and out. My body knows, but my head doesn't understand yet. I'm enclosed in a huge bubble. My arms and legs feel so heavy. I can barely lift them. Everything I do is on the verge of not happening. I'm waiting for the bubble to burst, to let me back into the world again. But it doesn't happen that way. It's like waiting for novocaine to wear off. Suddenly you realize that you're no longer numb.

Miss Rood kept repeating that it was a "terrible, unfortunate accident," like some kind of prayer. She was "shocked and dismayed" to discover that some of the girls had been walking along the roof gutters of the Residence. Then she asked us to talk to her if we saw or heard anything out of the ordinary last night. I'm not going to say a word about this. I'm scared of what Ernessa will do. I don't trust anyone.

No classes for us this morning. Miss Brody, the psychologist, is going to talk to the boarders later on. What can she possibly say? "Now, girls, I understand you've had a traumatic experience, but the healing process must begin. . . . " She can't pop my bubble. All around me, everyone was weeping. I thought Lucy was going to lose it. They had to carry her up to the infirmary this time. I walked straight out and up to my room. I wanted to write down everything in my journal. The only other person who didn't cry was Ernessa. But it doesn't mean anything. She's the kind of person who can laugh without being happy. So she can cry without being sad. I'm supposed to stay in my room until we meet with the psychologist in the library, but I have to see for myself.

Ten-thirty A.M.
The spot is directly under Ernessa's window, but far out. She missed hitting the roof of the porches, which might have broken her fall. Instead she landed on the pavement. She threw herself out. She tried to fly away. They roped off the area. There was reddish-brown blood on the cement. It's dried by now. I expected the pavement to be cracked or there to be a hole where her body hit, as if a meteor had collided with the Earth. I stood behind the rope and looked up to the

window on the second floor. The sun was out, and the black glass reflected back the blue of the sky and the wispy clouds, which flew across the window panes. Behind the sky I searched for a face, searching for me.

How can I ever talk to Lucy again? I'd be happy never to have to see her again.

Quiet hour
I don't think I've ever been so scared in my life.

They came and got me out of my math class. I panicked right away. Something terrible had happened to my mother. As I got my books together and left the classroom, I kept thinking, "How can you do this to me? How can you do this to me?"

It wasn't my mother at all. Mrs. Halton explained to me that a detective wanted to talk to me about Dora. I had already forgotten about her.

"There's no need to be nervous," said Mrs. Halton. "The gentleman wants to ask you a few questions. I'll be in the room with you the whole time."

But the way she said it, as if she were trying to talk a little child into doing something very unpleasant, made me feel that it was something to be afraid of. She was so pleased with herself. She had a smile on her face the whole time she escorted me along the Passageway to the Residence and up the stairs to the second-floor library.

The detective was waiting for me. He wasn't wearing a police uniform; he had on a regular suit, like an insurance salesman or a businessman. His overcoat was placed neatly over the chair next to him, and his briefcase was opened on the library table. He asked me lots of questions, and while I talked, he took notes on a yellow legal pad. No one has ever questioned me like that before.

"This won't take long," he began. "I just have a few things to ask you. One of your classmates said that you and the girl who fell into the courtyard this morning, Dora, used to walk along the gutters. She said she'd seen you outside her window."

"We all did it," I said. I heard Mrs. Halton gasp, for his benefit. "I've only done it once this fall. I think."

"When was that?"

"About a week ago. Maybe a little more."

"And where exactly were you?"

"I came out Dora's window. I just went down to the next window."

"And then?"

"I turned around. It was too cold."

"Was Dora out on the gutter that night?"

"Just for a little while. She heard someone in the corridor, and she came out to get me."

"And what about last night? Were you with Dora?"

"I was asleep in bed after lights out. I didn't wake up until I heard the sirens on the drive. I told Dora I didn't want to go along the gutters anymore."

"What do you think Dora was doing?"

"She was probably going to Carol's room, or maybe to Claire's, which is at the corner."

"You don't think she was going to the room next door? What was that girl's name? I spoke with her earlier today."

"Ernessa?"

"That's right, was she going to Ernessa's room?"

"I'm sure she wasn't going there. They weren't friends."

"Sometimes girls at this age develop very strong . . . feelings . . . for each other, good and bad. Things can seem more important than they really are. Did she ever mention being unhappy or talk about killing herself, even as a joke?"

"No. Never."

I answered all the questions, and he let me go. I said all the right things, and I think he believed me. Afterward I went straight to my room for the rest of the afternoon. I cut French and gym. I don't care what happens. I can always say that I was too upset about Dora. I want to skip dinner too, but I can't. Ernessa will see how upset I am. She sent the police to me.

While the detective was questioning me, I felt guilty about every horrible thought I've ever had. I kept reminding myself that just because I didn't always like Dora and I sometimes wished I'd never have to see her again and never laid eyes on her in the first place didn't mean that I wanted her to die.

■
December 18

Home. Safe for now. I panicked in the car when I thought I left my journal in my room, where anyone could find it, but it was in my book bag. My mother came to pick me up, and she was on time for a change. She comes through when she absolutely has to. She can sense when I need her. I couldn't stay around school after everyone left. Everything there is dead Dora.

Last night Sofia and Claire slept in my room. We were too scared to be alone. Lucy was in a daze. They gave her Valium when she went to the infirmary. She could hardly stand up. She wanted to sleep in her own room, with her stuffed animals, but she left the bathroom doors open all night and the light on in the bathroom.

Claire said that Ernessa was called into Miss Rood's office and that Mrs. Halton and the other corridor teachers were there. I'm so glad that Claire isn't in my math class. She still doesn't know what happened to me.

"Why'd they do that?" asked Sofia. She can be so dense.

"Dora's room was right next to Ernessa's, and she fell right below Ernessa's window. I guess they wanted to ask her if she heard anything," said Claire.

"Or did anything," I added. They didn't notice my remark. Lucy was in her room, so I let it drop.

Midnight

I didn't write about this earlier because I needed to think about it.

Somehow I got up the nerve to confront Ernessa after dinner in the Playroom. It annoyed me so much that she was so calm when everyone was distraught, even the girls who didn't particularly like Dora.

I walked right up to her and said, "Why aren't you upset about Dora like everyone else?" It's the first time I've actually spoken to her in weeks.

I thought she might get really pissed off, but she wasn't offended. She wasn't even surprised. Instead, she lit a cigarette and offered me one. I didn't take it. She spoke very slowly, as if she were speaking to someone who didn't quite understand her language.

"Why should I be sad? Everyone has to die. If you have a body, it's too late to cry. It's only funerals that I can't stand."

It's true I'm only partly afraid of dying.

I'm not ready to become like Ernessa. I have my journal, my books, my music, my friends, my mother.

When I came back to everyone on the sofa, they all stared at me as if I'd done something horrible. Sofia had her arm around Lucy. Lucy was whimpering. I'm too tired and confused to figure them out. I want to sleep for the next two weeks.

December 20

I made myself call Charley tonight. Someone had to tell her.

"Dora's dead," I said. "She fell from the gutter."

"This is a joke, right," said Charley.

"No. It happened on Wednesday night."

"You're telling me that Dora's gone to eternal dreamland?"

"Yes. Dora's dead. I told you."

"I can't fucking believe she fell from the gutter. What a klutz."

"I tried to stop her," I said. "I knew that it was a mistake, that Ernessa...."

I couldn't hear what Charley said after that. The television was on, really loud. Charley must have turned up the volume. That's the first thing she used to do when she came into the TV room at school. The canned laughter drowned out her words.

I would have had to shout to make Charley hear me. I didn't have the energy to explain to her that Ernessa had gotten rid of Dora. I don't know if she pushed her, but she made her fall.

"I've been tossed," shouted Charley. "I'm the only one. Kiki, Betsy, and Carol are coming back. My 'rents are totally pissed off, but it's like they've opened the door to my cell and thrown away the key."

"What are you going to do?" I shouted.

"Go to day school near home."

Now Charley and Dora are gone. I'm the only one left. The coward. I won't look through that window at night ever again. Ernessa understands that I won't come too close.

I could have gotten Charley to turn off the television and told her about Ernessa, but she doesn't seem to care about that anymore. She doesn't even really care about Dora dying. She's gone from school, from our world. Ernessa can stay out all night, every night. Ernessa can be whatever she wants to be. None of this matters. They won't be smoking dope together, so fuck it, as Charley would say.

—

December 24

My mother went to a party tonight. She asked me to come, but I told her I didn't feel like it. I was tired, and I wanted to go to bed early. I wanted her to leave, but the moment she closed the door behind her, every room fell silent. There's a wind whistling through the empty spaces. I wish Milou were still here, lying on the pillow by my head, purring gently and making little squeaking noises to let me know how happy he is. I'm all alone.

Ernessa is a vampire.

I haven't been able to write those words before tonight. I couldn't transform my fears into a conscious statement. She wants me, and only me, to see it. Her hand is guiding mine as I write these words.

December 25

If only I'd had a chance to see Dora's body after she died. Her parents were in Paris, and they had her cremated right away. They didn't even want to see her dead body. I wish I had. I would have checked her body to see if there were marks on it. Maybe something on the left breast, near the heart, or between the eyes. That's where they would be. Barely breaking the skin, like bruises. But they only want one kind of death.

What are they going to do with her unfinished novel, the dialogue between Nietzsche and Brahms? It probably wasn't any good. Still, it's sad that all those pages, covered with words, will disappear without anyone reading them. Someone needs to read them. I know her parents won't. Her father was always so critical of everything she did.

Maybe I should read her book.

I guess Dora was nice to me sometimes, but I couldn't stand the way she lectured me. I never forgave her for dismissing me like that. I was only friends with her because she was interested in Ernessa. She was only interested in Ernessa because Ernessa treated her the way Dora treated everyone else. Dora couldn't help herself. Her vanity was wounded.

Why am I writing such mean things about someone who has just died?

Her book would poison me.

> *I heard a Fly buzz—when I died—*
> *The Stillness in the Room*
> *Was like the Stillness in the Air—*
> *Between the Heaves of Storm—*
>
> *The Eyes around—had wrung them dry—*
> *And Breaths were gathering firm*
> *For that last Onset—when the King*
> *Be witnessed—in the Room—*

> *I willed my Keepsakes—Signed away*
> *What portion of me be*
> *Assignable—and then it was*
> *There interposed a Fly—*
>
> *With Blue—uncertain stumbling Buzz—*
> *Between the light—and me—*
> *And then the Windows failed—and then*
> *I could not see to see—*

Emily would have understood what interposed between Dora and her death, but I don't.

■

December 27

Last night I learned some interesting facts going through the books in my father's library. I knew he would have what I wanted. There are many ways in which a person can become a vampire, or a revenant (from the French for returning): (a) a bad person commits suicide under certain circumstances (What is a bad person? What are certain circumstances?); (b) a vampire visits someone while he's asleep; (c) a bat flies over a corpse, a cat or dog jumps over a corpse, or a person leans over a corpse; (d) a person dies unseen; (e) a person's shadow is stolen during his lifetime; (f) a corpse's mouth is open; (g) a person suffers a violent death; (h) a corpse is left unattended, not accorded proper burial rights, or not buried deeply enough; (i) a vampire bites someone, although sometimes the victim dies without becoming a vampire.

An open mouth, that's unfair. It's unfair to punish someone (or the soul) for something that happens when the person no longer has any control over the body. I laughed when I read about being born with two hearts, one of which is devoted only to destroying humanity.

My father wanted to die unseen, like an animal who goes off and curls up by himself to die. But Milou didn't need to hide from us. He wasn't ashamed of dying. There must be one final breath, like the last bit of air being squeezed out of a raft, the final heave of the storm, and then the living body gives up and the invisible soul is freed. Maybe someone does need to witness that.

December 31

I think I've convinced my mother to let me stay home and not go back to school. I told her that I feel partly to blame for Dora's death and that I can't get over it. Those are things she's tuned in to: grief, guilt, remorse.

JANUARY

January 1

I don't believe that my father is still around but in a different state. I don't believe I can communicate with him. I hate that about my mother. She takes her dreams literally and feels that she is still in contact with him. Even if he appears to her full of anger. Anything, just so long as he doesn't forget her.

I'm jealous of Ernessa. I'm jealous of Lucy's friendship with her. I'm jealous of her perfect body. I'm jealous of her piano playing. I'm jealous that she's never afraid. But that doesn't make her anything more than someone I don't like. That's too weak a word. Even hatred is. When I see her with Lucy, she fills me with disgust.

All that I've written about Ernessa has ruined this journal. It's not what I wanted it to be. I'm not the person I wanted to be.

After lunch

I put a strand of garlic around my bed, and I'm burning incense before I go to sleep. It's worked. I've been sleeping much better. If I go back to school, I'll have to keep doing it. Everyone will think I'm burning incense to cover up the smell of pot.

After dinner

Lucy just called to wish me a Happy New Year. We had a really good talk, finally. There were no closed doors between our rooms. Dora fell from the gutters. It could have happened to any of us. I dreamed the moths. I told her that I was thinking of not coming back to school after vacation. She couldn't understand why I would do that.

"When we get back, it won't seem so horrible," she said. "We will have forgotten about it a bit. I've already forgotten about it, just being away from school. It's beginning to feel like a bad dream. We'll just get back into our routines. It won't be the way it was right before vacation, when nobody could think of anything else."

"I guess," I said.

"You have to come back," said Lucy. "I would miss you too much."

I'm not going to read about vampires anymore. Mr. Davies should have known better than to expose us to things like this, even if he doesn't believe in them himself.

I could tear out some of the pages and start over again.

January 4

I've written much less in my journal over vacation than I thought I would. It wasn't a bad vacation after all. Tomorrow, school again. I'm going back.

■

January 8

Girls have moved into Dora's and Charley's rooms, and there's no sign that they were ever on the corridor. Lucy has come down to breakfast and eaten with all of us. The doors between our rooms are open, and she's been around for quiet hour. Nothing ever happened. She's trying so hard to be nice to me. We've been back for three days now, and I've hardly seen Ernessa at all. She hasn't even come to the Playroom for a smoke. She locks herself up in her room all the time. She probably smokes in there. She knows Mrs. Halton would never dare to bother her. Lucy is avoiding her too, I think. She waits for me now before she goes down to dinner.

It is a new year.

Once I saw a solar eclipse. The sun gradually darkened, until it was like dusk in the middle of the day. I knew that if I looked up at the sun, it would appear dark but it would actually be shining as intensely as ever. Its light would blind me. I had to hold my face between my hands, to keep myself from turning it to the sun. I had been told again and again not to look at it, but I still wanted to. The sun only appeared dark, just as the day only appeared to be night. The black sun burned.

Charley hasn't written or called at all. I'm almost glad they're not around anymore and that it's all over.

■

January 9

This morning Claire asked me at breakfast if I wanted to go with her to visit Mr. Davies this afternoon. She was going to call him and ask if we could come.

I'd never have the nerve to do something like that. I said I'd come along even though we have exams next week. I've already studied a lot. She only asked me because she knows he would never see her alone.

As soon as we got off the train, I wanted to go back to school, but Claire dragged me from the station to his house. It was only a few blocks away. It's a little white frame house, nothing much. Claire rang the doorbell, and while we waited for someone to answer it, we both burst out laughing, we were so nervous. I'm used to Mr. Davies in school, but I didn't know what it would be like to be with him in his own house. Maybe he would seem too ordinary.

His wife, Charlotte (we don't have to call her Mrs. Davies), answered the door. At first she was puzzled to see us there, and we couldn't stop laughing long enough to tell her who we were.

"Mr. Davies—" said Claire.

"Oh, yes," she said. "Nick's students. He's expecting you."

Nick. I know his first name is Nicholas, but Nick is too offhand for him. He must be another person at home.

Charlotte wasn't what I expected. (I don't know what I expected. Someone intense, intellectual?) She's a little chubby but very pretty, with light brown hair, which she wears up in a clip, gray eyes, full pink cheeks. She is always smiling and was incredibly nice to us. Even nicer than Mr. Davies. She served us tea and really good cookies: wafers with caramel filling. I ate too many because I was nervous. When I looked up from my tea, which I had balanced on my lap, Mr. Davies was staring straight at me. He started to laugh—because I ate so many cookies or because I kept spilling my tea? I looked over at Claire, sitting next to me on the sofa (an old sofa from the Salvation Army covered with an India print spread). Her hair was hanging in her eyes, just above her bony nose. Her face is so long and narrow, and her lips are thick and loose. She's ugly. Mr. Davies could never fall in love with her.

Everything is perfect. His wife works for Planned Parenthood. Claire asked her right away what she does. They have two cats: a calico cat and a gray and white cat. Their house is like a mini-commune. Charlotte's sister, her husband, and their baby live upstairs. We only saw the baby. They all share the shopping and cooking and cleaning. There's an old barber chair sitting right in the middle of the living room. It's so cool. Most of the time, the baby was with us, pulling himself up on the coffee table and taking a bite out of each cookie. No one else from school could understand how wonderful it was. All they understand is a fancy house, a new car, a stereo, nice furniture. . . .

Do they sit around on Saturday afternoon and have tea and talk about poetry? They probably talk about poetry all the time.

We didn't talk about poetry. Charlotte wanted to know about school and what it was like to be a boarder.

"How are you girls doing, after what happened at school? Nick told me all about it," said Charlotte. "It was so sad."

"What?" asked Claire.

"The accident with your friend," said Charlotte.

"Oh, that," said Claire. Charlotte doesn't understand how quickly everyone manages to forget about unpleasant things at school. "It was extremely traumatic for all of us on the corridor. But we're trying to put it behind us and get on."

I let Claire do all the talking. I was happy to observe Charlotte, sitting with her legs tucked up under her and her head resting on her hand. She was so relaxed.

Then she asked us if we missed our families very much. Claire loves to talk about how much she hates her stepfather and how strange it is to go home to North Carolina after being in school up North. How her stepbrothers say things like, "I'm gonna go out and find me a nigger to run over tonight."

Mr. Davies and Charlotte were both horrified.

"It's just talk," said Claire. "They never do anything. They're stupid teenagers."

"But that attitude is so disturbing," said Charlotte. "Those kids will grow up to be racists, like their parents, without thinking about what they're doing."

"That's why I can't stand it there," said Claire. "My stepfather's like that."

All this is a pose for her. She loves getting so much attention.

It was late, and we had to get back to school. The mini-commune with Salvation Army furniture and the India print spread and the two cats and the baby was so much more real. I used to live a real life at home. How can Mr. Davies stand to come from this to the Residence every morning?

Charlotte went to get our jackets from the closet. While she was carrying them, she dropped my purple scarf, the one my mother gave me over vacation. Mr. Davies picked it up and brought it over to me. He lifted the scarf over my head, wrapped it around my neck, and crossed the two ends in front. He was playful, but his actions were so precise, as if he'd planned each motion in advance. It made me think of a priest or a rabbi performing a ritual. He didn't let go of the scarf after he had arranged it so carefully. He pulled me toward him. I drew back. He pulled harder. The scratchy wool tightened around my neck, and he smiled, the way he does in class. If he had let go, I would have tipped over backward. He was doing this, in front of everyone, and I felt myself falling into him. It was so hard to hold myself back. The baby had pulled himself onto the sofa, where he sat, staring at us. Charlotte and Claire were standing by the front door, still talking about the South. Charlotte was telling Claire about going to Mississippi with the Freedom Riders when she was in college. I couldn't listen to them. Mr. Davies's face was so close to mine that I could feel the humid warmth of his breath against my cheek.

As she closed the door, Charlotte said, "You're welcome to come back anytime you want. Really. I enjoyed your visit." But another voice was hidden behind her cheeriness.

Mr. Davies's voice came from behind her. He sounded just the way he does when he dismisses us from class. "Remember, we're always here to talk to whenever anything comes up at school."

Claire and I walked in the cold toward the train station. It was dark out. I was soaked with sweat. The wind blew through my jacket, and I started shivering uncontrollably. Claire couldn't stop talking. His wife was so nice but she was sort of fat and the house was messy and when she went to the bathroom, she looked into his study and saw the desk where he sat when he composed his poetry and she was going to visit him again and did I want to come?

His house is not the house of a poet.

January 10

Lucy was annoyed with me for going out all afternoon yesterday, so I promised her I would spend Sunday with her. After lunch we rode on the train out into the country and went skating on Crumb Creek. It's gotten so cold this last week that the creek is frozen. Last year we did this practically every weekend in the winter. We were able to skate quite a ways down the creek. As we glided over the black ice, I looked up at the crisp blue winter sky, and I thought, I should remember this moment. My skates are a bit tight, and my feet ache. My fingers and toes are practically numb, but the sun is so bright that I'm sweating under my jacket. I feel perfectly happy right now.

We came to a bend in the creek, where it gets wider and a steep hill comes right down to the water. On the other side, the bare black branches of weeping willows brush the bank. Two boys were sliding down the hill on pieces of cardboard and what looked like a tray from a cafeteria. We slid down with them a few times, which was pretty hard since we were wearing our skates.

Lucy went down on the cardboard with one of the boys, and they fell off near the bottom. He was lying on top of her, and they stayed like that for a long time, not kissing, just lying together in the snow. When she got up, she was bright red in the face. On the way back, the day already seemed far away.

My mother's had affairs, even when she was married to my father, I think. She always makes fun of me and asks me when I'm going to get a boyfriend. I keep telling her that no one is ever interested in me at the tea dances. They always want to dance with someone like Lucy, someone with blond hair and pale eyes. "There's something so passive about her. She's not quite there," my mother once said of Lucy. "You're the real beauty, with your dark hair and lovely skin. One day the boys will grow up, and suddenly they'll notice you." It puzzles me when she talks like this.

Besides, the last thing I want is a boyfriend. Last year for the May Dance, Linda Cates set me and Carol up with her younger brother and a friend. I got the friend. I was surprised that Linda asked me. I had no idea why. I'm not at all like Carol, who has thick brownish-blond hair that curls up naturally at the ends and a little upturned nose. I was sure the boys would be sophisticated like Linda, and I was excited for weeks before the dance. Lucy and I went to a fancy shop and picked out a dress of green silk with big pink and yellow flowers. It's the only long dress I've ever worn. The boys arrived for the weekend, and we met them at the train station. My date had a greasy red face, covered with pimples. I could barely stand to look at him. I had absolutely nothing to say to him. We walked from the train station to their hotel, which was about a mile away, and my date carried his suitcase on his head, like a African woman with a basket of fruit. Carol and I kept looking at each other behind their backs and making faces. When they took their suitcases up to their room, we burst out laughing. We had to, otherwise we would have cried at the prospect of two days with them.

When I came to school in ninth grade, I was so excited before the first tea dance with Pottersville. Boys still interested me then. I wore a blue checked dress that I had bought with my mother at Saks. I hadn't wanted to buy it at the time because I was so annoyed with her for sending me off to school. But I was glad that I was wearing it the night of the dance. I stood with the knot of ninth graders, waiting impatiently for the bus with the boys to arrive. Finally, the boys marched into the dining room and went to stand along the opposite wall, so that we could eye one another across the empty space as they called off the names. Boys and girls would enter that no-man's-land alone and leave in pairs, matched up by height. They must think it's important for us to look into each other's eyes while we dance. It's an unspoken rule that you have to stay with your assigned date for the first half hour of the dance. After that, you're free to roam. I heard my name, and then a boy's name, Matthew something. As I approached him, there was a low murmuring in the room, and all the girls turned to stare at me. Matthew was older, at least a junior, and quite good looking. I had no idea why everyone was giving me dirty looks until Charley managed to whisper in my ear, "Watch out, he's Jill Ackley's boyfriend."

Even I, after only two weeks of school, knew who Jill Ackley was. She was a junior with bleached blond hair and large breasts, pretty much what I imagined the word blond bombshell meant. I looked around the dining room for Jill, but I didn't see her anywhere. That was why I had ended up with her date tonight. I couldn't believe my good luck at my first dance. In comparison, all the other girls in my class were with babies.

They all looked at me as if I'd done something horrible, but I didn't care.

Matthew danced with me all evening. We drank pink punch and ate cookies together. And even though he had a girlfriend, he took me out onto the shadowy porch, where couples went to kiss under the disapproving eyes of the chaperons, and he kissed me.

I don't know if it was the excitement of having such a nice time at my first tea dance, or the realization that as soon as his girlfriend came back he would forget that I ever existed. But after he had kissed me for a while, and he was just holding me, I leaned forward and bit him on the cheek, just under his eye. His flesh was resistant. My teeth didn't break the skin. They left a red welt and teeth marks. He pulled back, surprised.

"Hey! What did you do that for?" he asked.

I was so embarrassed I could barely speak. I wanted to run away. "I don't know. I really don't know."

I don't know why I did it.

Once when I was little, I ran up to my mother, sitting on the sofa, and sank my teeth into her thigh. I bit her so hard that I drew blood, and she had a bruise there for months. When I raised my head from her leg, I was laughing, and I was shocked to see the tears on her cheeks. I didn't mean to hurt her. I was just so wound up that I didn't know what to do with my body. It was the same impulse I felt with Matthew.

I never got another good date at a tea dance. I went to a lot last year, and they were all disappointments. I hated even more going to dances at boys' schools, where all the boys were waiting for the bus to arrive, and we had to walk into the room and suffer their stares.

Last year Lucy had a really nice boyfriend named Juan, whom she met at a St. Andrew's tea dance. They were only friends because Lucy was too scared to try anything, but she always had a date for the big dances. He graduated, and this year neither of us has gone to any dances.

January 11

Once I went home with Lucy for the weekend. It was a complete shock.

We arrived at night, and her father wasn't around. Her mother is incredibly sweet, very much like Lucy. As we drove through the night to her house and I listened to the two of them talking, I found myself wishing that she was my mother. She's so uncomplicated and straightforward. Lucy can tell her anything. Her mother never criticizes her or makes fun of her, the way my mother does. I never know quite what to expect from her.

Then there's Lucy's father. When we came down to breakfast the next morning, her father was sitting at the table in his boxers and an undershirt. The forehead of his fat flushed face was covered with drops of sweat. On the table in front of him, next to the milk and the boxes of cereal, was a rifle. He was bent over it, cleaning it I think. I had never seen a gun before.

He looked over at me without saying a word. Then he took Lucy in his arms and hugged her for a long time and demanded a kiss. I don't know how she could stand to kiss that steaming red face. After that, he turned to the dog, a little white poodle, on the chair next to him and fed him pieces of bacon. He wheezed while he did it. I could hear each separate breath. I started to count them. He sucked in the air, paused, and then released it, all used up and soiled. When he squeezed it out, he started up again. He was using up the air in the room, and there wouldn't be any left for us. Finally, he pushed himself up, groaning, took his rifle, and left the room. I was too embarrassed to look at Lucy or to speak. I wanted to tell Lucy that I didn't care what her father was like, but I couldn't because she was no longer ordinary, unless a father like that was ordinary. I longed for my father, to show her what a real father was like. I actually felt sorry for her.

We hardly saw him for the rest of the weekend. While we walked in the woods near her house, Lucy told me that he has a girlfriend in town and spends most of his time there. Her mother is happy about that. The problem is that he won't let her mother get a divorce. When she tried to bring up the subject, he put a gun to her head and threatened to kill her. Lucy was standing next to her mother, staring at the barrel of the gun pressed against her mother's skin.

Lucy said, "He was just kidding. The gun wasn't loaded."

But I know that Lucy was terrified. She thought her father was going to kill both of them.

I remember that afternoon in the woods so clearly. At school, everything was already in bloom, but there the trees looked dead. There was no sign of spring. The world was suddenly drab, finished. I walked behind Lucy, staring at the long blond hair that her father would not let her cut, and I kept saying to myself, "Why did I think she was so normal?"

Is it possible that all this has happened to Lucy? I look at her, and I can't see any sign of that terror. She insists that she's only going away to school because she comes from a tiny town where nothing ever happens. But that's not the reason. It makes me sick to think about him, with that enormous stomach hanging down over his pants. I don't know how he could manage to have sex, with that in the way. And who could bear to touch him? I look at my pen after writing this, and I can't stand to hold it.

Dora called Lucy a daddy's girl. Her father forces her to be what she doesn't really want to be.

Am I my father's daughter?

No more: I think Lucy just came into her room.

Lights out

I've got my fingers crossed that everything stays like this.

I should have studied tonight instead of writing so much in my journal. I've promised Lucy that I'll quiz her on her German vocab.

Exams. Exams. Exams. Exams. Exams. All week long.

Carol, Betsy, and Kiki came back on Sunday, so that they could take their exams. Everything is pretty much back to normal.

January 16

I'm never going to smoke dope again.

*

"The Black Spider": "As those sleep who carry the fear of God and an untroubled conscience in their hearts, and will never be awakened from sleep by the Black Spider, but only by the kindly sun."

What does Lucy carry in her heart? Can I really know?

January 17

It was supposed to be a celebration.

Lucy, Carol, Kiki, and I snuck into Claire's room late Friday night and smoked some hash that Claire brought back from home. She got it from her cousin. Ernessa was there, too. I don't remember whose idea it was. I've smoked a few times before, but I can't relax when I'm stoned. I always feel like I'm taking a quiz on a subject I know nothing about, where the questions keep changing before I have a chance to write down the answers. But I didn't think it could be this bad, that I could feel stoned to death.

Claire filled the pipe. "This shit will take you down the rabbit hole," she said. She sounded like Charley.

She held a match to the pipe, inhaled deeply, and passed it on. Then she arranged a few sticks of incense in a holder shaped like an elephant and lit a match. Ernessa was at her side, blowing out the flame.

"Don't do it," said Ernessa.

"Do what?" asked Claire.

"Light the incense."

"What kind of pill did you take?" asked Claire. "You're like Alice when she's tall. Or maybe when she's small. It hides the smell."

Claire started to laugh at her own joke as she picked up the book of matches. "Don't forget what the dormouse said."

But Ernessa held up her hand and said, "I mean it."

"I can't abide the smell. I won't be able to stay in the room. The smoke will suffocate me. It's unbearably sweet."

Claire shrugged her shoulders. "All right. Guys, open the window and hold the pipe outside. We'll all freeze our butts off."

We smoked a bit. I started to say, "I can't even feel a things . . ." when I couldn't finish my sentence. The last word was a million miles away, and I could only inch toward it. I stood up and started walking up and down the room, to try to escape that feeling, but the room wasn't big enough and everyone kept getting in my way.

"Stop it," said Claire. "You're driving me nuts. You're like the Mad Hatter."

"I can't," I said. "I can't. I can't. I'm losing all my words."

My heart was racing. I couldn't calm down. Carol got up and put her arms around me, but I pushed her away and kept walking up and down.

"She's getting really weird," said Carol, and I could tell that she was annoyed.

"What are we going to do with her? She's going to get us caught," said a voice.

Lucy was sitting with Ernessa on the bed. Lucy had a blanket wrapped around her shoulders, but even with the window open, I wasn't cold. Their heads were together, the black hair against the yellow, and they were whispering. They were alone. I couldn't hear anything. All the sounds in the room were going.

"I can't stand this feeling any longer." My words were muffled. They came from another room, from behind a closed door.

Ernessa looked up at me. Her body kept swelling and receding. The teeth were discolored and large, and her lips couldn't cover them. The red gums showed above her teeth. Her eyebrows were a black band across her forehead. Her face was ashen. As she pushed back her thick hair, I could see her white ears and the dark hair all over her hands. There was dark hair everywhere, on her cheeks, around her mouth. She smiled at me very calmly. She wasn't at all disturbed by what was happening to her.

"What's going on?" I demanded. But now I must have been whispering because no one listened to me, and no one noticed her. They were all laughing and eating cookies. The crackling of the cellophane each time a hand reached in the bag for a cookie was deafening.

I could hear Ernessa's voice, even though she was across the room and had lowered her head from my sight. "You can hear me. I need to tell you what it was like when I first came here. On the boat over, I looked down at the gray waves, and I kept saying to myself, 'Jump. Jump.' But it was too cold. I arrived the same way you did, with the same secret. I was ushered in by absence. Dusk was my escort. I checked into my own room, with my own bathroom and fireplace. It was fall. October 10. Brilliant sunshine. The Brangwyn Hotel. We took tea on the porch on the warmest days. Soon it became too chilly. They had to light the fire in my room. But I was still always cold. I lay in bed with hot water bottles, and my feet were blocks of ice. I couldn't warm them. We came here, my mother and I, to put at least an ocean between him and us. My mother managed to recover. In fact, she met another husband here. But to me an ocean was nothing. He reached out and took me with him. 'There's nothing for you here.' I could hear his words—"

Ernessa's old, old. Her life repeats itself like Lucy's horrible record, skipping over and over, always at the same spot. The moon shadow. She's waiting for my life to become stuck like that.

I ran out of the room, down the corridor to the back stairwell, down the stairs, and through the door out into the snow. Carol must have come after me, because she was there with me outside, trying to get me to put on a sweatshirt. I was only wearing my pajamas and slippers. It was cold outside, and there were several inches of snow on the ground, but I wouldn't wear the sweatshirt. I wanted to feel the frost on me, all over my skin. The cold always makes my hands and feet ache, but now I needed the cold. I ran down the drive. When Carol caught up to me, I was rubbing handfuls of snow over my face, my neck, my breasts. I was trying to rub something away that was clinging to my skin: the smell of hash.

We walked down to the Lower Field, around behind the Hut, and back up the drive. The hash started to wear off. I was shivering on the way back, and I put on the sweatshirt that Carol handed me. She didn't say a word. She just held my arm tight. She looked terrified.

When we got back to the door, I was ready to run up to my room and get into bed and sleep forever. I knew it would take hours to warm up my frozen body. I could barely stand up. But the door was locked.

"Shit," said Carol. "I jammed in the piece of wood. I can't believe the watchman came by and shut it. He never does."

"I'm sorry, I'm sorry," I murmured. "I didn't mean for you to die like this."

"What the fuck are you talking about? I really don't want to get caught. Not now. This is stupid."

I don't know how long we were out there, stamping our feet, walking in circles, cursing. Finally Claire came down to make sure I was all right, and she opened the door.

I slept. But when I woke up the next morning, I still felt stoned. I couldn't concentrate on anything. I'm not back to normal yet. I can't stand it when I lose control. I had planned to start reading *Bleak House* this weekend, but I can't think straight. There had to be something else in that hash. Hash isn't strong enough to make you hallucinate.

I know what was in the hash—the future. The hash was dipped in the future. The future when everybody changes and turns into someone different. I'll become a person I won't like at all. It won't matter because that person will have forgotten all about me. I won't exist anymore. It's worse than dying. It means my life now is not really happening.

Am I going crazy? How can I know the difference between losing my grip on reality and seeing things that are truly beyond reality? Everything is beyond reality. There's no one here to tell me.

Last year I watched Annie Patterson lose control. After that, she was changed. It was at a chorus concert. She was standing in the top row, at the back, because she was so tall. She kept shifting from one foot to another; she couldn't stand still. Her head was tilted to one side as she sang. It took too much effort to hold it up straight. Her long black hair, which had once been so thick, couldn't cover her ears. One ear stuck straight up. Her face was colorless, except for her nose, which was red and blotchy. She looked like a sick animal. After the concert, she stepped carefully off the risers, wobbling as she moved. It was incredible how thin she had become. I never imagined someone's bones were really that small. The old Annie was gone. Gone with the flesh and muscle and fat. And if the energy in the universe remains constant, where does that go?

She had fallen into a huge black hole, and she couldn't climb out. It was an accident. She was peering down into it to see what it was like, and then she fell. I never saw her again. At breakfast, I heard one of her friends say, "She lives her life as if it's a novel she's going to write some day."

After dinner

When I came down to supper, everyone laughed at me for freaking out. I wanted to run away and cry, but I was starving. I hadn't eaten a thing all weekend. I stayed in my room all day Saturday and Sunday and said that I was sick. I was so exhausted that I slept most of the time. It was Sunday night buffet, and I could eat quickly and get away. I ate ravenously. I couldn't get the food into my mouth quickly enough, and then I couldn't slow down enough to chew it properly before I swallowed. My hunger was unnatural. I ate two plates piled high with food, without speaking a word to anyone. Then I ran back to my room. I didn't go down to the Playroom afterward, even though we have an extra hour there on Sunday night and everyone goes. I closed myself up in my room. I'm convinced there was something in the hash. I don't understand why no one else had the same experience. But they love being stoned, and I can't understand that.

Lucy just stuck her head in to see if I was feeling better, and I told her I wanted to be left alone. I was lying on my bed, with my journal pushed under the blankets. I'm trying not to get violently sick. If I lie very still and let the waves of nausea roll over me, it will pass. I want to crawl into the back of my closet and hide behind the dresses, the way I did when I was a little girl.

This was why I didn't want to come back to school. I was afraid that it would start up again. I can't shut my eyes and will it away.

I want to be invisible.

January 19

There are no secrets in this school. Some girl always finds out. Or someone makes something up and convinces everyone else that it must be true. So in the end, it doesn't matter if it's true or not, or if there was a secret or not.

Claire was waiting for me when I went into dinner. She said she had to talk to me right after dinner. I knew it was about Mr. Davies from the way she pushed the ringlets out of her eyes so dramatically while she told me to meet her in the Playroom. I didn't want to go.

"I know you won't believe this," she said. She was standing too close to me, and I could feel her hot breath on my ear. I wanted to push her away. "Especially you. You only talk about poetry with him."

"Of course," I said.

"I can't tell you how I found this out, but I know it's true. Mr. Davies and his wife write pornography. They do it together," said Claire.

"You're right," I said. "I don't believe you. I think you're totally ridiculous."

"Ask Mr. Davies if you don't believe me," she said.

"What do you mean, they write pornography?" I asked.

"For a magazine," she answered. "They use a pseudonym, of course. He's not stupid. He doesn't want to get canned from his job."

"But how can you possibly know something like this?" I asked.

"I told you I can't tell you. Trust me."

"Why should I trust you? You'll have to prove this to me."

"Be patient," said Claire. "I'll have the proof."

I couldn't bring myself to walk away. "Have you seen the magazine?" I asked.

Claire squirmed, but she didn't answer my question. "Do you think he and his wife work it out in bed before they write it?"

"If they do it, it's for the money," I said. "I don't care if he does it." But I do care.

January 20

The day students never touch each other. They think it's queer when they see two boarders walking down the hall with their arms around each other. But that's the way we are. The thought of touching another girl disgusts the day students. They gab on the phone every night. They talk about boys and clothes and makeup. The boarders are with each other at night. We hate the phone. None of us wants to be reminded that she has a family. No news is good news. Everyone knows that most of the gym teachers and half the teachers are lesbians, but no one says anything. The day students are all in love with their new hockey coach, who's young and pretty. But everyone knows she lives with another woman. I don't care. I've almost never spoken to a day student, except for Dora when she was a day student. She was just boarding this year because her father went to Paris on a sabbatical. She was different because she wasn't stupid and blond. She was always more like a boarder, even though she wasn't the kind of girl you wanted to put your arm around. She was cold and stiff. The few times that we walked arm in arm, I felt uncomfortable and self-conscious.

I try not to think about Dora.

You can tell when there's something going on between two ugly, overweight girls. I'm glad all my friends are pretty—that's probably why I don't really like Claire.

Last night, after my bath, I was lying on Lucy's bed. We were both reading. I had my arm around her, and she had her head on my shoulder. I was playing with her hair.

At least she knocked before she entered this time.

I didn't bother to look up from my book. But Lucy had already jumped off the bed and was moving toward the door. Ernessa wasn't interested in her. She was looking straight at me, lying on Lucy's bed in my nightgown, my book on my chest. It frightened me. Lucy reached out for her arm, but Ernessa was gone without a word, and the door closed before Lucy had a chance to touch her.

When she was gone, Lucy and I had to look at each other and feel embarrassed.

Once Charley accidentally touched Ernessa's hand when she passed her a cigarette. Ernessa jumped back.

"What's the problem?" asked Charley. "I'm not a lesbo."

"Her hand was cold," Charley told me later. "Really cold. She freaks me out. She'll never bum another cigarette from me."

I could tell that Charley was really annoyed. She knew people thought she was a lesbian because she was so wiry and boyish looking.

Ernessa can't understand us.

It wasn't just because of Lucy and me. She's angry at *me*. I wouldn't listen to her story that night. I ran away. I won't listen.

■

January 21

There are places in this school that are beginning to feel unsafe, places where I'm used to being alone. If I think about it rationally, she has no reason to be there. But she has her own reasons.

I was on the fourth floor, outside Miss Norris's apartment, about to go in for Greek. She was standing right behind me. She just materialized.

"I thought about starting up Greek again," she said. "But the situation wasn't right."

I had no idea what she meant by that, but the tone she used was not at all nice.

"I used to study Greek and Latin. I wanted to be a classics scholar.

I was very serious, even though I was a girl. But then—other things intervened."

I don't believe a thing she says.

"I don't know if you could start in the middle of the year. You could ask Miss—"

"No, it's too late for that. Are you aware that Dora's death caused me a lot of trouble? It was very inconvenient. I had to have lots of discussions with the headmistress and the psychologist and the police. They wanted to know how it was that she fell directly under my window and I didn't know anything."

"It caused you a lot of trouble? What about the trouble you caused me? You told on me. You sent the police to me."

"They asked me if I'd ever seen anyone out there. I told them you and Dora liked to walk along the gutters. I didn't invent anything."

"Dora was probably going to Carol's room. We've done it for years," I said, trying to sound offhand.

"The hall is more direct," she said. "I'd never try the rain gutters. They're much too dangerous. Look what happened to Dora."

"It was an accident," I said. "Everyone knows that."

The door to Miss Norris's apartment opened, and she stuck out her head, wreathed in fine, white hair. "Ah, my delinquent student. I thought I heard you out there, dearie."

The light poured out of the open door, and it fell over the two of us in the corridor. I could hear the sound of the birds behind Miss Norris, a dissonant choir. Her white hair now glowed like a nimbus. Behind me, Ernessa stepped back out of the light. I hurried over to Miss Norris, and she pulled me inside.

She blames me for what happened to Dora and the fact that the accident, or whatever it was, has made them pay too much attention to her. I told Dora not to do it, and she didn't listen to me.

I found this in one of my father's books when I was home: "The vampire knows all secrets and the future." She doesn't need hash. We need it so that we can enter her time.

Someone is at the door. I'm going to put my pen and my journal away.

January 22

Mr. Davies stopped me in the hallway. I think he was looking for me.

"You didn't sign up for my poetry class," he said, as if he were accusing me of some awful crime.

"I'm not in the mood for writing poetry right now," I said. I never intended to sign up for that class. "I'm taking 'Responsibility in Literature.'"

"What are you reading?" asked Mr. Davies.

"*Daniel Deronda* and *Bleak House*. I'm in the mood for really long books. And realism. For a change."

"But weren't you the one who argued so convincingly in class that writers make their stories real? You can't get away from the supernatural that easily. The writer is always inventing, believing in the truth of the unseen," said Mr. Davies. "Dickens was fascinated by the supernatural."

I was surprised to feel that I had somehow disappointed Mr. Davies. "I'm sorry," I murmured. "I couldn't take your class. It didn't fit into my schedule."

"I'm sure you'll enjoy those books. Miss Watson is lucky to have you. But don't forget me just because you're not in my class anymore. Come visit, and we'll talk about poetry if you don't want to write it."

I smiled.

"I mean it," he said. "I miss you."

I have been avoiding him.

That day I was a spinning top losing momentum, wobbling on its axis. I felt myself tilting forward into him, then crashing back.

All my teachers have it out for me. Miss Simpson got annoyed at me for not being ready for my piano lesson. I used to get A's without even trying, now I can't keep up. I'd rather write in my journal than do homework.

Lucy missed assembly for three days, and she has a week's detention. She says she's too tired to get up in the morning. She sleeps right through morning bells. She can't understand why she's so tired all the time. This morning I went in to wake her up, and I couldn't get her out of bed. She seemed drugged. When I shook her shoulder, her head rolled back and forth on her pillow. Her eyelids fluttered like gray moths. She couldn't raise them. I went down to breakfast and signed her in. After breakfast I came up and dragged her out of bed so that she wouldn't be late for assembly again. I brought her up a doughnut, but she didn't eat it. I saw it, wrapped in a napkin, on her dresser an hour ago, when I looked in on her. She hadn't touched it. I didn't see her at lunch either. She was probably in her room, doing homework. She says she's gotten really behind, and we have a huge chemistry test next Wednesday. I'll have to help her study. I don't want to.

January 23
Yesterday I forgot to mention that I got my first-semester grades. All A's. Lucy did so badly that she won't even tell me what she got. I think she got a D in Chemistry. I feel so sorry for her. I wonder what Ernessa got.

I didn't feel the usual thrill when I took my report card from the envelope and unfolded the crisp paper. I didn't deserve those A's. My teachers gave them to me because they expect me to do well, the way Lucy's teachers expect her to do terribly. The comments weren't even that good. Everyone but Mr. Davies said I needed to participate more in class. I was embarrassed when I read what Mr. Davies wrote about me. My face got red, even though I was all alone in my room. It isn't true, but my mother will be pleased.

January 25
This morning in assembly, Miss Rood announced the names of girls who have to make up gym on Friday afternoon. Lucy and Ernessa were on the list. Lucy, the perfect daddy's girl who never gets into trouble, didn't seem to notice that Miss Rood had called her name.

Ernessa was furious. She turned around and stared at Miss Bobbie. Lucy had to nudge Ernessa to get her to stop. She noticed that.

I looked at the backs of their heads: the waves of Ernessa's black hair next to Lucy's straight blond hair.

Ernessa manages to get away with absolutely everything except missing gym. Miss Bobbie is the only one who makes her follow the rules. That's because Miss Bobbie hates her.

It's mostly the day students who hate Jews. I can always tell who would prefer not to sit next to me because I'm Jewish. There are empty chairs on either side of me until a boarder comes into class. I remember so clearly the shock I felt the first time something like that happened. I was going up to the drugstore near the train station to get a Coke and French fries after school. A group of girls from my class was on the platform with some boys. All the girls had shoulder-length blond hair, blue eyes, small noses—the kind who are stupid but good at sports, who wear their gym tunics really short to show off their tanned and muscular legs against their white socks. One of the boys was writing something on a post with a marking pen, and everyone was watching him write. The boy had curly reddish hair and dark freckles across his nose. He didn't look in my direction, but I caught one of those girls looking at me with her vacant blue eyes while the others laughed. On the way back to school, the platform was empty. They had all taken the train to wherever it is they live. I went over to see what the red-haired boy had written. He had drawn a swastika with the letters K-I-K-E in each of its four arms. There was a circle around it and a black line through the circle. They were black marks on a brown post, where the paint was cracked and beginning to show the silver metal underneath. I chipped the paint away.

I used to draw swastikas in secret, to see if I could force myself to do it. Then I would tear up the paper into tiny pieces before I threw it away.

They're pretty now, but they'll grow up to be just like their mothers: heavy around the middle, with dark leathery skin, going to the beauty parlor every week to have their hair frosted, driving around in wood-trimmed station wagons, and baking cookies to bring to hockey games. I'll still be thin and young-looking like my mother, and I won't have a family.

I never spoke to any of those girls again.

■

January 28

Lucy failed her chemistry test, even though we went over every formula together.

We spent so much time studying together in her room. It was just like last year, except that it wasn't any fun. I couldn't stop thinking, Lucy is using me. She's only being nice to me because she needs my help. When she's finished needing me, I'll cease to exist for her, at least in the way I want to exist for her. I'd look over at her staring with dull eyes at the study sheet, chewing on her pencil and trying to make sense of the words and numbers. She can't understand a thing unless I explain it to her. Then she forgets my explanation immediately. I wanted to leave the room. I tapped my foot impatiently. I opened my mouth to tell her that I couldn't do this. It wasn't like last year. She couldn't expect this any longer. But how could I explain to her that I didn't want to help her because Miss Rood had read her name on Monday along with Ernessa's?

Yesterday she fell asleep after lunch and missed two periods. Lucky for her, they were English and French, and when she explained to her teachers what had happened, they were very understanding. I've been signing her in for breakfast. Now I'll have to make sure she gets to class after lunch. She shouldn't be so tired, although she did stay up pretty late before her chemistry test. She's so worried about failing the makeup.

The others have finally noticed. We (Sofia, Claire, and I) have decided to take Lucy downtown on Saturday, just to wander around, look at clothes and records, maybe go to a movie. Anything to get her out. I'm going to call Charley tonight and ask her to meet us. The bells just rang for dinner, and I'm not dressed. I have to hurry. All my stockings have huge runs, and my clothes are dirty.

After dinner

Tonight I'm doing something I almost never do. I'm sitting in the library for study hour. Even though it's filled with old books and oak chairs and tables and reading lamps with green glass shades, I never read here. Usually, there are lots of girls sitting around, and they're all talking, and it's impossible to work. Tonight it's empty.

I like to do my homework lying on my bed, but I wanted to get away from Lucy. She'll never find me here. She'll have to figure out her formulas by herself. She's probably sitting at her desk staring into space and waiting for me to help her.

I'm annoyed at her for not eating dessert at dinner.

For a long time, I looked at the faded spines of the books and breathed in the dusty papery smell. I am happy. Lucy is in her room, far away from me. I can write about her without worrying that she'll see my journal.

The dessert isn't really important. She's stopped eating everything, and she's lost a lot of weight. We're together at Miss Meineke's table. That's by far the best table to be at. Miss Meineke's just like us. She lives up on the fourth floor, next to the infirmary. She walks down the corridor in her pajamas, and her room is a mess. She has stacks of books and uncorrected English papers on the floor, and she never makes her bed. It drives Mac crazy, but she can't say anything. At dinner, Miss Meineke makes fun of the corridor teachers and giggles all the time. That was how Lucy and I first got to be friends, setting up together at her table. Last week, when I saw the lists posted in the Cloakroom and our two names together, I was so happy for an instant. I thought, I have to go find Lucy and tell her. But then I didn't. Tonight we had our favorite dessert: caramel cornflake ring with coffee ice cream. At first, Lucy said she didn't want any, she wasn't hungry. Miss Meineke said, "How can you resist this?" and put some on a plate anyway. Lucy just picked at it. The ice cream melted into a puddle. I made a point of eating all of mine, even though I had lost my appetite watching her. She's not interested—

She came into the room without a sound and sat down next to me, as if I were expecting her. And I guess I was, in a way. For a long time, neither of us said a word. I didn't look up from my journal. I slid my arm over the page, to hide what I had written. I didn't want her to see the letters L-U-C-Y on the page. The black ink was still wet. I could feel it on the underside of my arm. My skin blotted the ink. I put my pen on the table, without closing it, even though I hate it when the nib dries out. From the corner of my eye, behind my glasses, I could see her arm resting on the table next to mine, inches away, but not touching. The hairs on her arm are long and black, and the skin underneath is so white. But thick. The veins are hidden.

"Do you think we'll be like that one day?" asked Ernessa, looking over at the portraits of the founder of the school and her first few successors, hanging on the wall directly in front of us. They are all in dark browns and grays and greens, very somber and stern. A smile could never soften those expressions. It would crack the paint of those lifeless faces.

"I doubt it," I said, laughing nervously. "Not my style."

"I don't mean dressed up. I mean grown up and desiccated, like Miss Rood and all the women here. I never wanted to grow up, really. I was content to be a child."

"So was I. But you don't become like that overnight. Unless you were born like that. The way Miss Rood was. It's probably less painful to get old than it seems. Everybody does it." It surprised me that I was actually talking to Ernessa.

"It happens faster than you can imagine," said Ernessa with the certainty that she always has when she's talking about life and death and all the other things that people don't know how to talk about.

"It seems so far away," I added softly.

"You wake up one day and you're just like them—amazed not to have lived the life you imagined you would. Do you think anyone is satisfied at the end?"

Ernessa waited for an answer that I didn't want to give her. I looked over at the door and prayed that someone would come in and release me. Why was the library so empty tonight? Her questions were like the moths' wings.

"I'd kill myself if I became like that," I said at last.

"They waited too long," said Ernessa. "They thought they would live forever." She pushed back her chair, got up, and walked out of the room. I looked at her for the first time just as the door closed behind her.

The words that drove me out into the snow that night in my hash-induced haze: "I kept saying, 'Jump. Jump.' But it was too cold."

■

January 31

Our expedition to town yesterday didn't work out the way we planned it. It was a disaster, like finding yourself riding in a stolen taxi. We met Charley at the train station downtown. At first everyone was excited to see her. It was a new Charley: she was wearing dirty bell bottoms, a faded blue jean jacket with an American flag sewn on the back, and a red bandanna around her head. It looked like she hadn't washed her hair since she left school, it was so greasy and stringy.

When she saw us, she raised her fist and shouted, "Power to the people—let's go to Wanamaker's." We ran along the wide sidewalks of Broad Street, shouting and jumping.

On the way there we passed by a big record store, and Charley called out, "Let's look at records" and was through the door before anyone had a chance to protest. We all followed her inside. I stood off to the side and watched the others flip through the records in the bins. Lucy was suddenly animated. As she looked at the albums, she started singing about being followed by a moon shadow. Cat Stevens again. She repeated the words over and over in a low, droning voice, like a chant. Moon shadow moon shadow moon shadow.

But by the time we reached the department store and all of us crowded into a dressing room with Sofia, Lucy sank to the floor in the corner, exhausted. Maybe it was the strange lighting in the dressing room that makes everyone look so awful, but Lucy's skin was gray, and her eyes were dull.

We hadn't seen Charley since before Christmas. She was telling us stories about her new school, especially how many different drugs she had sampled in the past month. "I've learned a whole new alphabet," she said. "LSD, MDA, DMT, PCP, THC. It's a total mind fuck."

I think we were all disappointed that she didn't miss us or school at all. We were silent. Only Claire wanted to hear more about the drugs. She wanted to know how she could get some.

"I don't know if I would try that shit at school," said Charley. "It's too spooky there. That was really freaky about Dora. She always talked about killing herself, but I never took her seriously. You know the way she used to go on about philosophy and books and things. I just used to tune her out. I mean like it's one thing to talk about it and another to actually do it. To snuff it."

Lucy had turned white and was breathing quickly. I waited for something to happen.

"No one wants to talk about her . . . about her accident," I said.

"Sorry," said Charley. "I didn't mean to bum you guys out. I'm cool where I'm at. I don't have to do a stroke of work. But I have to say the weed is not as righteous as it was at school."

Then she looked at the dresses Sofia had hung on the hook, for tea dances this spring, and said, "These are like totally capitalist old lady clothes. Come the revolution, you'll all dress like me!"

We laughed at her.

Sofia tried on the dresses, but she thought they were too short and made her look fat. She kept looking in the double mirrors and complaining about the cellulite in her thighs. What is cellulite, anyway? Does it even exist? Sofia is always rubbing Italian creams into her legs to make them smooth and firm, but it never makes any difference. She was born with dimpled thighs. She kept turning from side to side and twisting her head around, as if she were trying to imagine herself three months from now and twenty pounds thinner.

"Let's go," said Sofia. "These really are old lady dresses."

We pulled Lucy off the floor and dragged her out of the dressing room. Sofia and Claire wanted to look for bras, but Lucy didn't want to stay in the store. "It always makes me so tired to wander around big department stores," she complained. "My head hurts."

We went outside with Lucy and stood around on the sidewalk, trying to figure out what to do for the rest of the day. All of a sudden, we had nothing to do.

"I need to get some coffee," said Lucy. So we went into a coffee shop, and Lucy drank two cups of black coffee, no cream or sugar.

While Lucy drank her coffee, we decided that we would walk up to the park where we always sit and watch people. It was only ten blocks away, but we hadn't gone five blocks before Lucy had to stop and rest.

"I'm too tired. I think I'll go back to school. I just want to go back," she said.

I insisted on going back with her, and she sat down on the sidewalk and began to cry. "Let me go by myself. I don't want to ruin everything. Charley came all this way to see you."

I refused to let her go by herself. I didn't know if she could make it. In the end, everyone decided to come back with Lucy and me, and Charley went home early.

On the way back to the train station, Charley pulled me aside and asked about Ernessa.

"She's dropped out of the picture," I lied. "I hardly see her now. It's almost as if she's not at school anymore."

It is true that Lucy never goes into Ernessa's room now. She's too tired to do anything except lie on her bed.

"She's totally tight-assed," said Charley, "but she did me two big favors. She turned me on to some great shit, and she got me kicked out. Otherwise I'd have gone out the window like Dora. Headfirst into the ozone."

"Ernessa wanted to get rid of you," I said. "She thought you couldn't keep your mouth shut."

"Yeah, but it's not like it was a secret she was selling drugs to everyone."

"Did you ever see Ernessa get weird when she smoked?" I asked.

"What do you mean by weird?"

"I don't know. Kind of changed, different."

"I actually think she was immune to the stuff. It didn't seem to have any effect on her at all. Probably because she smoked all the time. Can you imagine, immune to pot? That would take all the fun out of life."

I wanted to tell her more, but Charley had lost interest in the subject. She was already talking to Claire about something else.

I turned and watched Lucy drag herself along the sidewalk arm in arm with Sofia. Her eyes were colder and more focused than I thought possible. She couldn't have heard our conversation.

In the end, I was relieved to say good-bye to Charley and to go back to school.

Lucy didn't say a word on the train ride. When we got back to school, she closed herself up in her room and didn't come out for the rest of the day. I didn't see her again until lunch today. She hasn't been to church for weeks, and she didn't go this morning. I used to tease her about going to church, but now that she's stopped going, I'm annoyed.

I didn't check on her the whole time. If she ate something, she wouldn't be tired all the time. When we got back to school, I asked her if she had her period, and she said that she hasn't had it for months.

FEBRUARY

February 1

If I approach Lucy, she pushes me away. If I avoid her, she comes to me in my dreams.

Lucy was in bed. I had gone in to get her up, but I couldn't wake her. She was lying on her side, and I shook her shoulder again and again, but it felt like wood. Finally, I pulled back the covers. She was naked, and her nakedness embarrassed me; it was different from her usual nakedness. She was completely stiff, with her legs tucked up to her chest. To get her up, I had to unbend her legs and spread them. Each time I forced them apart, she clenched them back together. At last I managed to turn her on her back. Between her legs was the cane of a rose bush, covered with green leaves and reddish buds and large brown thorns. She held it tightly between her thighs, and I had to rip it out, tearing the flesh. The blood ran down her thighs in rivulets and soaked into the sheets.

February 2

Last night Lucy passed out on the way to the bathroom. I heard her hit the floor, and I ran into her room. She was lying on the floor, barely conscious. She wouldn't let me take her to the infirmary in the middle of the night, and the next morning she insisted that she felt much better. I made her go anyway. I said I would tell the nurse what had happened if she didn't go by herself. She was really furious at me, but she went. I'm glad I forced her to go.

The nurse made her stay in the infirmary. The doctor examined her during the morning and said that there was nothing the matter with her that a little rest couldn't cure. She has to stay there for a few days. He really wanted to make sure she was eating properly. Mrs. Halton is going to talk to all her teachers.

After school I ran up to the florist and bought Lucy a bunch of red tulips. I bought the brightest flowers I could find. They cost a fortune, but I know how much Lucy loves flowers, and I think they will cheer her up. She was really upset when the doctor said she had to stay in the infirmary. They wouldn't let me be with her for more than ten minutes. I don't know why, if she's not really sick. She can rest in bed while I visit. They said it would be "stressful."

At least she appreciated the flowers and wasn't angry with me anymore.

February 3

Today I couldn't get to see Lucy until late, about half an hour before quiet hour, because Mr. Davies had arranged a poetry reading after school and asked me to come. He read two of his poems, and I actually thought they were good. They were simple, not at all what I expected. I guess I'd never really thought about what his poems would be like. One poem was about a thrush singing in a dead tree: the sudden and totally unexpected apparition of beauty in the middle of everyday life. Which is real, the bird's song or the dead tree, because they can't both be real?

I'm sure none of the other girls liked his poems. They are too quiet. They keep their meaning hidden. The girls want pain and angst, even from a man. There was plenty of that in their poems. Spiraling downward into dark pools of despair, being sucked under, suffocating. Everyone is misunderstood and moaning over some silly boy or some imagined pain. Living is a giant cliché. Even the desire for death becomes a cliché in their poems.

I'm so glad I didn't take that class. It's bad enough to have to think about yourself all the time, but then to waste poetry on yourself is a sin. There are so many things to write about, so many pure things, and that's what poetry should be about. But everyone loves to expose themselves in their poems and then to put on a show for the others. I only write "I" in my journal, where no one can see it.

By the time I got to Lucy, it was getting dark outside. I had two Hershey bars in my pocket and a copy of Hermann Hesse's *Demian,* in case she was bored. (She said she wanted to read it, but I doubt she will.) I opened the door and entered very quietly. At first, I thought she was asleep because she was lying so still on the bed, but when my eyes became accustomed to the light, I saw that her eyes were wide open. She didn't even blink. She was lying on her back, her arms pressed to her sides, and her face was as white as the covers on the bed. Even her lips were white. She was fading. Maybe it was the twilight, but neither of us raised our voices above a whisper.

"I brought you some chocolate and a book," I said.

"Thank you."

I noticed that an unopened book lay on the covers by her hand. It was a copy of *Jane Eyre,* in a pale green binding with gold letters. I opened it up and saw the name, Ernessa Bloch, written on an endpaper stained with spots in a black ink that had faded to brown. Even her handwriting is old-fashioned and formal; the E and the B were tall and elegant, and the rest of the letters tiny and almost illegible. It reminded me of the books in my father's library, old books that other people bought and signed and read years ago without giving a thought to what would happen to the books after they died. I used to look at the signatures and think about the people who first owned them, how they held the books in their hands and never imagined that one day they would die and the books would end up in my hands.

"Ernessa brought that for me. But I'm too tired to read. That book is so heavy."

"Don't you feel any better?" I asked.

"A little bit."

"Lucy, Lucy."

"I don't feel sick," she said. "Nothing hurts. It's not a bad feeling, being so weak. I'm not scared. All I have to do is lie here and think about breathing. I listen to the breath coming out of my mouth. Then there is one second, before I decide to take the next breath. I don't really decide. . . . "

Her voice trailed off. For a while we didn't say anything. I had never heard Lucy talk like that before. It frightened me. When the room had grown so dark that I couldn't distinguish her face from the pillow, I reached over and turned on the lamp beside her bed. The light from the lamp wasn't strong, but Lucy turned her face away and covered her eyes with her hands. Next to the lamp were the flowers I had brought her. The bright burning red had turned pink. The stalks and leaves had lost their green, but they hadn't shriveled up.

"What happened to your flowers?" I asked. "They're all faded."

I stood up and looked into the vase to see if the color had somehow run out into the water. But the water was clear.

"I guess they're starting to die," said Lucy.

"They were so fresh yesterday."

At that moment, the bells for quiet hour began to ring, and the nurse came. I knew she wouldn't let me stay any longer, so I kissed Lucy and left.

When I was halfway down the corridor, I realized that I still had the chocolate bars in my pocket and I was holding the book I had brought for her. I hated to leave Lucy there all by herself, thinking about each breath she took.

February 4

Lucy only has the energy to breathe. She is getting weaker, and Ernessa is getting stronger. Lucy's energy goes to nourish Ernessa. It's her food. They make Lucy eat in the infirmary, but she will waste away to nothing, while Ernessa becomes enormous and strong. I watch Ernessa during dinner. She pushes the food from one side of the plate to the other. But she looks so healthy. I need to keep her away from Lucy. I'm glad the nurses don't let anyone visit for long.

February 5

I've actually been much happier with Lucy in the infirmary. I don't have to look out for her all the time. The nurses do it for me. She's safer there. I love Lucy, but having her in the room next to mine was beginning to be a drag. I haven't enjoyed being with her except for a short time just after winter vacation. Even then, every nice time we had together was ruined for me.

In the last week, I've been very relaxed. I've practiced the piano for two hours each day, done all my homework, finished the second volume of Proust. I can write in my journal whenever I want to. It's been wonderful. I sleep well at night, and I'm not anxious. I've been alone most of the time or with Sofia. When Lucy is out of the picture, I can be with Sofia. Tomorrow we're going to take a long walk together after lunch. We like to walk past all the big houses with swimming pools and tennis courts and fancy cars parked in front. Some of the day students live in these houses.

Yesterday I had a good talk with Mr. Davies after school. I kept thinking about his poems and how surprised I was that I liked them. I didn't feel uncomfortable being alone with him. He asked me what I've been reading, and I told him that I want to read all of Proust.

"What about *Dracula*?" he asked. "That's been my favorite book since I was ten."

I must have looked disgusted.

"I promise you it's as good as Proust and much shorter. It's as perfect as a book can be. There's not a single word you would change."

"I can't read those books anymore. They ruined my fall."

Mr. Davis looked so disappointed that I added, "Maybe when I've finished Proust."

I told him about my father's set of Proust, which I brought back with me after vacation. There are twelve of them lined up on my desk: little blue books with turquoise and white covers. I'm reading them because I like the books so much. It makes a difference reading a book if I like the way it feels and looks. It's got to be a real book, which is usually an old book, with a certain smell, musty and vegetable. I don't like new things.

I love to read my father's books, to touch the pages he touched. The cells of his fingertips rubbed off on the pages, and they are still there. Sometimes my mother talks about getting rid of all his books. I've made her promise to save them for me, but I don't trust her. She could wake up one morning and decide she can't stand to have them around and call someone to come and take them away.

It was the baby sitting on the sofa staring at us and the sensation that his wife was watching me while she talked to Claire that made me so anxious. He was only playing, but I couldn't relax. I shouldn't have let Claire talk me into visiting him.

February 6

I've visited Lucy every day in the infirmary. Today (Saturday) I went after breakfast, and I'll go again after Sofia and I get back from our walk. She says she's not really bored and she doesn't mind being there. I don't know how she spends her time, since whenever I go in there, she's lying on her back staring up at the ceiling. I guess she's a little better, although she doesn't seem any different to me. Her eyes are red, as if she's been crying the whole time. She's probably getting out tomorrow. I brought all her schoolbooks today, because she has to try to catch up on her homework over the weekend. She's going to be so hopelessly behind. After she gets out, she's not going to have to take gym for a while.

I gave her the Hershey bars, but I doubt she's touched them. She used to be practically addicted to chocolate and had to eat some every day after school. It drove Sofia crazy that she could eat anything she wanted and not gain a pound. She says she doesn't have much of an appetite, but they make her eat at every meal.

It's lunchtime. I'm starving. I'll finish this later.

After lunch

I'm so angry. Sofia and I can't take our walk. I don't know what I'm going to do with myself until dinner. I was counting on being with Sofia.

Sofia came up from lunch, and she discovered an enormous pile in the middle of her room. Sweaters, bags, shoes, books, dirty underwear. She couldn't get in her room. For the last few months, she hasn't bothered to clean her room each morning. She shoves everything under her bed and pulls down the spread. Somehow her corridor teacher, Miss Fraser, discovered it this morning, and she pulled it all out. Sofia has to spend the afternoon cleaning her room. Miss Fraser is going to inspect it this afternoon. It really was incredible what Sofia had managed to stuff under her bed. I don't know how she found anything to wear. Claire and I stood in her doorway and stared in amazement. Sofia sat on the mound with her legs crossed and did a perfect imitation of Miss Fraser with her long, drooping fingers and drawling voice: "My dear, someone like you with an artistic temperament finds it hard to bother with the mundane details of life. I understand so well. But we have to. Rules are rules."

We all laughed, but Sofia has to clean her room, and my afternoon is ruined. "I don't blame her," said Sofia. "It's a mess."

She can't help feeling sorry for Miss Fraser. She says Miss Fraser once dreamed of being a modern dancer, and she feels that she's never been able to fulfill her artistic potential. Miss Fraser is a frustrated artist.

I think it's a different kind of frustration: sexual. Isn't purple supposed to signify desire? Sofia says that Italians think it brings bad luck and death. Anyway, absolutely everything in Miss Fraser's suite is some shade of purple. The bedspread is a rose purple. The curtains are a bluish purple. The throw over the sofa is lavender. The rug is a black purple. I once went in there when Sofia needed her to sign a permission slip. Miss Fraser sat at her desk, her tight black skirt creeping above her knees, flat shoes like ballet slippers on her feet, her reddish hair pulled back in a bun. Her hair is so thin that I can see her pink scalp underneath. She always has the same white roots. She must dye her hair from time to time, but it's permanently grown out. When she reached for her pen, I noticed that her perfectly painted nails (a pale lavender) were so long that they were beginning to curl up at the ends. They didn't look like part of her body any longer. It would be impossible to hold a pen with those pearly nails. That was probably why she wrote so incredibly slowly. As she traced each letter on the little white slip, she would whisper it aloud. S-O-F-I-A C-O-N— She paused and stared down at the paper through her half glasses. Then she scraped it up with the nails of her other hand, crumpled it into a ball, threw it into the wastepaper basket, and reached out for a new slip. She started writing again, making huge loops with her hand as she went. Each letter had to be attached to the one before it and the one after it. When she finished each word, she went back and carefully dotted the i's and crossed the t's, just so. Finally, after three tries, she handed the completed slip to Sofia.

Sofia got angry at me when I made fun of Miss Fraser. She thinks she's sweet and harmless and the best corridor teacher. If Sofia had been on our corridor, Mrs. Halton would never have noticed a thing. We agreed that Miss Fraser is sad.

After dinner
I saw Lucy for a little while this afternoon and helped her with her homework. She is definitely getting out tomorrow. I really don't want her back.

■

February 8

Lucy is back, and she seems much stronger. She got up this morning and came down to breakfast and actually ate. She's a bit like her old self.

Charley may come down on Saturday. We're trying to figure out what to do. I think Lucy's coming along.

At breakfast, I overheard a conversation between Lucy and Kiki. I was sitting at the other end of the table pretending to talk to Carol, but all the time I was really listening to what Lucy was saying. Carol had to keep repeating herself. Lucy was complaining that Miss Bobbie is always after Ernessa; she used the word "persecute." That's a big word for her.

"Ernessa hasn't been feeling so good lately. After about ten minutes of calisthenics, she's completely exhausted. She can barely move. But Miss Bobbie won't let her sit out, even for five minutes, without a doctor's note."

"So, why doesn't she go to the infirmary and get a note? Everyone does it."

"She doesn't want to go there. She's afraid they'll make her stay. It's not like she's sick or anything. She's just feeling worn out."

"Well, Miss Bobbie'll never lighten up. She doesn't like her type."

"But it was so easy for me to get excused from gym, and there's nothing really the matter with me. It's not fair."

I don't believe any of this about feeling exhausted. Ernessa is incredibly strong. She just wants to get out of gym. And Miss Bobbie doesn't fall for it. Lucy buys into everything Ernessa says. Everyone does. It's ridiculous. Lucy's so concerned about Ernessa being tired when she's the one who was in bed for a week and still isn't completely recovered.

Lucy is no longer the helpless victim lying on her white bed in the infirmary, counting her breaths and weeping. She doesn't have to let Ernessa take anything from her. She can resist. And if Ernessa takes, it's because Lucy has offered.

February 11

The night is so long. In the middle of the night, I'm certain that it will never end. I usually fall asleep as the sky begins to lighten, and when the bells ring for breakfast, I'm sound asleep. My head feels so heavy and dull all day long. It's a struggle to hold it up.

Lucy is all right. Some days she's stronger than others, but basically she seems okay. Having her in the next room makes me edgy. I'm up all night long, listening for noises, tossing from my back to my front and then to my back again, trying to get comfortable. I can't. I must get up to pee five times a night. It's like a nervous tic.

When I was a little girl and woke up during the night and was scared, I used to get my father. I would go and stand by his bed. He was always lying on his back. He looked so peaceful asleep that I didn't want to disturb him. After a little while, he would open his eyes, sit up very slowly, and follow me silently down the hallway to my room. His feet shuffled on the rug in the hallway as he walked behind me because he was half asleep. When he lay down next to me on my bed, I instantly calmed down and fell asleep. I didn't like to do this too often, only when I was desperate. I was afraid he would say something during the day. He might tease me about being such a baby. But he never did. And when I awoke in the morning, he was gone, back in his own bed. Only the impression left by his sturdy body convinced me that he had really been there during the night.

Now there isn't even an impression.

After my father died, my mother took me to a psychiatrist a few times. I told him that what I missed most about my father was that if I wanted him during the night, he couldn't be with me. Even though I hadn't gotten him out of bed for years, I needed to know that I could do it. The psychiatrist said that he felt it was inappropriate for my father to share my bed. He spoke about him as if he were still alive and his real crime were helping me to fall asleep rather than killing himself. When the doctor said that, I wondered if he had forgotten the reason why I was there. He had so many patients that he might get their problems confused. After that, I wouldn't speak to him anymore. I refused to tell my mother why. I didn't know if she ever noticed that my father was sometimes absent from their bed in the middle of the night. She sent me off to school anyway. I didn't want to think about my father sleeping in bed next to me ever again. The doctor ruined it.

Last year at this time, I was getting ready for the spring dance and secretly dreaming that I was going to fall in love with my date. I never told anyone. And then he was so ludicrously boring and pimply faced. I kept thinking what a waste it was that I had bought such a beautiful dress. But still I was much happier then.

▬

February 12

Can anyone know the exact point where reality ends and something else, completely unfathomable, takes over? If you look at two parallel lines, you know that you'll never be able to see to the point where they actually touch, only the point where they appear to converge. But that point exists, theoretically, and there everything is possible.

This morning we were supposed to go to the library to research our history term paper. I decided to practice instead. If I sit down in one of the comfortable chairs in the library, I fall asleep right away. At least in the practice room, there's no place to sleep except the floor. I played for a while, but the smell coming up from the basement was bothering me. Again. I'd forgotten about it, but today I couldn't stand to be in the room. I decided to look for the janitor and had just opened the door, when I saw someone coming out the basement door. I caught a glimpse of a navy blue sweater and a long gray skirt at the end of the hallway. I pulled the door half shut and waited for the girl to pass. I already knew who it was before I actually saw her face. She passed by quickly, not exactly running, rather skimming over the ground. Her face was dark reddish-purple and bloated. Slick with wet. She tried to wipe her face with her sweater sleeve. It was awful.

When I was sure she was gone, I walked down the hallway to the basement door. I was afraid to touch the knob. I was afraid that it would scorch my skin. The door was locked. I'm sure I saw her coming out of the basement. She's managed to get a key. Or maybe the door was left open. That still doesn't explain anything.

Last fall, I let myself get sucked into stories, and the stories killed Dora. I won't let that happen now. I won't let myself believe things that I don't think are possible. I skipped class and snuck up to my room and crawled under the covers of my bed. I needed to be in my own room, on my own bed, with my own smell around me, not the wretched basement smell. If Mrs. Halton caught me, I was going to tell her that I had terrible cramps. When I calmed down a little, I forced myself to read. I held the little turquoise book open under the covers and looked at the words on the page. I have no idea what I read.

When I saw her later on this afternoon, just before dinner, she looked normal. I made a point of looking straight at her and meeting her eyes. She acted as she always does, basically ignoring me, so I don't think she knows that I saw her this morning.

February 13

Today I didn't go into town with the others to meet Charley. I didn't feel like it. I was tired, and I was getting the kind of headache that I sometimes get before my period. There's a tightness in my head, and my tongue is thick and swollen. It's a strange feeling for which there are no words. It used to frighten me when I was little.

I have to lie down in a dark, quiet room. I can't even read. All I can think about is my headache. The whole world is my throbbing head. Sometimes, it's so bad that I have to throw up. I sleep for hours, and I wake up tired. When my headache goes, the tiredness is almost pleasurable. My arms and legs are too heavy to lift. Everything flows out of me. I never dream when I have a headache.

As soon as I could stand to sit up in bed and to let some light into my room, I got my journal and pen to keep me company. I feel so alone with my headache.

Lucy didn't seem to care that I wasn't coming.

I don't have the strength to fight Ernessa. She goes where she pleases. She appears unhoped for, uncalled for. She moves through doors and walls and windows. Her thoughts move through minds. She enters dreams. She vanishes and is still there. She knows the future and sees through flesh. She is not afraid of anything.

■
February 14

Today my headache is even worse, and I'm spending the day in bed again. Sofia came and visited me and brought me something to eat from lunch. She's going to see her father over spring vacation. He's taking the kids skiing in Vermont. Skiing in Vermont—that sounds so normal, even though her parents are divorced and live three thousand miles apart. At least they inhabit the same planet. She's really excited about seeing her father. I can't write anymore.

■
February 15

Last night after dinner, Lucy came into my room.

"Sofia said you were really sick," she said. "Are you feeling better?"

"A little. At least I have my period, finally. I'd rather have cramps than a headache."

"I've never had cramps," said Lucy, as if she were missing out on something. "When I have my period, I hardly even bleed. And I haven't had it since last fall."

Lucy sat down on the edge of my bed and stroked my cheek. I wanted to tell her to go away, that I had been sick for two days before she even noticed and the only reason she noticed was because Sofia told her. I wanted to tell her that I knew she didn't really care how I felt. I'm so weak. I didn't say any of the things I felt. I let her stroke my cheek in the dark.

February 17

I couldn't get to my journal until now. I skipped lunch and came straight to my room. I'm afraid I'll forget something of what happened last night. It already feels like a dream. I'm beginning to lose it. My cramps were really bad, like nothing I've ever felt before. The blood poured out of me. I pulled back the covers, and there was a huge dark stain spreading over the white sheet. I stumbled into the bathroom and sat down on the toilet. That felt better, so I stayed there for quite a while, just letting the blood run out of me. I rested my head on the back of a chair and dozed. There was low droning sound coming from Lucy's room. I didn't pay attention to it at first, but then it became louder and more insistent. It separated itself from the night's silence. It rose and fell of its own accord. When I stood up, I felt dizzy. I had to lean against the wall as I turned the doorknob. The door to Lucy's room swung open. The moonlight was streaming in, the blinds were up, and I could see everything clearly. Lucy was lying on her bed, on her back. Her skin was silver. I could see that her eyes were closed and her lips parted, exposing the tips of her white teeth and her pointed tongue. She was so still she might have been asleep if it weren't for the sounds coming from her. Those were her moans, rising and falling with her breath. Alongside her lay Ernessa. There was no distinction between the two bodies. They touched from head to foot. Ernessa was propped up on her elbow. She brought her head down, pressed her lips around Lucy's nipple, and began to suck hard, pulling the flesh into her mouth. Lucy's nightgown was open to the waist, baring her other breast, with the skin pulled back tautly and the little bump of a red nipple. Ernessa's arm was wrapped around Lucy's naked waist. Their bodies, their hair were mixed up, black and silvery gold. The moon passed behind thick clouds, and the room grew dim. I was afraid I would pass out. I couldn't focus on the bed any longer. It disappeared into the night. I shut the door quickly and hurried back to my room.

This is what Lucy and I always used to make fun of. We were

always so careful not to be like that. Girls who go too far. Girls who pretend the rest of the world doesn't exist. Girls who can't grow up.

Are they happy? Does that word describe them? Blissful? Ecstatic? Oblivious?

What is love?

After dinner

Lucy never got out of bed this morning. I was late for breakfast myself. Mrs. Halton brought her to the infirmary, and later on, when we were all in class, an ambulance came and took her to the hospital. She was so weak that she couldn't walk. They had to carry her up to the infirmary. Of course, Claire found out everything, and she told me. I could barely make it through dinner. I was too upset to eat anything. I know I should only be worried about Lucy. But all I can think of is the two of them, bathed in that moonlight, like dust. Tonight at dinner Ernessa looked fine. Her face was a little flushed. She came down to the Playroom after dinner for a smoke, but she sat off by herself and didn't speak to anyone. We all sat together on the sofa and talked about Lucy. Ernessa held her cigarette up to her mouth and puffed on it without stopping, as if she were too keyed up to put it down for an instant. She was alone with her cigarettes. Ernessa has made Lucy sick. It's so clear. It's been her all along.

I didn't tell anyone what I saw last night. They wouldn't want to believe me. It doesn't matter anyway. All that matters is that Lucy is in the hospital. I looked back in my journal. Just a week ago I wrote that Lucy was much better.

▬
February 18

I went to Mrs. Halton's room during quiet hour to ask if she had any news and when I could visit Lucy in the hospital. She said that Lucy is very weak and they are doing a lot of tests. No visitors are allowed for now. Her mother is with her. She promised she would tell me as soon as she heard anything. She only pretended to be nice to me.

Midnight

There's no moon tonight. There are no clouds. The sky is black. But the moonlight was streaming into Lucy's room. It was so bright I could see the pores of her skin.

February 19

Still no news about Lucy. I thought about calling her house to find out what's happening, but I don't want to talk to her father.

I know that something killed Pater. I know I saw a cloud of moths swarming in Ernessa's room. I know someone walked along the gutter the night before Dora died. I know Charley is gone and Dora. One by one. I know the person leaning over Lucy was real.

Those are facts.

After chemistry, it was snowing hard, and everyone wanted to walk back in the snow. Ernessa headed in the opposite direction, toward the Passageway. Kiki called after her to come with us. She's the only person, other than Lucy, who gets along with Ernessa and spends any time with her. Ernessa is always getting stoned with Kiki now that Charley is history. She seems to like blond, shallow Waspy types.

Ernessa said, "No, I don't feel like it," without even turning around and pushed open the door that leads to the Passageway. No one thought that was strange.

I've hardly ever seen Ernessa outside. One time Lucy mentioned that Ernessa's skin is extremely sensitive to the sun. She has some strange skin condition. But it was snowing. No one's going to get a sunburn in the snow.

I started to walk toward the Passageway, too, but Sofia grabbed my hand and pulled me out into the snow with the others.

We scooped up handfuls of freezing snow and stuck them down each other's backs and shrieked. We lay on our backs and swept the snow away with our arms and legs and made snow angels. The snow was soft and thick, and the wings of the angels were perfect. We made up snow dances. Everything was white, dim, veiled.

I stood up, and the wet snow clung to my clothes in clumps. I realized I had forgotten all about Lucy while I played in the snow.

In the Passageway, there was a face pressed close to the window. She was watching us play in the snow. Through the thick glass, we must have looked like ghosts.

I remember the time she turned away from the sun when Miss Norris opened her door.

February 20

Finally, Mrs. Halton has some news about Lucy. They've done all kinds of tests, and the only thing the doctors know is that she is incredibly anemic. They think it's some kind of blood disorder where the immune system turns on the red blood cells. Mrs. Halton said that Lucy's blood cells were immature. It sounds like some kind of character weakness, not an illness. She has been getting lots of blood transfusions. They are basically replacing all the blood in her body. As soon as they can stabilize her, her mother wants to take her to a hospital near home. She can't have any visitors now. It's not just that she's very weak and needs to rest. It has something to do with her being very upset and crying all the time.

Lucy's not the type to have a nervous breakdown. She's not complicated enough for that. And before this year, she was always happy. I'm the one who's always anxious and upset. Even if she knows I saw her with Ernessa, shame can't affect the blood cells.

I wish I could see her, just once, before she goes home. She might never come back to school again. That would be the best thing. I just need to see her once more, to look into her face, to see if there's a sign of anything there, or if it's blank.

February 21

Wordsworth: "'Oh mercy!' to myself I cried, 'If Lucy should be dead!'"

I thought of Lucy when I first read that line.

Today I begged Mrs. Halton to let me visit Lucy in the hospital. I said I was so worried about her that I couldn't concentrate on anything. I couldn't sleep or eat. I could see her relenting a bit, so I poured it on.

"She's been my best friend since I came to school," I said. "She's helped me so much with my own problems." Then I began to cry. She said she would talk with Lucy's mother tomorrow.

It's true; I can't concentrate on anything. I spend most of the time sitting in my window seat and looking outside. I'm not even thinking about anything. I'm studying the bare branches of the oak tree that grows in front of my window: the forks in the branches, the twisted shoots that meander into nothingness, the dark furrows in the gray bark. The glass in the window is very old, like everything in the Residence, and it twists the images on the other side. It's like looking at the world from underwater. I'm looking up through green water at the trees and sky. The sounds are muffled. The light is liquid.

I have lost interest in my books. Before I couldn't live without them. There's a pane of glass between me and everything.

February 22

I was supposed to go see Lucy, but last night she got much worse. Now it's impossible. As far as I can tell from what Mrs. Halton says, which I don't entirely believe, the doctors don't really know what's the matter with her. They just keep doing the same thing over and over, giving her new blood, and hoping it will work. She's better for a while; then she gets weaker. Today I realized that Mrs. Halton enjoys telling me bad news. It makes her feel important.

I need to see her. Who knows what she'll be like now, with the blood of so many other people in her body. No longer Lucy. I tried to imagine what that must feel like. Your blood is such a personal, intimate thing. Now she's being kept alive by other people's blood.

February 23
When can I see Lucy? That's all I want to know.

February 24
Every day it's the same: I can't see Lucy. I don't need to ask anymore. When Mrs. Halton sees me waiting in her sitting room, she just shakes her head and says, "Not yet. You just have to be patient."

"But when am I going to be able to see her?"

"Soon, I hope. She's getting a little stronger each day."

February 25
I'm beginning to give up on the idea of seeing Lucy again before vacation. I know for sure that she isn't coming back to school. She's going straight home from the hospital. I would have to go to her house, with her father and the dog. I don't know if I could stand that.

February 26
I stare at the blank page, and I leave it blank. No news. No new thoughts. My journal has abandoned me when I need it most. I have no desire to write.

February 27

I can't be patient any longer. I haven't thought about anything but Lucy for ten days. I have to see her.

February 28

Maybe I should just go to the hospital and try to sneak into Lucy's room. I don't think Mrs. Halton is ever going to let me visit her.

MARCH

■
March 1

I want to kill Mrs. Halton. The old witch. The next time I see her, I'm going to put my hands around her neck and squeeze until her eyes turn white. All this time, when I've been begging her to see Lucy, she's been letting Ernessa visit her. I overheard Kiki at breakfast this morning telling Claire and Sofia that Lucy was much better. I asked Kiki how she knew. It was obvious she'd made a mistake letting me overhear this.

"I don't know," said Kiki. "I just heard."

Then Sofia said, "Oh, stop it. Ernessa told her. She visited Lucy in the hospital."

Kiki had to come out with it: Ernessa had been there several times last week because she was, as Mrs. Halton puts it, "Lucy's very special friend." What does Mrs. Halton know about anything?

"She makes Mrs. Halton feel sorry for her," I said. "That's why she's allowed to do whatever she wants. Mrs. Halton lets her get away with everything. My father died too. Has everybody forgotten that?" I shouted the last words. They all understand that kind of manipulation. I was so embarrassed that I ran up to my room and slammed the door behind me. I sat on my bed and cried.

■
March 2
It's too late to see Lucy, ever.

I don't think I can cry anymore. There are no tears left.

When Mrs. Halton came out to check on us at quiet hour, I was waiting for her outside her sitting room. At first she tried to deny that anyone had been allowed to see Lucy, but when I said that I knew Ernessa had been to the hospital, she admitted that Ernessa had visited, but only twice, and very briefly each time. "Lucy asked for her." She said it in a very mean way. She knew she was hurting my feelings. When I insisted that she allow me to see Lucy, she said, "If we must continue this conversation, come into my room."

She closed the door behind us. "It is not appropriate for you to talk to me in this tone of voice," she said. "These things do not depend on you."

I told her that she was dishonest and I intended to speak to Miss Rood about it.

"There's no point in doing that," she said. "I wouldn't have told you this because I was sparing your feelings, and I know how emotional you are, but Lucy has taken a turn for the worse. She's very, very ill. The doctors don't think she'll last the next few days, she's so weak. The school is extremely concerned."

"Then I need to see her one last time. To say good-bye. It's absolutely necessary," I shouted.

"Out of the question. Only family members can visit her."

She actually smiled as she told me this.

I picked up her porcelain shepherdess from the table, the one with a pink dress and long blond hair and a crook in her hand, and before Mrs. Halton had a chance to ask me what I was doing, I threw it on the floor in front of the door. We both watched it explode into pieces while the head, still intact, rolled to the edge of the rug. I would have thrown everything on the table after it, but Mrs. Halton grabbed my arm, twisted it, and shouted, "You disrespectful girl! I should have you expelled!"

I turned and ran out of her room and down the corridor. I've been crying for the past three hours. I didn't come down for dinner. I don't care if I get into more trouble. Mrs. Halton hasn't come looking for me. She's staying away. She thinks I'm going to talk to Miss Rood.

Ernessa is killing Lucy. She wants to turn her into something like her, to consume her completely. Killing means nothing to her. It's just a means to an end. Death is where she's taking her. And Mrs. Halton is holding the door open.

March 3

Lucy is lying on her bed in the hospital. She no longer has the strength to lift her hand or to raise her eyelid, but that doesn't matter because she has no reason to do it. She no longer cares. She is perfectly calm. She is ready.

I'm waiting to hear that Lucy has died. I haven't heard anything. Maybe Mrs. Halton only told me that to torment me, to play a sick joke on me. Lucy must still be alive; otherwise we would have heard something. Someone would find out. They can't keep that secret from us.

March 4

I haven't been punished for smashing the stupid shepherdess. When I pass Mrs. Halton in the corridor, she looks away. She knows I know. She's afraid to meet my gaze.

I can't ask her about Lucy. All I can do is wait.

March 5

I waited for her for a long time. I skipped breakfast. I was afraid I would miss her. The other girls on the corridor came and went while I stood silently by my doorway. No one said a word to me. The bells for assembly rang, and she still didn't appear. She's the kind of person who leaves everything to the last minute, even past the last minute, and manages to get to assembly or dinner or classes just before the door shuts.

When her door opened and she walked out, I was surprised to see her, even though I had been waiting for her for an hour.

She looked at me as she pulled the door closed behind her. "You overslept?" she asked.

"Why her?" I asked.

She didn't answer me. "Why not Kiki or Carol or Betsy?"

"I could ask you the same question," she said.

"Because she's my friend."

"If she's your friend, why are you standing here, waiting for me?"

"You and Mrs. Halton are trying to keep me away from her."

"Mrs. Halton? What can she possibly do? Lock you up and throw away the key?"

"I'm already in enough trouble with her."

"No one is stopping you. You can do whatever you want."

Ernessa started to walk down the corridor. "What does she look like?" I called after her. My voice was so desperate I could no longer recognize it.

"It's time for assembly. I'm already late. So are you."

She continued to walk away. I ran after her and grabbed her arm. I wanted to make her stay and answer my question. She always comes and goes exactly as she pleases. No one can make her do a thing she doesn't want to do. She flung me away. I hit the wall so hard that I couldn't breathe for a moment. She pushed up the sleeve of her sweater and showed me her arm. "Look what you've done," she shouted.

I could see the imprint of my hand on her forearm, as if I'd grabbed onto clay rather than flesh. The skin was red and swollen. The sight of what I had done made me sick.

She made it to assembly, but I didn't go. I'm going to be in so much trouble.

■
March 6

■
March 7

■
March 8

I just talked to Lucy! If someone can talk to the dead, that's what I did. She sounded like someone far, far away. Mrs. Halton wasn't lying about one thing. She was really sick, and the doctors did think she was going to die. Her heart and lungs were filled with fluid, and they had to drain them. She had a breathing tube down her throat until yesterday. Even today, on the phone, she could barely speak.

Carol called me to the phone. She had a queer look on her face when I passed her in the corridor. I thought, this is probably my mother, calling to tell me that she won't be able to pick me up on Friday. I don't want to talk to her, to pretend. I picked up the black receiver, lying on its side on the telephone table like a little animal.

"Hi, it's me," came the voice through the telephone lines. I had to strain to hear her, and she had to rest between each word to catch her breath. Her voice was different. I couldn't recognize it. I kept staring at the telephone, in disbelief, convinced it could communicate with the spirit world. I realized that I had already begun to think of Lucy as dead, even though she hadn't died. The thought came to me that I could call my father on this little black telephone.

Really? I kept thinking. Really?

"I wanted to visit you," I said, "but Mrs. Halton wouldn't let me. She let Ernessa, but she wouldn't let me."

"Ernessa hasn't come. For a while," said Lucy.

"You don't sound like Lucy."

"It's too hard to breathe. Force the air into my lungs. The doctors think I'm a miracle."

"Well, they would, considering the fact that they couldn't figure out what was the matter with you in the first place."

"I miss you. I miss school," said Lucy.

"You sound so far away."

"I am so far away. Tell me I can come back."

There was a long silence, broken only by Lucy's harsh breathing.

"Were you scared?" I asked.

"Only at first," said Lucy. "I got used to it."

She needs me to pack a bag and collect her schoolbooks and try to get her homework assignments. Her mother's coming to get her stuff tomorrow or the next day. She's being transferred to another hospital near her home at the end of the week, if she continues to get better.

"In an ambulance. The whole way," she said. "Do you think they'll keep the siren on?"

She didn't call Ernessa and ask her to get her things together. I feel like telling that to Mrs. Halton.

I've already told everyone that Lucy's much better. We're all so happy about it.

—

March 11

I don't have time to write now. It's ten o'clock, and I still have lots of homework to do, and I have to pack for tomorrow. I'll be able to catch up over vacation.

March 12

Spring vacation. I'm home. I'm tired.

I got so behind in all my classes and had to spend the last week working all the time.

Lucy's mother came on Tuesday to pick up her stuff. Until I saw her, I wasn't sure that I had really talked to Lucy. She gave me a big hug. Lucy is much stronger. It was hard for her mother to believe that a week ago the doctors said she was about to die. She was taking Lucy away on Wednesday, and she thought Lucy might only have to stay in the hospital for a few days before going home. She's going to try to do all her schoolwork over the vacation. And then she's coming back to school, if she's completely recovered. Now they think it was a virus and the body got rid of it by itself.

I told her that I begged my corridor teacher to let me see Lucy, but she refused.

"Lucy was really too sick to see anyone," said her mother.

"But Ernessa was allowed," I replied.

"What a mistake," said her mother. "I shouldn't have let her talk me into that. Those visits were too emotionally draining for her, but Lucy kept insisting that Ernessa would help her get better. Ernessa would make her so afraid. It was always Ernessa. I finally gave in. I didn't want to upset her. But after each visit, Lucy would weep for hours, and then she got sicker. It was just too much. . . . "

I didn't say anything. There wasn't any point. They can look through microscopes for viruses all they want. They won't find any.

We all left this week—Lucy, Ernessa, me—and it would be best if we never saw each other again, ever. I'd be willing to give up Lucy just to keep Ernessa away from her.

I need to go to bed. I'm going to sleep for the next two weeks.

March 13

I have to put everything down, just in case I need to look back. . . . I need to leave a precise record. I can't rely on my memory.

For the last two nights before I came home (Wednesday and Thursday), I woke up in the middle of the night. I sat up in bed, suddenly wide awake, but when I got out of bed, I felt as if I were still lying in bed and dreaming myself moving across the room. There was a noise on the drive outside my window, of dry leaves and acorns being blown about. I looked out. Someone was walking back and forth under the windows of our suite. So this is what she does every night, I thought. She watches us sleep. I wondered why I hadn't bothered to look outside my window before. The noise stopped when I got to the window, or I didn't notice it anymore. She moved like an animal in a cage, ten steps in one direction, then exactly the same number in the other direction. The whole world is too small for Ernessa. She's trapped inside it. Why did she come back to this boarding school? Here everyone is in boxes inside boxes — the iron fence, the Residence, the second floor, Mrs. Halton's corridor, the room, the bed. Boxes for girls who are not ready to face the big world of men and sex. I know how unreal it is. I'm not a fool.

She was making me aware of her. I almost felt sorry for her. If only she hadn't ruined my life. I watched her pace for two nights, for hours. She moved with the same anxious energy that makes her practically inhale her cigarettes. She never slowed down. And then the sun started to come up. I closed my eyes for a few seconds, and she was gone.

I'm sitting at my father's desk. His books are all around me. They have the answers to her secrets.

March 14

She changes everyone around her. She finds out who they are and turns them into something else.

In September, just after school started, Dora and I were kind of friendly with Ernessa. We even spent an evening together. Lucy wasn't there. It was a Saturday night. She must have gone home for the weekend. She was going home practically every weekend then to be with her mother. I looked back through my journal, and I can't find anything about that evening. That's strange, because I remember quite clearly what we talked about. Ernessa asked us about Miss Bobbie, who was already on her case after two weeks of school. I said that I didn't take her anti-Semitism in a totally negative way. I didn't mind being excluded. It meant I was different from the rest of them.

Ernessa laughed at me. "I don't have your sentimental feelings about being Jewish. The religion is a burden, a cosmic joke. If Jews *are* chosen, it's only for special punishment. The whole world is their graveyard. Any Jew who thinks differently is demented."

"Is that how you can stand to speak German?" I asked. "The language of murderers."

"You know some German, I think. The language of Rilke and Heine," said Ernessa. "Of the greatest lyric poets. Besides, every language is the language of murderers. It's only fitting that the language with the most deaths should have the most sublime poems."

I was shocked. I hardly knew her then. She was a girl from some strange country who had materialized out of nowhere and ended up across the hall from Lucy and me. She and I were the only real Jews in our class. I looked over at Dora. She was scowling. For her, being a Jew was just an intellectual pose. She dropped it whenever it got in her way. She unjewed herself. When Dora was around Ernessa, she needed to feel Jewish, even though Ernessa didn't take her own Jewishness seriously. In the end, Miss Bobbie hated all three of us.

It's always described the same way: a long black animal that resembles a cat, four or five feet long. The animal paces the room faster and faster as everything whirls around and grows darker. It's like a terrifying ride in an amusement park.

But it's not true.

Has anyone ever really seen a vampire?

Can anyone stand to see it?

Ernessa always shows herself to me in human form. And yet, I always have the sense that she's trying to confuse me, to trick me. I felt this way when my father died. Why deceive me?

March 15

I am a coward. All the evidence was right in front of me last fall when Dora died, but I refused to do anything about it because I was scared. Ernessa only cares about Lucy. She doesn't even see the rest of us. We are only annoyances. Our lives have no more value than that of a fly you swat without thinking. She wants a companion in her existence. One companion, all hers, forever.

Remember: It is not love. It is passion. And the vampire needs the consent of the victim.

March 16

The books are all wrong. Most of the writers don't believe in vampires. They're always trying to come up with a scientific explanation for everything. It's like writing a book about Jesus and then concluding at the end that he couldn't possibly have existed because there was no street address for him in Nazareth. Why bother? Montague Summers even says there is "the philosophy of vampirism." Philosophy?

I have to figure out a way to protect Lucy. If she can just make it to the end of school, I think it will be all right. Just another three months and maybe Ernessa will give up and go back where she came from. I don't know if I'm strong enough, or brave enough. I didn't save Daddy.

March 17

I think it would be better if Lucy didn't come back to school, although I wouldn't be able to keep an eye on her then. I called her last night, and she said she feels fine. She's already beginning to forget how sick she was. She's been to the doctor, and he can't find anything wrong with her. She's had so many blood tests they can barely get any more blood out of her arm. It's black and blue from the needles. There's no sign of any blood disorder or virus. The doctor thinks she may have had severe mono. "I don't see how I could have had mono, since I haven't kissed a boy in ages. And I never had a fever or anything," said Lucy. She went out shopping with her mother for a whole afternoon and didn't feel at all tired.

I have to remain vigilant.

March 18

So this is what my father was thinking about before he left us. How long had he been doing this? He went through and marked all the passages about suicide. And there are a lot. All that time we were walking together, he was thinking how and when he would end it. He had forgotten all about the girl hanging on his arm.

Suicides were not buried in churchyards because they could return from the dead and pull others into the grave with them.

My father left very careful instructions about what my mother was supposed to do after his death. He wanted his body cremated, thoroughly (he underlined that word, I saw the note), and he asked us to go to the top of Mount Washington (where they had recorded the highest winds on the planet, he wrote) and scatter his ashes. "Make sure the ashes scatter to the winds." His other request was no memorial service. (Also underlined.)

My mother did everything he asked. He knew she would.

Lack of a proper burial and not living out one's allotted years put you in peril. If you die too soon, if you commit suicide or are killed, then your spirit might remain on Earth until you reach what should have been your seventy years. I don't know if cremation absolutely keeps the spirit from returning, but I'm glad that both Dora and my father were cremated.

There is a passage in Montague Summers's book that is blocked off in blue pen. My father never would have used pen in a book, only pencil. He considered it a crime. Usually he didn't even buy a book with markings in pen. I guess whoever owned this book before my father marked this passage about the Baganda (a tribe in Central Africa):

The body of a man who has destroyed himself is removed as far from all human habitation as possible, to waste land or to a cross-road, and there is utterly consumed with fire. Next the wood of the house in which the horrid deed has been done is burned to ashes and scattered to the winds; whilst if the man has hanged himself upon a tree this is hewn to the ground and committed to the flames, trunk, roots, branches and all. Even this is hardly deemed to be sufficient. Curiously enough there is a lurking idea that the ghost of a suicide may survive after the cremation of the body, so horrible is this crime felt to be and so eradicated the taint that this terrible deed establishes.

My mother was completely wrong about my father's suicide, but I'll let her think what she wants.

I'm finally in direct communication with my father, through his books. My own black telephone to the spirit world. He's telling me things that he never told anyone when he was alive. He didn't want me to know about them unless I needed to.

■
March 19
This morning, I came into the kitchen and found my mother sitting in front of her bowl of cereal and cup of coffee, sobbing. I sat down next to her and put my arm around her shoulders.

"I'm not crying for myself, darling. I'm crying for him."

"Why?" I asked.

"He's been visiting me every night, in my dreams. I think he's lonely. And last night, he was so angry. He couldn't even speak. He just pressed his face down toward mine, so that I could see his anger."

"It's just a dream," I said.

"Is he angry that I'm here? Or does he realize he made a mistake?"

"You can't talk like that."

I hugged my mother until she calmed down enough to eat her breakfast. I have to go back to school. I remind my mother of him.

If I told her what's been going on at school, I know she would get really annoyed and tell me not to talk that way. Other people's encounters with the spirit world are preposterous. Only hers are real.

March 20

Lucy just called me with questions about chemistry. I was on the phone with her for ages, trying to explain orbitals. I think she got it. She told me about all the new clothes her mother bought her and the stuffed animals she got in the hospital. She sounds exactly like Lucy again. It annoys me. If you've come that close to death, how can it not turn you into a different person? You've had a glimpse of something (who knows what it is, a flash of light or the memory of a flash of light) that it's impossible for the rest of us to know. That knowledge has all washed off her. Maybe Dora was right, and all these years I've made myself think that she's somehow different from what she really is—a vacant page. She's not the girl who lived in the light blue room flooded with sunlight.

All Christians are uninteresting because they will all be resurrected.

March 21

Today my mother was much better. No sobbing in front of her cereal bowl. That was yesterday. This morning at breakfast, she asked me why I never see any of my old friends.

"We don't have that much in common anymore," I said. "I've hardly seen them for years."

"Just last summer you used to call them up."

"I've gotten a lot closer to my friends at school. You should be glad."

"It would be good for you to get out, that's all," said my mother. "You spend all your time behind the closed door of your father's study."

"I've been working on a project for school," I said. "I have lots of work to do over break."

I have to keep everything hidden from her, especially this journal.

She wouldn't understand it. It scares me to hide things from her. Now I'm doing exactly what she does.

Either tonight or tomorrow, we are going to a movie with my aunt. I think my mother's doing this to get me out of the house.

Midnight

I thought she only existed inside those gates. I used to feel safe here.

I went to the Met after lunch so that my mother wouldn't have to think about me shut up in my father's study with his books. I wandered through the museum until I came to the Flemish painters. I read the names beneath the paintings—Dieric Bouts, Petrus Christus, Hans Memling, Jan van Eyck, Quentin Massys. Those harsh syllables had twisted my tongue years before when my mother dragged me through the galleries on the way home from school. For a while, we went practically every day. They sounded so Christian and so devout. I used to study the feathers of the angels' wings and the sad, resigned faces of the women.

I passed by all those paintings. The familiar faces bored me. Instead, I stood in front of a portrait of a young Austrian princess that I'd never noticed before. I stared hard at her face, framed by an ornate scarf and a fringe of brown hair, at her bulging wide forehead and bony nose and pouting red lips. She stood in front of a window, opening onto a long landscape of castles and clumps of trees and blue hills, but her gaze was caught somewhere in between that landscape and me. I thought of Ernessa staring out the window in the Passageway, as if the Science Building and the girls running up and down the Middle Field and the cars going by outside the iron fence were just an illusion she could look right through. Devotion, obsession—try to tell them apart.

I saw Ernessa on the steps outside the museum. She had on her black coat with the velvet collar, the one I was so envious of when I first saw her wear it. I was jealous of everything about her last fall. She wore a navy blue beret, and a small brown pocketbook hung from her shoulder. I picked her out of the crowd immediately. She turned her head just enough that I could see her face and know that it was her. She told me in that instant that she was in the world, wherever I was.

I want to know if she tracked me through the museum and stood behind me while I studied the head of the young princess and thought about her.

When I got home, I went straight to my room. I wanted to stay at home, but I had to pull myself together and go out. I couldn't let them see how upset I was. I kept splashing cold water on my face, but my cheeks burned my fingertips.

We went to see the new Truffaut movie, *Bed and Board*. My mother and I love to see those movies together. It's our romantic side. We both adore Jean-Pierre Léaud as Antoine Doinel. In this movie, Antoine has a job dyeing white carnations. He mixes buckets of dye and fills them with flowers. The dye runs up the stems and into the petals. The plants drink, and they are transformed from the inside out. I wonder how long it takes to turn a flower from white to blazing red.

I kept thinking about Ernessa all during the movie.

March 23

As far as I can tell, apotropaics (from the Greek, to avert) fall into three categories: (1) crosses, (2) sharp objects, (3) strong odors.

Garlic, incense, perfume, green nutshells, cow dung, feces, juniper. These repel vampires. You can place a silver knife under the mattress or a sharp object under the pillow and draw crosses over doorways. In my drawer, I found a necklace of dried juniper berries that my father gave me years ago, after he visited New Mexico. He told me that they would keep away bad dreams. That's what the Indians used them for.

Will I be able to convince Lucy to do any of this? I don't think so.

The words used to describe vampires are incredibly sad: a "disconsolate person" who is "inaccessible to salvation." Why would Ernessa want to turn Lucy into someone like that? Lucy's a happy person, no matter what happens. Bad things don't leave a mark on her. That's why everyone likes her. Why not me? I'm a much better victim. I'm already halfway there. But she won't touch me.

Every place and time has had vampires, going back to the earliest times: all across Europe, Assyria, ancient Ireland, Russia, Hungary, Transylvania, Greece, India, China, Java, etc. Do human beings make up the same stories everywhere because they have the same fears?

March 24

I called Lucy today. I didn't want to, but I couldn't help myself. I picked up the telephone and dialed the number. She answered the phone. There's nothing wrong. We couldn't talk for long because she was going over to her cousins'. The cheery person was back. She's putting off doing her homework, and school is starting again in a few days. Before she hung up, I asked her, trying to sound casual, if she knew what Ernessa was doing over the vacation. There was a long pause before she answered.

"No. Why?"

"I think I saw her a few days ago on the steps of the Met, and I wondered if she mentioned anything about being in New York."

"I really don't know," said Lucy. "She might have relatives there. Did you talk to her?"

"No. I only saw her from a distance."

"Maybe it was someone else."

"I'm certain it was her. I could never—"

"I've got to go now. My mother's calling me."

She hung up without waiting for me to say good-bye.

Underneath that friendly exterior, she's suspicious of me. She's trying to protect Ernessa from me. What did I ever do to Ernessa except complain to Mrs. Halton about her putrid room?

■

March 25

Today I went into a store and bought straw crosses that look like Christmas tree ornaments. That made it a little less horrible, but it was still queer to buy them. This is much worse than singing hymns in assembly. It must be a sin for a Jew to buy a cross. I'm going to feel uncomfortable walking into my room. I'll have to keep telling myself that I'm not trying to be a Christian. I've always hated that about the girls at school, even Lucy, their smugness and superiority at being Christian, as though I were secretly dying to be just like them. No one really believes in that religion. Saying that you're a Christian is no different from saying that you like to wear a certain kind of clothes. Their churches are like Mrs. Halton's sitting room; you're afraid to sit down or to touch anything, to leave your sweat and fingerprints behind. My favorite churches are the ones that are in ruins, with grass and dirt for a floor and sky for a ceiling.

■

March 26

I'm sorriest for the children who become vampires through no fault of their own, rather through their parents' guilt. They are the unknowing victims — conceived during holy week, the illegitimate offspring of illegitimate parents, the seventh child, the baby born with a red caul over the head or some other flaw. Children born on Christmas Day are fated to become vampires to atone for their mother's vanity in conceiving on the same day that the Virgin Mary conceived the Lord.

Why should children pay for the sins of their parents? Isn't it bad enough just to be born?

Lucy gives in to everyone. She's weak, and now I have to watch over her.

March 27

Am I any worse than all those people who go to church and pray to the Holy Trinity? To ghosts? Christ rose from the dead. Believing in something that can't be proved makes it more beautiful. Even though it's terrifying, you feel free. Your mind is made up.

March 28

I'm furious at my mother. I had wanted to get back to school before everyone else. She had errands to do, a phone call, all kinds of stupid little things. By the time I got back, everyone, including Lucy, was already here. It was too late. Her room was full of girls. Everyone wanted to be with her. Ernessa stayed away. I don't know if she's back yet from wherever she went. Do they know that I saw them together that night? Do they care?

When I walked into her room and saw her, sitting on her bed surrounded by girls, laughing at their stupid jokes, I thought, she is exactly the same as always. But when she got up to go to the bathroom, I realized how wrong I was. She only appears to be the same. Everything about her is faded. Her skin is so pale and smooth that it has a bluish tint. She doesn't have a single pimple on her face. She moves slowly and deliberately, as if she has to think where to put her foot before she takes each step. It made me impatient to watch her.

I didn't have a chance to do anything except give Lucy the necklace of dried juniper berries. She didn't seem at all interested in it, but I insisted she hang it from her bed. Actually, I put it there myself. I don't think she would have let me do it, except that I made a big deal out of the fact that my father had given it to me.

I stayed in her room to make sure she didn't move it.

■

March 30

The spring has been ruined. Nothing can save it, not even the weeping cherry trees.

Last year, I looked forward all winter to the time when the trees along the Upper Field bloomed. That was the joy of my first year: the spring. I let it give me joy. I knew my father wanted that. Nature was his religion. One morning, I came out after breakfast, and the cherry trees were all in flower, their tight buds released during the night. That afternoon I went outside and sat under the trees and read for hours. I wanted to spend as much time as possible under the pink veil. I sat there every day, until all the flowers had fallen and the thick mat of pink had turned to a rotting brown. One day it was windy, and the petals fell on my head like pink snow.

Last year Lucy used to get me up at six to practice lacrosse before breakfast. She was convinced that I could make it onto A squad with her if I practiced because I could run so fast. I never understood how someone like me, who had always had such a hard time getting out of bed in the morning, could leap out of bed and run down the stairs to shoot goals at dawn. Lucy has become so fragile and awkward. I can't imagine her ever running up and down the field cradling her lacrosse stick, her blond hair streaming out behind her.

It's all that new blood in her body. She's changed from an athletic, healthy-looking person into someone who is weak and hesitant. Everyone has gotten used to this Lucy. They don't really understand how different she is.

APRIL

April 1

Now Sofia is changing, too. When she was skiing in Vermont, she met a boy named Chris. She says she's not in love with him, but she's decided to lose her virginity with him. He's going to come down for a weekend, and she's going to meet him over at the College and spend the night with him. She asked me if I would come with her to keep watch. Carol's going to go, too.

All I could do was shake my head yes. I hope she gets it over with soon. She was always so prudish. Now it's all she can talk about. I'm disappointed in her.

I wake up exhausted.

I can't sleep at night. I need a pill to make everything go away.

My first year we crowded into the bath stall after study hour ended, put a towel under the door to the stall, and turned on the boiling hot water. The steam rose from the bathtub up to the ceiling in white gusts. When the room had filled with steam, we lit a cigarette and passed it around. The steam ate up the cigarette smoke. We smoked until we were dizzy. Then, one by one, we opened the door to the stall and ran down the corridor to our rooms. I got into bed, still dizzy. The instant I closed my eyes, I went right to sleep without a thought. It was like taking an oblivion pill.

April 2

I couldn't help getting drawn into an argument with one of the day students this morning. That awful kind of argument where the other person doesn't even listen to you.

I was standing outside the Math room with a bunch of girls, waiting for Mrs. Hutchinson to open the door and let us in, when Megan Montgomery said, "I think we should just go in there and bomb the hell out of them! We could level Hanoi in a couple days."

Megan wasn't talking to anyone in particular, or maybe the remark was directed at me. How could I keep my mouth shut?

"What a horrible thing to say," I said. "So many innocent people will die."

"It's us or them," she said. "I don't think that's a very hard choice. Let's bomb them back to the Stone Age and get the rest of our troops out of there."

"You're just repeating what your parents say."

"What about you? Your commie parents . . . or mother. She's probably at a protest march right now." Megan laughed at her joke, and I could see that the other girls were trying not to laugh, too.

My face got hot, not from embarrassment but from anger. "At least my mother, my commie mother, hates murder. What does it feel like to want to kill another human being?"

My voice was rising, and the circle of girls had stepped away from me. At that moment, Mrs. Hutchinson opened the door, and her gray head emerged. "What's all the commotion out here, girls?"

Everyone else hurried into the classroom, eager to get away from me. I stayed out in the hallway, trying to calm down, but I couldn't get rid of Megan and her smug, self-satisfied grin.

I should feel sorry for someone who can't think for herself and is trapped by her parents' stupid ideas. The exploding bombs are as unreal to her as a Buddhist priest setting himself on fire was to me. I watched the transparent flames nibble at his robes and suddenly shoot straight up in the air. The body collapsed, and the black smoke of the priest's burning flesh billowed around his still frame. I wasn't even sad; it was taking place only on the television set. That was how we could stand to witness a scene like this.

For the first time in months, I missed Dora. The only girl who could have understood what I was feeling, my moral indignation, was dead.

Maybe I'll call my mother after dinner. She's the one who sent me here in the first place to be with girls like that.

April 4

Sunday is a lost day. I don't know if it's the beginning or the end of the week. Even when I was a little girl, Sunday always pulled me down. Now it's much worse. I never know what to do on Sunday.

I'd thought about doing this for a long time.

It was the middle of the afternoon, and no one was around. The corridor was deserted. It was so still. I was sitting in my room, staring out the window. This was what I had been waiting for.

There was no answer to my knock. When I turned the knob, the door swung open partway. No one stood in my way. If Ernessa surprised me, I would say that I was looking for Lucy. The dresser was still pushed right up to the door. I moved a few steps into the room and closed the door behind me.

Nothing had changed since the last time I was there. The room was bare. No books, no pens and paper, no hairbrush and shampoo, no photographs or letters. Only bed, dresser, desk, chair, lamp, the basic furnishings listed in the brochure. If Ernessa had packed up and left during the night, it would look the same. There was no longer the horrible smell that used to seep into the corridor. The window was closed. It was very stuffy. The stuffiness grew more oppressive. Something was drawing the air out of the room.

"She doesn't breathe the same air as the rest of us." I said it out loud to remind myself that I could still speak.

Tiredness, heaviness inside me. They were so inviting. "Là, tout n'est qu'ordre et beauté, / Luxe, calme et volupté." I wondered if I had the strength to make it to the door and turn the knob. No matter how I gasped for air, I needed more and more. It wasn't at all what I expected.

There was a slight murmur that made me turn my head. Then it grew louder and became the sound of water rushing over the rocks in a streambed, throwing up white foam.

The room was crowded with people. So crowded that they merged into one another. They had no substance yet they pressed against me. I couldn't recognize any of the faces. I was dizzy, and everything was blurred by their sound. I wasn't sure that they had faces or even bodies. They gave off a feeling of despair that was as strong as the smell of sweat in the locker room. There were so many of them, and they kept coming.

In time, Lucy was going to end up there. My father might already be there, welcoming me. If it no longer frightened me, why wait? I was among them. I could hear my father's voice clearly. "I had not thought death had undone so many." He always used to laugh when he recited those words. It was one of his favorite lines.

I forced myself across the room, through the pressing bodies, and fell against the door. Out in the hallway, I gulped the air in huge mouthfuls, greedily. I locked myself in my bathroom and sat on the cold tile floor for a long time. In the mirror, my face was still a deep red, and my ears ached with the deafening rushing of my blood.

April 6

Mr. Davies stopped me again in the hall to ask how I was. He wanted me to come visit him. I asked him why. He looked pained and said, "To chat. Talk about books."

All around me, in the hallway, were clumps of girls, talking, swinging their book bags, eating and drinking. No one noticed Mr. Davies and me standing off to the side. No one noticed the way he looked at me.

▬

April 8

I forced myself to go to Mr. Davies's room. Claire was waiting around afterward to find out what we talked about. "Death." That was all I would tell her. She crinkled up her big bony nose in disgust.

The door was closed, so she couldn't possibly have seen Mr. Davies lean over and put his hand over mine.

I could make him fall in love with me, if I wanted. I could make him do anything. He looks at me for a long time. He can't stop looking at me. What is he looking for?

He was telling me this afternoon that his poetry class is reading Emily Dickinson.

"Why?" I asked, annoyed. "Her poems weren't written for stupid girls like that. Those are the girls who used to avoid me because I reminded them of something unpleasant. I frightened them." I imagined the girls reading the words and heard their embarrassed laughter. "Let them have Sylvia Plath and Anne Sexton. Insanity, failed love, suicide. That's good enough for them."

"Whom were those poems written for?" he asked. That was when he put his hand over mine. He pressed down hard; he was trying to restrain me.

"For me."

"Just for you?"

"Yes. Not even for you. They're mine."

I was upset when I left his room. I could have cried for hours. Instead, I had to deal with Claire.

Next time I see him, I'm going to tell him that I don't need Emily Dickinson's poems anymore. He can have them. Even the stupid girls can have them.

April 9

This morning in assembly, Miss Rood read Ernessa's name again, for the fourth week in a row, for cutting gym. Miss Bobbie is out to get Ernessa. Miss Rood tolerates Jews, even though she doesn't like them, but Miss Bobbie hates them. She'll go after Ernessa. She's done the same thing to Dora and me. For a while, Dora stopped wearing a bra, and Miss Bobbie used to come up behind her and run her finger up her back to check for the strap. She gave her so many comments for not wearing a bra. I don't even think there's a rule that says we have to wear a bra. Once I didn't have a clean white shirt, and I just wore a sweater on top. Lots of girls do that. She caught me first thing in the morning and gave me a comment for being out of uniform. She's given me so many comments on Monday morning for dirty shoes. That's her life.

Maybe Miss Rood makes sure there are always a few Jews at school to keep Miss Bobbie occupied.

I looked at Ernessa after Miss Rood called her name. As usual, she turned to glare at Miss Bobbie, who always sits next to the doors to the assembly room. She was furious. She refused to stop staring at her. After assembly, Mrs. Halton pulled her aside to talk to her. I couldn't hear what she said to Ernessa.

April 10

No one ever talks about Ernessa in front of me. Sometimes they even stop talking when I come into a room. I know what they've been talking about. This afternoon, when I was in Sofia's room, I overhead a conversation between Sofia and Carol about Ernessa. I was reading in Sofia's big chair, and they were lying on her bed. They forgot I was in the room. I stuck my head deeper into my book and held my breath. I was afraid they would remember I was there and stop talking.

"Miss Bobbie is making Ernessa swim laps every day after school next week. It's punishment for cutting gym," said Carol. "Lucy says that she hates to swim. It's a torture for her."

"Why doesn't Ernessa just say she has her period and can't swim?" asked Sofia. "I'd do that."

"She doesn't want to go to the nurse and get a note. Then she has to deal with the nurse, too. Besides, Miss Bobbie will just make her do it the next week. She can't have her period forever."

"Then she should say that she can't swim."

"But she passed the swim test last fall. Otherwise she would have had to take a class."

"She could say she isn't very good."

"Apparently Miss Bobbie told Ernessa, 'If you can swim one lap, you can swim ten. This will be good practice for you.' What a bitch that woman is!"

Miss Bobbie has tortured me plenty; now it's Ernessa's turn. But I can't enjoy it. Lucy's sympathy infuriates me.

I imagined Ernessa going into the locker room next to the pool, where all the bathing suits are arranged on shelves according to size. It doesn't make any difference what size you choose, because once you get into the water, the cotton loses its shape immediately and hangs from your body. Some of the suits are newer, a deeper blue, and others faded almost to white, but they are all like bags, exposing your breasts and the pale skin under your arms.

There are always girls changing in the locker room. There's no place to hide. She'll have to change in front of them, to show them that she has a real body underneath her long sleeves and long skirts and long socks. She even wears her gym tunic down to her knees. No one does that. She'll have to expose her nipples, her pubic hair, her belly, her ass, if only for a few seconds while she pulls on the suit. Someone will be sure to see her nakedness as she struggles to pull up her suit. That's the torture for her. The other girls will see that her breasts are completely flat like a little girl's. The nipples don't even rise above the surface of the skin. They barely make a mark; they look like a shadow on her skin. It won't be a secret any longer. They will be forced to admit her strangeness.

In ninth grade, when I had to change with older girls for swimming, I couldn't help staring at them. My eyes were always drawn to that dark curly patch of hair between their legs, above the soft flesh of the thighs. On a little girl's body, the smooth fold of skin is no different from an eyelid. It's the hair that transforms it. The coarse hair hides the entrance to a secret place. My breasts were pathetic little mounds, and some of these girls had big round breasts with huge nipples that were pink and purple and brown. They had the bodies of women. They would catch me looking and accuse me of staring at them. Then everyone would look in my direction and see my puny body.

April 11

It's the second day of Passover, and I've pretty much stopped eating. I haven't told anyone. I just say that I'm not hungry. The only other person who would keep Passover is Ernessa, and she never eats anyway. Certainly not sweet things like cinnamon buns and angel food cake with whipped cream. There is something pleasurable about giving up what you want. My father always kept Passover and fasted on Yom Kippur. He loved to observe any kind of ritual, even though he didn't believe in religion.

I'm drinking a lot of coffee and water.

April 12

New tables. For the first time, I'm at the same table as Ernessa, with Miss Bombay, no less. They put the two Jews at the same table during Passover.

April 13

After dinner

Another dinner with Ernessa. It's hard not to stare at her the whole time. It's either that or watch Miss Bombay shovel the food into her mouth. She's even bigger than she used to be, like a beached whale. After dinner it takes her forever to get up from the table and walk over to the elevator. Without the elevator, she wouldn't make it back to her room. All the time that she's eating, she's looking around the table to make sure that we are all eating well and drinking milk. Tonight she noticed that Ernessa was only pretending to eat and that she hadn't touched her milk.

"Is there something the matter with the food, Ernessa?" she asked her. "It doesn't suit you?"

"I'm not in the least hungry tonight," said Ernessa.

"But we must eat to keep up our strength. Especially growing girls. We're in no hurry at this table. We'll wait for you to finish."

"I don't want any more," said Ernessa.

"But you must eat unless you don't feel well. In which case you'll have to report to the infirmary after dinner."

"What about her?" asked Ernessa, pointing her finger at me.

Miss Bombay followed her finger, along with everyone else at the table. They all stared at me and my plate, which was piled high with spaghetti. I had eaten the meatballs and finished my milk.

"Well, what about you? We'll wait for you too."

"I have a reason not to eat this," I said very softly.

"And what is the reason?" asked Miss Bombay.

"It's Passover."

"Yes . . ."

"Well, I can't eat spaghetti on Passover. It's not allowed. I ate my meatballs. See?"

It was embarrassing to have to confess this in front of all the other girls. My face was burning red. But no one paid any attention to me. They were concentrating on Miss Bombay's efforts to get Ernessa to eat some of her dinner and to drink milk. Ernessa took a few bites and some sips of her milk, and that seemed to satisfy Miss Bombay, who only wanted to see some food go into her. Ernessa put down her fork, and Miss Bombay told the clearers to take away the plates. There was a huge clatter of dishes, since everyone was in a hurry to finish by now. Most of the other tables were already dismissed, and girls were drinking coffee. The two of us were no longer the subject of everyone's attention. I turned to look at Ernessa. This was the first time I had ever seen her eat or drink anything.

"Don't you feel better now?" asked Miss Bombay.

"No," answered Ernessa. "I wasn't hungry."

I looked over at her as she spoke, and there were drops of sweat on her forehead. When she spoke, I saw that the inside of her mouth was bluish black, even the bottom of her tongue, and that her teeth were stained the same color, especially the tips of the teeth. She looked the way we do in the summer when we eat fresh blueberry pie.

■

April 14

After dinner

Ernessa wasn't at our table tonight. She managed to get herself switched with a tenth grader who was at Mrs. Halton's table. I've never known anyone to get out of sitting at a certain table. You can't even get out of setting up if you play sports and have a late game. But I guess no one ever tried before. I wonder what excuse she used. No one even commented on it. The other girls acted as if it were perfectly normal. I asked the tenth grader why she had switched places with Ernessa, and she said something about a "conflict."

She didn't look well tonight. I watched her as she left the dining room. She looked weak. She reminded me of Annie Patterson.

It's the swimming, I'm sure. Today was her third day.

This afternoon after last period, I saw Ernessa go into the locker room by the pool. I waited awhile at the water fountain, pretending to drink, before I followed her in. She was already gone. I walked through the showers, across the damp, mildewy cement floor, to the stairs that lead up to the pool. Sometimes we go through the pool to get to our lockers by the gym when we don't feel like going outside, if it's raining or cold. It's not an unusual thing to do. The smell of chlorine had seeped into the shower room, but when I opened the door to the pool and stepped out into the warm, humid air, it made me gag. Ernessa was standing by the window, carefully placing her tiny white towel on the sill.

"Shower!" shouted Miss Bobbie.

We have to shower in front of the gym teacher before we are allowed in the pool. I hate that jolt of freezing cold water. I always run in and out of the water without really getting wet. Ernessa walked over to the shower, pulled the chain, and stood under the stream of water without flinching. The water ran off her body onto the floor, and her faded bathing suit turned a dark blue. She would have stayed there much longer, but Miss Bobbie interrupted her: "Now into the pool!"

Ernessa let go of the chain and walked slowly to the end of the pool. She hugged herself tightly. Lucy was right. There is something the matter with her. Her face was flushed a deep red, but the skin of her upper arms and thighs was very white, as if it had never been exposed to the sun, and it was covered with little brown splotches. It looked like the skin of a snake.

She didn't look over at me as I walked along the pool. There was only the water.

"Into the water. We don't have all afternoon," barked Miss Bobbie, even though she was standing right next to Ernessa. Her voice hung in the air. I waited for a shrill blast from the silver whistle that hangs from a chain around her neck.

Ernessa dropped off the edge into the water. Her arms were still crossed tightly; her fingers dug into the skin of her upper arms. She barely made a ripple in the surface. Her body sank right to the bottom of the pool and remained there, immobile, for a long time. It was too long. Miss Bobbie was unconcerned as she watched Ernessa rise slowly, slowly up toward the surface, as if she were caught in thick, heavy oil. I thought she would never break the surface, but her head, covered by a white bathing cap, finally rose above the water. She tilted it to one side, to breathe. After a few seconds, she started to move forward through the water. She flailed her arms and flung her head from side to side. She wasn't swimming. She was panicking.

Miss Bobbie acted as if nothing were happening. She walked over the slick green tiled floor, close to the edge of the pool. Water splashed onto her white sneakers and navy blue knee socks, but she ignored it as she leaned over the water and called out useless instructions: "Keep your legs up. Head down. Bend your elbows. Point your toes." Ernessa continued to thrash.

Is this her weakness? Is water the medium that pulls her down? She is used to having the advantage. Dora had no wings, and she was facing someone with wings. Wings are useless in water.

April 15

Today is Sofia's birthday. She's seventeen. I gave her a carved wooden box from India, lined with purple velvet. I bought it when I was home over vacation. Carol ordered a beautiful birthday cake decorated with flowers from the bakery store in town. She asked Mrs. Halton if we could all have tea and cake in the kitchen during quiet hour. Sofia didn't want to eat the cake. She said it would ruin her diet. She picked at the white cake and left a huge pile of frosting with pink roses and green stems on her plate. I looked around at the crowded little table, and I realized that no one was eating their cake. At least I have an excuse. I ate one of Sofia's pink flowers. It was too sweet and buttery. No one was even talking. Everyone looked glum and tired. What's happening to us?

April 16

I was swimming. The pool was long and narrow, and at the end the sunlight came through tall windows and splashed into the water. The surface had been warmed, but underneath, in the depths, it remained chilly. I could swim forever and never tire. The water supported my buoyant body like a hand. It was impossible to sink into it. I opened my eyes and watched the arrows of light pierce the murky green liquid and leave shadows along the bottom. My arms had taken over the rhythm of the stroke. I didn't have to do anything but float. There was nothing to be afraid of.

April 18

Early morning

When I opened my eyes, I found myself humming "Morning Has Broken." More Cat Stevens. The words of his songs are beginning to make sense. Only I'm not convinced that every morning is a new beginning, like the first morning in the garden of Eden. I've lost that innocence. Memory has replaced it.

Last night Carol and I snuck over to the College with Sofia at midnight, finally. It was dark out, and we kept tripping over roots and stones. Chris was waiting there, just as Sofia had arranged, and the two of them went off together. It was too dark to get a good look at him. We all brought sleeping bags. Carol and I slept together under a weeping willow. Before we fell asleep, Carol made a lot of crude jokes about Sofia and sex like, "The fucking you get isn't worth the fucking you take," and we laughed so hard. I kept thinking, her life is changing forever, and all we can do is laugh.

As we were walking back to school early this morning, I asked Sofia how it was.

"Not what I expected," she replied.

"What do you mean?" I asked.

"Well, it was kind of nothing. I feel exactly the same way I did before, except that now I'm worried about getting pregnant. And I'm sure I'm not in love with him."

"Well, did you at least enjoy it?" asked Carol.

"Not really. Maybe I will after I get used to it."

We walked a ways in silence.

"I'm glad it's over with," said Sofia. "I'm glad it was the first time for both of us."

Probably Lucy and Ernessa are the only girls left on the corridor who are still virgins, besides me, of course.

In English class, when we read *Iphigenia at Aulis*, no one could understand why the Greeks sacrificed beautiful virgins to the gods. In the middle of our discussion, Kiki shouted out, "All the girls must have rushed off to lose their virginity when it was time to make a sacrifice." We all laughed at her, even Miss Russell. But Sofia is rushing off like that to lose her virginity, as if she's afraid of something.

Is it worth sacrificing your life to remain pure?

I'll finish this later.

Or maybe I won't write another word.

After dinner

I'm ready. Here goes. I'm doing this for Sofia.

I went right to sleep last night. I was tired, and I didn't want to listen to them. They weren't very far away, just up the hill behind the tree. I woke up a few hours later. It had grown cold and damp. I was shivering. There was mist everywhere, rising out of the ground and floating away. I wondered how we would ever manage to get back to school if we couldn't see a thing. I'm sure I was awake, because by then I was much too cold to sleep. I thought about waking Carol and telling her that I wanted to go back to school, but she was sound asleep.

I must have dozed off, even though I was sitting up. I was standing by Sofia and Chris, but they couldn't see me, because I was hidden in the mist. There wasn't much to see. They were in a sleeping bag, and he was lying on top of her and moving back and forth slowly. There was a faint rustling, and Ernessa was standing next to me. She smiled at me like a conspirator.

"You need to look more closely," she said loudly. I was sure they could hear her and would know that we were watching them. "Can't you see their hovering spirits entwined? Throughout eternity, like a poem. Don't see them yet? I don't believe in spirits, but I believe in eternity. For all I know, they feel eternal."

I turned to her to tell her to be quiet, not to talk to me anymore, ever, but she was gone.

They had thrown off the sleeping bag and were lying on the damp ground, completely naked. Still, they didn't seem to realize that I was practically standing over them. Sofia was underneath, whimpering and flailing her hands, then sinking her nails into his back, and on top Chris was rising up and crashing down on her, while he held her shoulders against the ground, at first with his hands, and then with his knees, as he slid up her body. He looked over at me, when he had pushed himself into her mouth, and I could see him: his short fair hair, his wet blue eyes, his pink complexion with pimples on the forehead. He looked just the way Sofia had described him.

His knees rose up and down, while he braced himself with his hands. From Sofia came choked screams. Each time his knees came down, he pushed Sofia a little farther into the earth. The ground broke open under their weight. The soil was loose. It crumbled. Sofia sank until she was completely out of sight and I could only see her arms, the hands grabbing at the air. His broad back was white against the black earth.

Midnight

I asked Sofia, "Did he hurt you very much?"

"A little bit," she said, slipping her arm through mine. "It was uncomfortable, not really painful. He was sweet about it. I don't think I bled much. I couldn't tell. I just wanted to get it over with as quickly as possible. It's not as bad as I thought it would be. You shouldn't be scared."

"Was that all he did to you?" I asked.

"What do you mean, all he did?" Sofia looked at me suspiciously.

"I don't know," I said. "Forget it."

—

April 19

This school is finally finished. A lot of the day students stayed home today. Between classes, the halls were empty. "The handwriting is on the wall"—my father's expression.

Miss Bobbie died.

It happened over the weekend, but somehow the day students already knew about it. Miss Rood announced it in assembly this morning. She wanted to keep it a secret from us, but she had to tell us. She can't hide something like that. All however many hundred girls gasped in unison and turned to each other and started to whisper. It was like a dream. Immediately, the row of teachers sitting in the very back began their shushing.

"Girls, quiet. Assembly is not over. You have not been dismissed," said Miss Rood.

We went on with the rest of assembly as if the school weren't coming to an end. That was her intention, to let the news sink in before she let us go. Miss Rood wasn't going to tell us anything more about Miss Bobbie. She seemed less upset than when Pater was found. Her nose wasn't red this time. She was perfectly calm. I wondered if I'd misunderstood her words, and she'd only been announcing the names of girls who had to report to Miss Bobbie after assembly.

"Let us turn to hymn fifty-one," said Miss Rood, and she signaled the music teacher to start playing the piano. The opening bars were drowned out by the sound of us reaching for the hymnbooks. I found myself singing along with everyone else, without any hesitation: "Oh, God, our help in ages past, our hope for years to come." It's my favorite hymn, and Miss Rood always chooses it when something bad has happened. She made us sing every verse. A fierceness settled over her face while she sang: "Time, like an ever-rolling stream, bears all its sons away: They fly forgotten, as a dream dies at the opening day."

After the hymn, Miss Rood made all the announcements for the coming week, and then she said, "You may go now," just as she does at the end of every assembly. The teachers all stood up at once in a line at the back and tried to usher us out. "Don't run! Don't talk! Stay in a line!" they shouted. But they couldn't stop us. As soon as we left the assembly room, we all broke into a run and headed straight for the doors to the Passageway. The roar of voices surged up and carried everyone along on it. My ears are still ringing.

In the Passageway, I caught up to Claire, who had already managed to get some details out of a senior who had talked to someone who knew firsthand what had happened. She said that Miss Bobbie's body was found on the Upper Field. The top part of her was in tatters. Those were the words she used. In tatters. Just blood and shreds of flesh with broken bones sticking out. The lower half, with her plaid kilt and navy blue knee socks and brown tie shoes, was untouched. That was how they identified her. A wild animal had chased her and then attacked. She tried to run away. Imagine Miss Bobbie running. It pinned her against the iron posts of the fence. It was hungry.

We're not out in the wilderness. The wildest thing I ever see is a squirrel.

I should be terrified, but I'm not at all. I'm flattered. Ernessa has something else in mind for me. I am the one she has chosen to see everything. Lucy could never do that. She is the victim, which she plays so beautifully. Iphigenia, the virgin sacrificed to Artemis by her father to win a war. Lucy's saving the rest of us.

I used to feel that my parents could protect me from anything. If I boarded a boat, the swelling of the waves was like the gentle rocking of a cradle. Now those same waves crash against the boat's side, tossing it about like a toy.

Thank you, Daddy, for preparing me to be Ernessa's witness. Thank you for bringing me her poison apple.

I'm not the same person I used to be. That person would have felt sorry for Miss Bobbie. Maybe she did die in that horrible way. As I walked down the Passageway to class, I tried to feel what it would be like to have your throat torn open, to drown in your own blood, while the thing that attacked you just kept at it, relentlessly, impersonally. But I don't feel the least bit sorry. I keep seeing Ernessa rising up through the water, pushing her way through the heavy liquid, digging her way out, while Miss Bobbie ignores her and keeps walking along the side of the pool, shouting instructions. The loose skin above her knees shakes with each step. Her navy blue kneesocks slip down around her ankles. After a week of swimming, Ernessa was so weak she could barely walk. She was drowning right in front of everyone. She could sleep so peacefully under a heavy blanket of earth, but being under water was like being buried alive. She slipped down so quickly, and each time she barely made it back up. She's so strong. So weak.

April 20

Everyone has told their parents about Miss Bobbie. It didn't even cross my mind to call my mother. Miss Rood is sending out letters to all the parents, explaining that there's no cause for alarm, even though two people and a dog have died at school this year. One by one. She'll say, "The Brangwyn School has experienced a series of unfortunate events, but the administration has complete control of the situation. You can be confident of your child's safety." That won't do it this time. No one wants to come back next year, and every day there are more empty seats in the assembly room. They'll empty out one by one.

Today when I walked up the drive to the Residence after gym, I saw Betsy coming down the stairs with her mother. She was carrying a suitcase. She put the suitcase down and ran over to me.

"My mother's taking me home," she said. "I told her that I didn't want to go, but she's making me. I shouldn't have called her last night, but I was upset."

"You'll be back next week," I said.

I watched her get into the yellow station wagon with wood trim. Her mother backed out, and as they drove away, Betsy turned and waved to me.

She's the only boarder who has left so far, but most of the others are talking about not coming back next year. Now they can hate school in a new way. They think that something horrible is going to happen to them here. I know that nothing is going to happen to any of us, not even to me. Only to poor Lucy. "'Oh mercy to myself!' I cried, 'if Lucy should be dead!'"

After dinner

Tonight everyone could only talk about Betsy leaving. They couldn't decide if it was really stupid or if they wanted to go home, too. Beth, the mouse, who never says a word, who was sent home for a month after she tried to cut her wrist, announced that she heard there was a police detective walking around the Upper Field on Sunday.

"Oh, shit!" shouted Carol. "What if they question us, the way they did with Dora? Sofia, you'll never pass a lie detector test. Everybody will find out what you did on Saturday night."

"Do you think they'll make us all take lie detector tests?" asked Sofia. She was about to cry.

"Cut it out," I said. "Nobody's going to be questioned. Miss Bobbie probably just had a heart attack and died in her sleep. Or she slipped, hit her head, and fell into the pool." I saw Ernessa standing at the edge of the pool now, watching Miss Bobbie sink. "Why is everyone trying to turn this into something?"

Sofia looked totally confused. "We have to lie, or we'll all be kicked out."

"No, we won't," I said. "We'll be the only ones left."

I would do anything to keep from getting kicked out. If I were the last person left. I don't ever want to leave. I belong here.

Lights out

They feed on each other's fear, and they can never have enough. No one wants to think about anything else. They're like children huddled under a blanket with a flashlight telling ghost stories. Tonight

Sofia was crying right before lights out. She said that she was too upset to sleep. Carol was sitting on her bed, trying to comfort her. She was constantly sweeping her blond hair out of her eyes and back over her shoulder and twisting her head to the side. It drove me crazy. I wanted to grab her hand and twist it behind her.

I broke my promise never to mention her name. It's time they understand what's going on. They have to see the difference between what's real and what's imagined. She's around the corner, behind her door. They need to realize that.

Carol got up and left the room right away. Even Sofia was looking at me strangely.

"She doesn't eat anything," I insisted. "Have you ever seen Ernessa put food in her mouth?"

"I don't know," said Sofia impatiently. "I can't remember. What does it have to do with anything?"

"How can she survive? She needs some kind of nourishment."

"Just because I never see her put food in her mouth doesn't mean she doesn't eat, ever. Besides, look at Annie Patterson, she lasted for a long time without eating a thing. Nobody noticed for months."

"She was a skeleton in the end. Look at Ernessa—"

"I'm not as fascinated with her as you are. I don't study her eating habits. You're not eating either."

"Don't you think I'd eat if I could find food I liked?"

"I can't talk about this anymore," said Sofia. "I need to go to sleep."

I finally got Sofia's attention. The subject of food always does.

■
April 21

Lunch hour

Lucy slept through breakfast this morning and said she was going to get a note from the nurse to excuse her from gym. I can't bear to go through this again. I told her to call her mother and tell her she wasn't feeling well. She got furious.

"My mother would come and get me this afternoon," she said. "I'm not sick, and I don't need to go home. I don't want to go home. I'm just a little upset. Everyone is."

We have been getting along pretty well since vacation. I've avoided her. I don't even like being around her. I've spent a lot of time with Sofia and Carol. I thought it would go on like this forever.

Ernessa was just playing the game we all play. It gives her pleasure to deny herself something that she wants, the way we push away a plate piled with angel food cake and whipped cream. We can do it a few times, but we always give in and gorge ourselves in the end. You feel that you can't live without that piece of cake.

Sometimes Ernessa got up from the chair in her corner of the Playroom and started to walk toward Lucy, who was in the middle of a group of girls. Lucy would pretend not to see Ernessa, but I knew that she did. There was something wrong about the way Ernessa moved. She was being pulled toward Lucy by a winch. And then halfway across the room, she put up her hands to stop herself, turned to the door, and walked out. No more of that game.

If Lucy starts to get sick, I'm going to call her mother. I don't care if she never talks to me again. I don't want to talk to her anyway.

There's someone in Lucy's room. I have to put this away.

Quiet hour

I got *Strange and Fantastic Stories* from the library. I wanted to write down a passage from "Carmilla" so I can study it.

The vampire is prone to be fascinated with an engrossing vehemence resembling the passion of love, by particular persons. In pursuit of these it will exercise inexhaustible patience and stratagem, for access to a particular object may be obstructed in a hundred ways. It will never desist until it has satiated its passion, and drained the very life of its coveted victim. But it will, in these cases, husband and protract its murderous enjoyment with the refinement of an epicure, and heighten it by the gradual approaches of an artful courtship. In these cases it seems to yearn for something like sympathy and consent. In ordinary ones it goes direct to its object, overpowers it with violence, and strangles and exhausts often at a single feast.

Someone got there before me. In the margin of the book, she wrote: LIES!

I am an obstruction, a tree that has fallen across the road and must be removed or stepped over.

■
April 22

Can a vampire feel?

Can you be evil if you are alone in the world?

What is death to someone who has died and held on to that memory?

If you know everything, can you desire anything?

I look inside myself, and I know I can't feel what Ernessa feels, not even a tenth. And I love Lucy.

This is all Lucy's fault. It's her fault for being such a weak person. She could have saved Ernessa from this. And now I'm forced to save Lucy.

The juniper berry necklace is gone. I have to find a way to protect Lucy without her knowing it.

In Romania, at construction sites, they measure a person's shadow against a wall and fix it with a nail to the head, to protect the building from earthquakes. But a person who loses his shadow becomes a vampire. How cruel to steal a shadow. Even when the Greeks sacrificed young girls to placate the gods, they never took their shadows, only their lives.

It's warm outside today. My window is open for the first time. Everything is full of life when the wind blows through the world.

Later

It's a false spring. I closed the window and lay down on my bed to take a nap. It was so quiet that I could hear the air moving through my throat. But the sound, growing louder, was not inside me. It was all around me. The room was full of flies, and their buzzing was everywhere. Fat black flies bumping against the windowpanes, stupid insects flying straight into the glass over and over again. Clusters of flies thick as grapes. I don't know where they came from. They've been torpid all winter. Now they're roused to a frenzy by the sunlight. When I shut my eyes, the sound of the flies was right there, pushing out every other thought.

■

April 23

After breakfast

I want someone else to call Lucy's mother. I want someone else to take care of her. Everyone keeps telling me not to interfere. There's nothing the matter with her. No one will talk to me. No one will sit with me at meals. Even Sofia, who's never deserted me before. I'm not going to go to lunch from now on. I never really got back my appetite after Passover. I'll go straight to my room after class and take out my journal. I know that no one will disturb me then. They are all downstairs eating. The lunchroom is so noisy with the sounds of chewing and clattering dishes and loud voices that I can't hear my own thoughts. After dinner, I'll sit by myself in the corner of the Playroom and smoke.

Only Lucy can stand to be with me because she doesn't care about anything. She's sleeping through morning bells and can barely drag herself out of bed when I wake her up. This morning she said to me, "I'm too tired to eat breakfast. It would take too much energy to move my mouth." I dragged her down and forced her to drink some coffee. She's much better during the day, once she gets out of bed. Even though she says that she sleeps at night, she wakes up exhausted.

Is everyone totally blind?

I couldn't believe what I was hearing at breakfast. I still go to breakfast because I need the coffee to get through the morning. Not the rolls, though. That food is too cloying. All these girls make me sick. I'm surrounded by people I don't know. They have all decided that Miss Bobbie was killed. And now they need to believe that a man did it. They're making up all kinds of stupid stories about the old negro janitor who doesn't have a name and the night watchman who's also a mortician and eats crackers in the back of the kitchen.

I know she was killed, but I could never explain to them how it happened. It's better for them to think whatever they want.

They can't see what's right in front of them. They have to make things up. It's just like what happened with Ali MacBean last year. First the tires of her green VW Bug were slashed, and then hate notes started showing up every day on the Athletic Association bulletin board. One morning she opened her locker, and a jar filled with acid fell out and burned her hands. She was almost blinded. The twisted psycho who had done this had to be found. Her friends, all day students like her, immediately suspected the girls who weren't just like them. Ali sat up on the stage during assembly, her hands wrapped in white gauze, and she smiled smugly while Miss Rood talked about her tormentor. I looked at her freckled face, her brown hair pulled straight back in a ponytail, her slightly protruding teeth, and I felt sick. I knew then what everyone found out later. She was doing all this to herself. They made her leave school just a month before graduation. And all those friends who had wanted a psycho now only wanted to talk about how she had destroyed her life for no good reason.

I've got to go to assembly. The bells rang five minutes ago.

Lunch hour

I never got to the most pathetic part of this morning's breakfast conversation. I was about to leave the table when I heard Claire say, "What about Mr. Davies?" She was sitting at the other end of the table, but I knew the question was directed at me. I didn't bother to answer her. Instead, I pushed out my chair.

"What about him?" asked Carol.

"Well, he's a man," said Claire. "And he's kind of . . . weird. You have to be to write the stuff he does."

I knew the conversation would turn to Mr. Davies in the end. There are no more men left to fantasize about.

"You have to be weird to write poetry?" I asked. She was baiting me, but I couldn't keep quiet.

"Not that," said Claire. "The other stuff, the stuff for porno magazines."

"Look, you made that up in the first place," I said. "But even if he does write it, which he doesn't, what does it have to do with anything?"

"Plenty," said Claire. "If you can imagine such twisted shit, you can do it. And I don't think he even likes women. I think he hates them deep down, and he could get off on making them suffer."

"This is ridiculous," I said.

"I knew you would stick up for him," said Claire. "Frankly, I wouldn't want to be stuck alone in a room with him."

"Why are you doing this?" I shouted. "You make me want to throw up!"

I got up and ran out of the room. If I'd had to listen to another word from her, I would have clawed her face.

April 24

This afternoon I went down to practice. I haven't touched the piano in so long. I need the music more than ever.

I was alone. No one else would dare to come down there by herself. Girls are crying during classes. They don't want to stay after school for gym. If they do stay, they all walk up to the train station together. Even Sofia, who has always adored school, is talking about leaving. It's getting worse and worse every day. That's because they'll never find what they are looking for.

There's been a lot of rain, and the practice rooms are clammier than ever. My hands are so stiff that they ache when I play. I tried hard to concentrate and to follow Miss Simpson's instructions. That's why I keep making mistakes, she says, because I can't concentrate. I have to use my will to conquer the mistakes. While I'm playing, someone should be able to come up behind me and slap me on the back, and it shouldn't make any difference in my playing. I should continue without a pause. That's what they do to you in music school.

I gave up. I couldn't play.

The door to the basement was open. I tried it, and the knob turned. I won't go down there yet.

Every door is my door, just for me. Eventually, I always go through the door, whether or not it is locked. I had to push hard with my shoulder to open the bathroom door. My father's leg was pressed up against it. The white tiles were covered with dark, sticky blood. His head was slumped over his chest. He could not move his leg. He sat and sat. One breath left, just for me. The last bit of air seeping out of the deflated raft with a faint hiss. He was waiting for me to come. The sunlight streamed into the room, and it was so warm. I wanted to curl up and go to sleep right there next to him. Instead, I had to scream and scream and scream even though there was no one to hear me. And the sound went nowhere; it just swirled around and around in that little room.

If I know something, I am not a victim. Victims don't know the meaning of their suffering. I am an enemy or a collaborator, not a victim.

April 25

Ten A.M.

Sometimes I forget that other people can't hear my thoughts. I sit at breakfast drinking my coffee, and I look around in a panic. All the girls at the table must know what I think of them, my total and utter disdain for them. I can't hide it.

Claire's made them all obsessed with Mr. Davies. They don't talk about the janitor or Bob anymore. It's all Mr. Davies. He's their favorite monster. They whisper to each other and stare at me when I sit down by myself. I know what they're saying: "You think he did it to Miss Bobbie first? Or did he tear her to shreds and then do it?"

I don't stick up for him anymore.

April 26

I went to see Mr. Davies after school today.

I wanted to tell Mr. Davies what they were saying about him, but I couldn't. I talked about the girls instead.

"They'll calm down," said Mr. Davies. "Eventually the school will get back to normal."

"They can't calm down," I said. "They can't because the person who is doing this hasn't finished yet. She still has one more victim, the one she came for. The others just got in her way."

"The person doing this?" he asked. I'm sure he wasn't really puzzled.

"Ernessa Bloch."

"One more victim?"

"Lucy Blake."

He waited. I knew he knew what I was going to tell him.

"Lucy's getting sick again. The way she was before spring break. She's very weak. She can't get out of bed in the morning. She can't eat. Last time, they almost didn't save her. Ernessa won't let them take Lucy away from her again. I want to call Lucy's mother, but no one wants me to. They tell me not to interfere in something that's not my business. They think Lucy's death is nobody's business but her own. They don't care what she becomes after that."

I should have kept my mouth shut. But I couldn't. The words forced themselves out of me as though they were alive. He looked scared. I'm sure he understood, no matter what he said.

"You know what you're saying can't possibly be true," he said very quietly. "Perhaps Ernessa is a thoroughly repulsive person—certainly she is to you—but she's only that. She's a girl just like you, not a spirit. You can't let yourself become trapped by these fantasies. You've got so much creativity. Draw on it. Write. You have poetry in you. Let it help you."

"I know it seems crazy," I pleaded. "But I have to believe it."

"This has been a difficult year for you. You're still coming to terms with what happened to your father, and on top of it all the chaos at school hasn't helped. Two people die; your best friend gets sick. But you can't blame everything bad that happens on a person you dislike. If it weren't Ernessa, it would be someone else."

"It is Ernessa. I hated Miss Bobbie too, but I didn't need to tear her to pieces."

"Ernessa doesn't exist for you. She's become your poem about death."

"My what?" I said.

"You need to try to think about other things. You're too young to think about this stuff all the time."

He doesn't believe in another level of reality. He doesn't believe in the imagination. He's not a real poet.

"What else can I think about? Boys? Clothes? Food?"

The conversation felt finished, used up. I would never come to talk to Mr. Davies again. Those hours in the empty sun-filled classroom talking about books were over. I stood up to leave, but I didn't move. Mr. Davies came over to me and stood directly in front of me. Slowly, deliberately, he undid the top three buttons of my white shirt, underneath my pleated gym tunic. Then he pulled down the straps of my bra, very gently, with such consideration, and placed his hands over my breasts. His hands were so cool, so smooth, against my hot skin. What he was doing was meant to soothe me, to calm me. Each hand covered a breast. Beneath them, my heart was racing. I couldn't help it. Then he leaned over me and took my mouth in his. He kissed me for a long time.

An incredible lethargy came over me. I would never be able to move again, to free myself from him and walk across the room, through the door, down the hallway to the outside. Claire was posted by the door, trying to look through the frosted glass window. When I walked out that door, I wouldn't be able to hide what had happened to me. I would be her proof about Mr. Davies, even though it was really the opposite.

The kiss was long. It was sweet. It would never end. Somehow I left that room. It took all my strength to do that.

An hour later, it is already vague. I put a gray sweater over my white shirt, which was soaked with sweat, and buttoned it up all the way. The wool scratched my damp skin. I'm certain that I dreamed it, along with the pleasure that I felt. His hands. Isn't it worse to dream something like that?

I never trusted Mr. Davies. He was trying to get to my father through me. Something of my father must have rubbed off on me, and he wanted to get as close as possible to that something. What rubbed off? Did he get what he wanted?

I can't imagine what would happen if someone found my journal and read this. I don't want anything bad to happen to Mr. Davies.

I've pushed the dresser in front of the door and locked the bathroom door.

After dinner

I have no time for homework today, only for my writing.

Thank God I didn't tell Mr. Davies much, just enough to get him upset. I could feel his resistance to what I was saying, even before he heard the words. Everything will be in my journal. My journal will protect me.

Sunday morning (yesterday) I got up at about eight thirty. I looked in on Lucy, and she was asleep, so I went down for a cup of coffee. When I came up, she was still asleep. I decided not to wake her, even though I know she has tons of homework. She used to be the first one up on Sunday morning and in church before the rest of us got out of bed. She wasn't the type to sleep late. I was. Now she needs to save whatever strength she has left for the coming week. I went into my room, straightened up a bit and made my bed, then sat down to work on my history paper. I went to the bathroom; I brushed my teeth; I washed my face. I wrote for a little while in my journal, but it made me too sad. I kept getting up and opening the door to her room a crack and looking at her. Finally, I went in and sat down on the bed next to her. Her face was colorless, and her breathing was so shallow that it barely lifted her chest. Her hand was lying outside the covers, and when I touched it, the skin was cold, like marble. She hadn't changed her position since I first looked in on her. I panicked. She was dead. But when I placed my hand on her heart, her breast was warm, and there was a fluttering under my palm. She still had her smell, that moist powder smell.

I had to leave her room. I went down the corridor clutching a pile of books and my notebook and pushed open the swinging doors to the library. On a Sunday morning, it was quiet. Everyone was off doing something else. I was all alone. I was away from Lucy. The light was streaming into the room through the high windows in sheets.

How surprised the others would be to know she confides in me. Friendless with no need for friends, she tells me everything. The most surprised would be Mr. Davies, who doesn't believe in books, who turns them into bad dreams. I hadn't even opened my books. I was waiting. There was one more thing she wanted to tell me.

"Books won't save you," said Ernessa. "Your writing won't save you. The past won't save you. Mr. Davies won't save you. Daddy won't save you. You could try a crucifix. The star of David never saved anyone."

"My father wanted to save me," I said. "I'll believe that to the end. He will be my final thought."

"He's the one who caused you all this trouble in the first place. Parents give you a disease: they infect you with life. Your father made it possible for you to see me as I am and to hear my words."

"You're wrong. That was what happened to you. That was your

death. The walks we took, the poems, the searching in the dark with a flashlight. They happened. We were together, for a while."

"He read you other fairy tales that you've forgotten."

She began to hum softly, then to sing, in a whisper, a familiar song.

> *My mother she butchered me,*
> *My father he ate me,*
> *My sister, little Ann Marie,*
> *She gathered up the bones of me*
> *And tied them in a silken cloth*
> *To lay under the juniper.*
> *Tweet twee, what a pretty bird am I!*

I put my hands over my ears, just as I did whenever my father sang that song to me. I used to be relieved that I didn't have the baby brother I wanted so much. I could never be like Ann Marie and box his ears and see his head fall off and roll over the floor and into the corner. My father would never eat his child and beg for more. My mother would never be a witch.

"Time to free yourself," she said.

"I am free."

I expected her to be angry with me for defying her, but she wasn't.

Ernessa pushed back the heavy wooden chair, and it scraped against the floor, just as it would for a real person. With one long motion, she pulled something out of her pocket and dragged it across her left wrist. She held it out, as if she were offering me something. A moment passed. Nothing happened. Then the skin split open, exposing the red flesh, a laughing mouth of a wound. Blood sprayed out with the force of water from a hose. It splashed over her clothes, fell in pools on the floor, rained down in dark droplets on the table in front of me, over my book and notebook. It kept pouring out. There was no way to stop it.

She reached over and dropped the razor blade on the table. When she stood up straight, she blocked the light coming through the tall windows. The room grew dim for a few seconds; outside, a dense cloud had passed quickly in front of the sun. Her skin absorbed the light spilling over her the way a sponge soaks up liquid. When her body had taken in as much as it could hold, the light passed straight through her flesh and began to dissolve it, from the tips of her fingers up through her hands to her arms. Their shapes lingered in the air, like a faint halo, then vanished along with the blood.

I turned away. I refused to watch the rest. The breasts, the ass, the legs, her face. When I looked back, she was gone among the particles of dust in the air. A fly began to buzz and bang against the glass of the window.

To sublime: to pass directly from the solid to the vapor state.

To sublimate: to divert the expression of an instinctual desire or impulse from its primitive form to one that is considered more socially or culturally acceptable.

Sublime: of outstanding spiritual, intellectual, or moral worth.

I took the razor blade back to my room. There was no blood on it. I put it in my desk drawer, along with my photographs and letters. I moved the dresser away from the door. It won't do any good.

—
April 27

Six A.M.

I am standing under an enormous tree. The trunk is so thick that I can't get my arms around it. The wind soughs through the treetops, catching on the needles. It sounds like heavy rain, but I am dry. I stretch my head back, but I can't see to the top of the tree. I count the soft needles in each bundle: five. I examine the long, curved brown cones and the gray, furrowed bark. It is a white pine. I turn to tell my father. He'll be so pleased that I know.

Lunch hour

During break I snuck into the upper school office and looked through the binder with the schedules of all the girls. I waited outside in the hallway until Miss Weiner left the office. I had to hurry. My hands were shaking so much that I couldn't turn the pages. She has no classes until eleven every day. She has to show up for assembly before school, but after that, she is free for two and a half hours. That's when she sleeps. She doesn't need much sleep.

Quiet hour

All day I walked down the hallways and looked only at the ground directly in front of me. I didn't want to see him. A meeting of our eyes and he would abandon everything: the cheerful wife who works for Planned Parenthood and went on freedom marches, the gray and the calico cats, the Salvation Army furniture, the baby who watched us from the sofa, his poetry. He would leave it and take me away.

April 28

Lunch hour

After breakfast, while I was making my bed, Mrs. Halton came to my room and told me that I had to see Miss Brody that afternoon, immediately after classes ended. Mrs. Halton talked to me from outside my doorway. She was very careful not to set foot in my room. She looked angry and disgusted. She didn't bother to hide it.

They've been trying to get me to talk to Miss Brody for years, and I've always refused. Now they are ordering me. She's a complete fraud. All she ever does is talk in platitudes about getting in touch with our inner selves, when she has no idea what's there. Why is she a school psychologist anyway? The only person who likes her is Sofia, who will talk to any adult about her problems. Miss Brody loves it when girls confide in her. She doesn't really listen to what they say.

Quiet hour

At first, it was pretty much what I expected. Miss Brody wanted me to talk about my father's suicide, about my unresolved feelings for him. She seemed so eager to hear. How did he do it? "He slit his wrists. Both of them." How did you feel? "Strange." There was another woman, wasn't there? "No." And who found him? "My mother." Did you see him? "I was kept away."

Lies, the truth. She couldn't tell the difference between the two.

Then she asked me about the other times I've seen psychiatrists. The time right after my father died, and the other time, when I was much younger. How does she know about that? My mother would never have told the school. I didn't want to talk about those things. I've told her enough. Let her peep through her own keyholes. I never wanted to talk to the doctors in the first place. I kept saying that I was just anxious, that there was never really anything wrong. But that didn't satisfy her. She kept asking more questions.

Miss Brody is a thoroughly conventional person. She was wearing black pumps, a navy blue dress with gold buttons, and a blue and gold flowered silk scarf around her neck. Her dark hair is always perfectly in place, and she speaks very slowly and carefully, as if everyone else has trouble understanding the simplest things.

"We have to come to terms with our deepest feelings, to accept them even if they cause us pain. It's hard work, but it's the only way we can move beyond them. Otherwise they'll keep tripping us up again and again."

But she didn't really care about feelings and how they "trip you up."

"It's come to our attention, actually several girls reported it, that you have done something inappropriate. In fact, unacceptable. You placed some . . . some excrement outside your roommate's door. Is this true?"

No one had seen me do this. I was sure of that. It was the middle of the night. And it had barely smelled. It wasn't noticeable. Just a trace, that was all that was needed. All around the doorway, along the wooden floor, not an inch left untouched. Only someone with an oversensitive sense of smell could detect it. The ammonia they used to clean it up left a worse smell that made everyone hold their noses when they passed Lucy's room. I looked down and smiled uncomfortably. I wanted to act exactly as she expected me to.

"It was a joke. Between Lucy and me," I said very softly. "I shouldn't have done it."

"A joke? What kind of joke could it be?" asked Miss Brody.

"I made a mistake," I said.

"When you feel those impulses, you must work to sublimate them and behave in a socially acceptable manner."

Pearl necklaces instead of rosary beads, that's the school's real religion. I didn't tell her that late at night, I had finally realized that only the most extreme actions could save Lucy. And that she would never agree to anything I suggested. How could I live with myself if I was too cowardly to do everything possible to protect her? Even something so repugnant that I couldn't defile my journal by writing about it. And it worked. For the two days that the barrier remained around her doorway, Lucy was fine. On Monday and Tuesday, she got up in the morning, went to breakfast, went to her classes. She was alive again. No one said anything about how well she looked because they don't notice when she drags herself through school with sunken eyes and gray skin and uncombed hair. They never notice anything.

I smiled at Miss Brody and nodded my head in answer to her questions. I admitted my guilt. Why not? I even admitted that I had never really come to terms with my grief for my father. "Grieving is hard work," she said. "Harder than studying for an exam." She was talking in a dull, droning voice. I lost interest. My mind started to wander. Then she wasn't talking about guilt or grieving. "Some people find great joy in the prospect of death," she said. "Just thinking about it can be a comfort, like lying down in your own bed and pulling up the covers. It's a liberating experience, not a fearful one. The moment before dying is ecstatic, the most joyful sensation. One is being born into a new existence." At first, I thought she was joking. I couldn't understand what she was trying to say. But she went on.

"You read a lot. It's like reading a book and skipping to the end because you can't wait to find out how it will turn out. The suspense is unbearable. I'm sure you've done that sometimes, taken a peek at the ending. What a relief that knowledge can be."

She paused and said, "What do you think about this, what I've been telling you? Does it help?"

I finally looked up. She was sitting sideways, with one side of her face turned to me. I could see the powder covering the pores of her skin, the fine lines emerging around the corner of her mouth, the skin beginning to sag under her chin. She was older than I thought. Then she reached across her desk for a pencil and a pad of paper and turned her other side to me. It was so smooth and pink that it didn't look like flesh. This face was without a single wrinkle or blemish or hair. It belonged to another person. The sides of her face were completely different, and I couldn't remember what she looked like in the first place. The left? The right? I couldn't fix that image in my brain.

"Do you think your conversation the other day with Mr. Davies was simply an expression of deep-seated fears? You don't really believe what you told him, do you?" asked Miss Brody.

"I don't believe any of it," I muttered. "I was upset. Like everyone else here. There's nothing the matter. Really."

"I'll talk to the doctor about this. Maybe Valium would help you to calm down, to get you through this difficult period."

How could I defend myself if I no longer had any secrets? I only wanted to get out of there, away from Miss Brody, to get the two sides of her face to come back together, for everything to look normal again. I was excused. I ran up to my room, got into bed, pulled the covers up over my head, and put my pillow over them. I was beyond trembling and crying. I was frozen.

April 29

Lunch hour

I have detention for one month: no more weekend privileges. Mrs. Halton told me this morning after breakfast. She smiled while she spoke and then added, "Consider yourself lucky, young lady. You got off easily. You seem to want to add to the misery at our school."

Everyone is avoiding me, even Sofia in her nice way. I can feel it. They all know what happened, but they won't say a thing. Of course, they are disgusted. One good thing, though, they've suddenly forgotten about Mr. Davies and Miss Bobbie. It's all me.

Sofia has finally managed to lose weight, the twenty pounds that dimpled her thighs. She's gone on some kind of macrobiotic diet, and she eats nothing but toasted brown rice, which she cooks in the kitchen on weekends. After a month of that, she's lost her appetite. So now she's thin, the way she's always wanted to be. She looks gaunt and anxious.

This morning, again, I couldn't get Lucy out of bed. I gave up and went down to breakfast by myself.

"What's with you?" asked Kiki.

I looked up, surprised that someone was talking to me.

"Me?" I asked.

Everyone's gaze was fixed on me, even though I wasn't doing anything. There used to be a girl called Margaret Rice who walked around as stiff as a board. She always looked straight ahead, with the same blank expression on her face. I never saw her speak to anyone else. I never saw her smile. We used to call her the Zombie. Now I'm the Zombie.

"You've been staring at your coffee for at least ten minutes," said Kiki. "Drink it already."

"I was thinking about Lucy," I said, encouraged to speak because of Kiki's attention. "She's acting the way she did before she got really sick. She's too exhausted to get out of bed in the morning, even though she's slept for hours and hours. Someone needs to call her mother."

"Oh, drop it," said Kiki. "She seems fine to me. She can call her own mother if she wants to."

"But she doesn't realize how sick she is. She looks so awful."

"Leave her alone. She can take care of herself," said Carol. "Now she's got a great bod. Not an ounce of fat. Even her little belly is gone. I wish I looked like her."

I looked into that circle of annoyed faces. They have no idea that something terrible is about to happen. Or they already know. They are willing to sacrifice Lucy to protect themselves.

I wish, for once, someone else would mention Lucy's name first. Those two syllables, Lu-cy. I only want to hear another girl talk about her in front of me, say her name like a charm to ward off spirits. They used to look at me first for approval when they talked about her. She belonged to me more than to anyone else.

I got up and took my coffee cup to the cart and dropped it in. The brown liquid splashed everywhere. All those eyes turned to stare at my back as I walked away. The Zombie.

When I got back upstairs, it was almost time for the last bells, and Lucy was still in bed. I left her alone, just as they told me to. Let her get into trouble for missing assembly. Let her get angry at me.

Everyone abandons me in the end. My mother and father were too wrapped up in themselves. All those indistinguishable gray ladies who are supposed take care of us at school. My teachers. Miss Brody, the confessor. Even Mr. Davies, the poet, who I thought was different from all the rest. The eyes of all those stupid girls follow me everywhere.

Study hour

After Greek I had tea with Miss Norris. She could tell that I didn't want to go back to my room. She invited me to spend quiet hour in her apartment. I ran down to my room and got some books. I wish I could move into her room. I love her.

During tea, I talked to her a little bit about Lucy. She kept nodding her head while I spoke. She knows Lucy. I brought her once to have tea with Miss Norris. I wanted to show Lucy the birds. She was concerned about Lucy.

Then I told her that Ernessa is a bad influence on Lucy. She encourages her not to take care of herself. To ruin her health.

"That girl came to see me once, in the beginning of the year," she said. "Her Greek is very good. I told her that I had nothing to teach her in that regard. But if she wanted to read the Greek historians, we could. She turned up her nose at that."

"I'm afraid of what she's doing to Lucy. Lucy's too weak to stand up to her. She doesn't think she's sick. All the girls keep telling me not to interfere. That it's none of my business."

"You have to follow your instincts. You are a good person. Do what you think is right. Ignore what the others say. They will never listen. The opinion of the crowd is often evil, and, as Sophocles says, 'Nothing evil ever dies.'"

Today we started translating a passage from the *Odyssey*. It was too hard for me. Miss Norris did most of the translating. Odysseus calls up the ghosts from the underworld and gives them the blood of black rams. He pours it into a deep trench, so that they can recover the power of speech. I have the English translation with me. The meeting with his dead mother was just as I might have written it.

> *I bit my lip, rising perplexed, with longing to embrace her,*
> *and tried three times, putting my arms around her,*
> *but she went shifting through my hands, impalpable*
> *as shadows are, and wavering like a dream.*
> *Now this embittered all the pain I bore,*
> *and I cried in the darkness:*
>
> *"O my mother, will you not stay, be still, here in my arms,*
> *may we not, in this place of Death, as well,*
> *hold one another, touch with love, and taste*
> *salt tears' relief, the twinge of welling tears?"*

Everything is unfair. The body and spirit separate and disappear, like mist. There is no way to hold on to either one or to reunite them. How I've longed to fling my arms around my father and give him back the power of speech, but even in my dreams, he always drifts away without saying anything.

April 30

After dinner

I had a huge fight with Lucy, and I am finally free. Free of the dream of a perfect friendship. I never wanted it to come true. I wanted it to remain a dream and vanish the way dreams do. One day I would find I no longer dreamed about the girl in the light blue room. I had some other dream.

During quiet hour, I went into her room. She was lying on her bed, her eyes half-closed. She doesn't have the strength to open them or to close them. I sat on the edge of the bed and pushed the hair off her forehead, the hair that's as smooth as metal. Her skin was moist with sweat, and loose strands stuck to it. She tried to smile.

"Lucy, I know you're getting sick again. I'm worried. I need to call your mother."

"I'm not sick, really. I know I'm not sick. It's something else. It makes me seem sick, but I'm not."

"Don't you want to leave here? To get away from this place? Don't you want your mother to come get you?"

"No. I'm not afraid. You can't call her. She'd come right away. In the middle of the night."

"I don't understand."

"That's because you want to believe I'm still the old Lucy. That's the sad thing. You were friends with the old Lucy, not with me. You don't care about the new one, the real Lucy. You don't even want to know her."

"It's all Ernessa's fault," I screamed at her. "She's turned you completely against me. That's why you say this."

"She's never said anything mean about you. I've just changed, that's all. Why do you always want to blame her for everything?"

"Because she's to blame for everything. If she hadn't come here, we would have had a wonderful year. She's ruined everything for me. I hate her so much I would kill her if I had the chance."

"You make me sick, the way you talk," said Lucy, pushing herself up, suddenly energized.

I grabbed her arm and pulled her off the bed toward the bath-room. She was so light, but I struggled to drag her across the room. We stood side by side, barely able to fit into the narrow mirror on the bathroom door. She leaned heavily against me.

"Look at yourself," I shouted. "Tell me that you don't look sick. You can barely stand up."

"Look at yourself," whispered Lucy.

In our white shirts, our long blue skirts, with our pale skin and our eyes rimmed with red, we were both ghostly, only partly present. She wasn't pretty anymore, but her prettiness never really interested me. My face was wet with tears. I didn't know that I had started to cry.

"Leave me alone, please," said Lucy. "I can't stand having you around me all the time, wanting me only for yourself. You are a fuck-ing drag. You pull me down. All that pain."

"You never said anything."

"There's only a month and a half left of school. We should be able to make it without changing rooms."

I left her room and closed the door to the bathroom behind me. I'll never speak to her again. Never. I don't even understand what happened. She was so sweet the whole time, gazing up at me with that stupid smile of hers.

I forced myself to go down to dinner. I didn't want her to see how much she had hurt me. How much she makes me suffer. At dinner, she seemed livelier. My pain has given her strength. I feel desperate. I won't call her mother. I'll stay out of the whole thing. I ate dinner without once taking my eyes from my plate. I didn't want to see Lucy, at the next table, laughing and talking as if nothing had happened. She feels relieved to be rid of me at last. I was just the friend she took under her wing, like an injured bird, because she felt so sorry for her, but who turned out to be too much trouble in the end. I ran up to my room after a quick cup of coffee and sat down at my desk with my journal. But I couldn't write. I listened to the girls coming up from dinner and going to their rooms. Their voices in the corridor sounded so happy! They weren't worried about anything. Some of them were laughing. They all left me alone. Lucy only said what everyone else thinks.

I've been here for three years, and I feel exactly the way I did my first week at school, when I hurried up from meals, shut myself up in my room, and listened to the girls outside my door. All the other doors on the corridor were open. Only mine was closed. They inhabited a world I couldn't enter. How could I ever learn to be like them? I would be locked up in my room by myself, day after day, reading my books, listening to the rising and falling voices, wanting only my father. She had the key, and she unlocked my cell. That was why I loved her so much.

I cried when I saw our reflection in the mirror because we are both so changed.

If I am no longer the person I once was, then I no longer know any of the people around me.

Lights out

After study hour, I snuck downstairs to the pay phone in the back of the Cloakroom. My pockets were full of change. My fingers shook as I dialed the number. They kept getting stuck in the holes. I prayed that no one would see me. The phone rang four, five times before someone finally answered it. A pause, a heaving breath, a hoarse voice. I didn't expect him. I was sure her mother would answer. He was standing by the phone in the kitchen in his underwear, panting, his face a deep, glistening red. The dog was jumping up and barking by his side. "Hello. Hello? Hello?"

I hung up.

MAY

Seven A.M.

> I heard a Fly buzz—when I died—
>   The Stillness in the Room
> Was like the Stillness in the Air—
>   Between the Heaves of Storm—
>
> The Eyes around—had wrung them dry—
>   And Breaths were gathering firm
> For that last Onset—when the King
>   Be witnessed—in the Room—
>
> I willed my Keepsakes—Signed away
>   What portion of me be

Assignable—and then it was
There interposed a Fly—

With Blue—uncertain stumbling Buzz—
Between the light—and me—
And then the Windows failed—and then
I could not see to see—

Why does she keep lecturing me? It's like a sermon. Preacher Emily converting the Jew. I cover my ears. I close my eyes.

Nine P.M.

I can't find the right pen to write this. Nothing feels comfortable in my hand. I picked up my fountain pen, but it's clogged. The nib scratches the paper and makes little tears. I can't write quickly enough to keep up with my thoughts. I went through my desk and my book bag and tried every pen. Nothing is right.

I'm going to write the words: Lucy is dead.

She's been dead for more than a day.

Finally, I understand my part in the tragedy. Is it a tragedy? Or a story that came to a close while I was still telling it? I have so few blank pages left anyway. I've almost filled my journal. That was what I set out to do.

I am still alive. My hand holds my crimson pen, my most treasured possession. And it moves. I am amazed by that. My hand trembles, but it still moves. The blood continues to flow through my body, without my having to tell it what to do. I breathe in and out.

They've taken her body away. The dead body. The no-longer-alive body. Her mother sobbed uncontrollably as she hugged me. The nurse, the doctor, everyone has questioned me, over and over, about what happened. Lucy had another attack, and this time she stopped breathing. They don't need me to tell them that. They have ordinary truth. What would they do with my extraordinary truth?

If only her mother had answered the phone.

Lights out

I passed Mrs. Halton in the corridor, and she was so excited. She knows how much I am suffering, which makes it even better for her. She has so many details to take care of. She's incredibly busy. She has to talk to all the girls and comfort them, to help Lucy's mother with the wake, to arrange for all of us to go, to order flowers, to bring her trunk up from the basement and pack up her room. There's so much to be done.

May 3

I open the urn with my father's ashes. White bones are sticking up out of the soft gray ash. I throw out the ashes in handfuls. I am eager to be rid of them. The wind blows them back in our faces. My mouth is full of his ashes. They dissolve on my tongue. My hands and mouth are stained black. "Get rid of the bones," shouts my mother. She is impatient with me. She grabs the urn from me, pulls out a long bone, and hurls it up into the sky. Then another and another. The white bones fly up and out into the sky in an arc. They don't come down.

After they took Lucy away from me, I got in bed and went to sleep. I slept for most of the day. I had no trouble sleeping. At the end of the day, I went down and ate dinner. I didn't cry. All the girls huddled together in the Playroom after dinner. It was a different kind of silence this time. No one knew what to say. From time to time, someone began to whimper a little, and then a few others started up. Everyone took turns crying. I didn't even cry when Lucy's mother hugged me. I whispered in her ear, "Cremate the body." She looked at me in amazement, then she started to sob again.

I'm sure Ernessa didn't cry either. Lucy's special friend. I saw her this morning in assembly. She was red and swollen, like a pregnant woman.

Sofia and I helped Lucy's mother pack all her clothes this afternoon. Her mother needed to do something to keep herself occupied.

Before she put Lucy's jewelry box in the trunk, she opened it and held it out to us.

"I want each of you to pick out something of Lucy's."

She began to cry as Sofia and I emptied the box on the bed. Those were the only sounds in the room: the soft sobbing and the tinkling of silver and gold. It embarrassed us to disentangle the necklaces and bracelets and pins. Sofia chose a silver charm bracelet. Lucy was just the kind of person to have a charm bracelet. She had probably been adding to it for the last ten years. Bells, hearts, stars, horses, dogs, skates. I took her gold cross. It had been resting on the dark green velvet of her jewelry box all this time. She could have put it back on anytime. The girl who went to church every Sunday and dressed up on Easter with her hat and little pocketbook and matching patent leather shoes knew where it was.

—

May 4

Dawn

I thought I would do anything to save her life. That was before I was put to the test.

That night I went to bed early. My argument with Lucy had exhausted me. It wasn't even ten o'clock. I could still hear noises from her room. Lucy was talking to someone. I lay in bed and knew that I didn't want to have to save her. I closed my eyes and fell asleep. My dream started so slowly that it never felt like a dream. I awoke and walked toward Lucy's room. The bathroom door opened, and I passed through it. Lucy's bed was empty. The covers were thrown back. The mattress was still warm. I hurried into the corridor, around to the back stairs, down to the ground floor, through the door. It had already been propped open with a stick. I ran down the driveway, past the wide staircase that leads up to the Residence, past the weeping cherry trees that line the Upper Field. The pink flowers were gone; dried brown blossoms matted the ground. The new leaves were a silvery green. Little stones and sharp sticks stuck into my bare feet as I ran over the scruffy grass at the crest of the hill. The moon had just risen full above the tops of the trees on the far side of the field, and it was enormous. Its light was so bright that it threw deep shadows across the grass. It could have been the middle of the day. There was no longer any connection between the two: no way to go from night to day and back again. I stood at the top of the hill. Lucy and Ernessa were on the field. Their white nightgowns glowed.

"Lucy," I shouted. "Lucy!"

I could never make them hear me. Ernessa was behind Lucy and above her. She had grabbed hold of Lucy's hair and was pulling her up off the ground. Lucy's hair shone like solid gold in the moonlight. They hovered, as weightless as angels. The carefully arranged folds of the nightgowns hid their feet. Angels don't need feet. It annoys me when their toes peek out beneath their robes in old paintings. Lucy held her arms out to the side, bent at the elbows, with fingers and thumbs straight, as if she were pressing hard against something.

I ran down the hill toward them. It took a long time. The air was as thick as water, and it pushed against me. My legs went up and down, but I couldn't move forward. I'd had this dream my whole life, and I was always too late.

Lucy's body lay crumpled on the ground. Ernessa was gone.

I gathered Lucy in my arms and pressed my face against her. The sound of her breath was a faint gurgle.

"Lucy, don't leave me here all alone. I won't let you do this to me."

She stopped breathing, and her mouth became rigid. I began to shake her. A little at first, then harder and harder. I banged her head against the ground. Her hair was a tangled mass. I could still shake her back to life. I was furious at Lucy for being able to die just by closing her eyes.

Then I searched her neck, the space between her eyes, the skin over her heart, her nipples for marks that would tell me how to go from life to death. There were none. The books were all wrong. The marks are invisible. Not even a microscope could find them.

I awoke from my dream in my room with the moonlight pouring through the uncovered window. At first, I thought someone had come into my room and switched on the overhead light. Charley had crawled in through the window and was playing a stupid joke on me. But Charley was long since gone.

I jumped out of bed. I ran into Lucy's room. The door opened for me. The bed was empty and warm. Everything happened exactly as it had in my dream.

They found me sitting on the ground with Lucy's head on my lap. It was just dawn, and the grass under us was damp and cold. My legs were numb.

After dinner

This afternoon was the wake for Lucy. Tomorrow they are taking her body back home to be buried. Her father didn't come.

The white coffin was all alone in the middle of the room. The people in their dark clothes were pushed back against the walls. At both ends of the coffin stood tall urns with white flowers spilling out of them. She looked dead, truly dead. Her greenish skin would convince anyone that she was dead and not just sleeping. Her eyes were closed, her golden hair beautifully arranged, her face made up, her lips pink, her body perfumed, her hands clasped under a pile of white roses. She was wearing her white commencement dress from last year and the matching white shoes and lying on white satin. Everything was white, white. And all the perfumes thick and dizzying. The embalming fluid had the sickening smell of overripe fruit. I leaned over her for a long time, and no one dared to stop me. I was the one who found her. I felt her last breath. I had her all to myself. From my pocket I took a tiny silver knife and the strip of black and white photos of Lucy and me. I slipped the knife between her stiff hands. I pushed the photos under the folds of her dress. There were four images, and in the last one we were laughing uncontrollably, pushing each other out of the tiny frame. Our arms were wrapped around each other's necks.

It won't keep her from becoming what she'll become, but perhaps the knife will protect her and the photos will remind her of me in the lonely place where no one feels anything except hunger.

I stood up and looked around the room. Everybody had turned

away. In the corner stood her mother, dressed in a black suit, black pumps, black handbag, talking to Mrs. Halton. She was totally composed. What was she really thinking while she talked and smiled sweetly? About taking Lucy back to the house with her husband's rasping breaths sucking up the air and the little white poodle that barks all the time? I went over to say good-bye to her. I wanted to tell her mother that it was my fault. I wanted to tell her that Lucy had stopped confiding in me, that we weren't friends, that I didn't know her anymore, that I didn't want to know her anymore. What could I have done to save her when she was so determined to go? I couldn't bring myself to say a word.

The girls from the corridor were standing in a corner, clumped together, crying, afraid to go near the coffin. I wanted to tell them that they shouldn't be frightened. Lucy was beautiful. Even Sofia had come, at the last minute. Someone had talked her into it. Only Ernessa had stayed at school. I know how much she detests funerals, that cloying smell.

When Sofia saw me near the door, she ran over and grabbed my arm.

"Are you going now?" she asked.

We walked back together. The funeral home is only about ten minutes from school. We used to pass it when we walked around town after having French fries and a Coke in the drugstore. We'd joke about Bob being in the back, dressing the corpses. Lucy was superstitious. She loved to look at the flowers in the window of the florist next door, but then she always insisted on crossing the street. She wouldn't walk in front of the funeral home. It gave her the creeps.

We walked most of the way in silence. I thought Sofia was too overwhelmed to speak, but she was only working up the courage to confront me.

"I think you should know what the others are saying about you," she said. "They think you caused her death."

"What do you mean?"

"You dragged her outside in the middle of the night."

"I went out to find her. I wanted to save her. You were the ones who kept insisting that there was nothing the matter with her. You told me not to interfere."

"They blame it on you."

"I don't care what they think. What about you? What do you think?"

"Honestly? I think you've been obsessed with Lucy and with Ernessa for a long time. You couldn't accept their friendship. I'm afraid you'll turn Lucy's death into something that it isn't."

"I've known all along what Ernessa was doing to Lucy. I don't need her death to show me the truth. It doesn't convince you of anything. You don't want to know."

Sofia made a feeble attempt to smile, but she couldn't hold on to the smile.

"I'm trying to help you," she said.

I gave her back the smile.

—
May 5

Dawn

I want to give Lucy back her death. I want to prevent Ernessa from turning her into a creature. Unhappy. Despairing. Without hope. Lucy is floating through eternity with a blank expression on her face. She doesn't understand what has happened to her. She will be a victim forever.

I wake up in the morning, go down to breakfast, go to classes, practice the piano, go to gym, do my homework, eat dinner, have a bath, sleep. How can I change it all back? If Ernessa controls the future, can't I control the past?

Quiet hour

This morning I practiced the piano before lunch. I can't play. I stumble over passages that I used to play without any trouble. My hands tremble when I hold them out in front of me. I have no control over them. They are leaves quaking in the wind. There is no wind.

The door to the basement was ajar. I pushed it open with the tips of my fingers and walked down the stairs. The strange smell coming from the basement has been gone for a while. Today it was only dry dust. There was a light on, a bare bulb hanging from the ceiling that lit up a circle of gray cement beneath it and left splotches of darkness in the corners. At the top of the walls are small, dirty windows that let in a weak light. I passed stacks of old furniture. Our trunks are arranged in rows along the back wall. They store them here during the year. Rows of black boxes. Her name was on the front, under the lock, in gold letters: E. A. Bloch. The trunk was covered with labels— Cunard Line, Holland-America Line, Compagnie Générale Transat-lantique. The red and blue labels were tattered and rubbed away; a skin of paper adhered to the black surface. The newest, brightest label, with the school's name, was the only one with a legible name and destination, except for one on the side. In faded, sloping hand-writing, I could make out most of the letters: Bloch, Brangwyn Hotel. There was dirt in front of her trunk.

When she returned, everything was familiar: the wide porches that encircled the hotel, the red tiled roofs, the downstairs sitting rooms, the dining room, the grand staircase, the ballroom. Had she stayed in the same room, overlooking the back courtyard? She had taken a picnic out to the Hut, near the woods, and sat on a blanket on the side of the hill. She had taken afternoon tea on the porches and gone for a pony ride on the Upper Field. Were the weeping cherries planted along the drive then? They would have been small, their branches hanging down like spindly arms. Her mother recovered, but she never did. Her mother found a new husband. She composed her face, but inside her thoughts bumped up against each other. She filled the long tub with warm water. It was less painful underwater. The dark curlicues of color floated around her. By the time all the water had turned red, she could no longer see.

Dinner bells. Something always interrupts me.

After dinner

The heavy brass lock hung open against the trunk. It was so easy to unfasten the two clasps on either side of the lock and push up the lid. I let out the smell of the woods the day after it has rained: damp, mushroomy, rotten. Crumbs of black earth still clung to everything. Stones, sticks, scraps of leaves, pieces of decaying wood, mounds of moss, lichens, husks, straw, grasses, flowers, winged maple seeds, birch catkins, horse chestnuts, tattered moths, dried spiders, gray wasps' nests, clumps of matted feathers, tufts of fur, yellowing bones, a snake's jaw, snail shells, animal droppings. The matter had been scooped up from the ground in armfuls and tossed into the trunk in a heap. In the middle was a hollow that marked her body, a body that was weightless and a burden at the same time. For a pillow, there was a thick notebook. I lifted it out of the trunk and carried it over to the window to read. It must have had hundreds of pages of stiff blue-lined paper. Every line was filled on both sides of the page. There was an entry for each day: a time, a place, a brief description of the weather, never more than two or three words, not even filling an entire line. The days ran into one another. Snow. Rain. Sunshine. Frigid. Westerly winds. Sleet. Hot. Cooling. Boring and meaningless. I looked and looked. Seventy years without a pause. There were no secrets to her existence.

Ernessa was passing through time, quickly, searching for others like her. She was here, now, where she had begun.

I turned to the most recent entries, near the end of the book. May 1, Brangwyn, warming. That was all there was to it. The weather is the only thing that affects her. She's sensitive to sun, rain, snow, wind. No mention of Lucy's stiff hair in the moonlight or the silver leaves on the weeping cherries. "I believe in eternity; I don't believe in spirits."

I tore the pages out of her journal and scattered them over the trunk. The white paper floated down like huge fluttering moths.

She had only a few pages left. She managed to cram so many years into one book.

I'm running out of room, too. The words are spilling off the page, into the top and side margins, between the straight lines. My handwriting is tiny, impossible to read.

■

May 6

Lunch hour

I cut Math today. I got to the practice room at exactly 10:45 and waited there until she came out. She came down the corridor at 10:53. That gives her seven minutes to walk down to the Schoolhouse and get to her class on time.

After dinner

As soon as class was over, I went up to my room. I cut softball practice, which starts at 3:15. I put on my raincoat, to hide my uniform, and walked up past the train station into town. I stopped at the first gas station I came to. It was next to the supermarket where Lucy and I always went to buy the frozen honey buns that we used to eat on weekends. I told the attendant that my mother had run out of gas a few blocks away. He sold me a gallon of gasoline and lent me a plastic container to carry it in and a funnel to pour it into the gas tank. I promised him that I would return everything. I gave him two quarters. Then, before I left the gas station, I carefully wiped the container with paper towels so that I wouldn't get the smell of gas on me. The container is behind the bushes along the far side of the Residence. No one ever goes there. It was easier than I thought it would be. I was afraid I wouldn't be able to ask the attendant for the gas, but I had no trouble.

Midnight

The days are false. The nights are true.

During the day, I drive them away, but at night they return. They slip under my doorway and into my dreams. I see Lucy again, and I sigh with relief to discover it is all a dream. Nothing really happened. Then we reach out to embrace one another, only to discover that each of us is clutching at nothing. Lucy wants me to save her. I can tell from the way she stretches out her arms and refuses to give up. She sucks in the air noisily, as if she's not used to breathing the strange atmosphere where she is now. Ernessa always appears, her eyes dark, with thick circles around them. She stands off to the side, observing, amused. Each night Lucy grows dimmer. Soon even in my dreams, I won't be able to convince myself that nothing has really happened.

May 7

Friday, the end of the week

Miss Norris wasn't the least bit surprised to find me standing at her door with my notebook and pen under my arm. I have been carrying them around in my book bag all day. She's been here all morning long. She's probably the only one who didn't leave when the alarms went off. She ignored them and the trucks.

"I didn't see you outside with everyone else," I said.

"I knew I would be safe up here," she said. "I didn't want to abandon my birds. If I needed to, I could always open the window and let them fly away."

I am sitting at the table where we translate Greek together. There are no books or notebooks or pencils. There is only a cup of tea on the table, with a silver spoon lying on the saucer. She has left me alone. She is in the other room reading. Even the birds are quiet. I told her I needed to write in my journal for a while today.

After they put out the fire, we weren't allowed back into the Residence. All the girls, standing outside in solemn groups of blue and gray, were herded back into the Schoolhouse. I slipped into the Science Building and walked through it to the Passageway and from there past the Playroom and up into the Residence. It was absolutely silent. I looked for Miss Olivo, her head shaking on her skinny neck, humming tonelessly to herself, but her chair was empty.

She should have been in her trunk in the basement this morning, the way she is every morning until 10:53. I should have opened the lid to make sure she was lying in there, neither dead nor alive, vulnerable and weak, and I should have thrust something into her heart or severed her head, the way they do in books. I didn't want to look at her.

The force of the explosion took me by surprise when the match touched the gasoline. The flames encircled Ernessa's trunk with a flash. The heat was sudden and everywhere, and the flames sucked the air out of my lungs. I wanted to see the fire consume it, but I panicked. I didn't want to go with her.

Outside I joined the other girls on the driveway, and they backed away from me. I smelled bad. The fumes clung to my clothes. I tried just now in Miss Norris's bathroom to wash the smell off my hands, but I couldn't. I washed and washed, but the smell has seeped into my skin. They could see from my smudged face and my singed hair that I was the one who had started the fire. My eyes were stinging and full of tears. My throat was burning. I couldn't have spoken a word if someone had spoken to me. They let me pass. Only Sofia looked directly at me. I stood off to the side, my arms folded and watched them watching me. Who can judge me?

The fire engines arrived. There were four of them. Everyone turned to look at the men in their black suits and helmets. They unwound the thick hoses, smashed the basement windows with their axes, sprayed the flames that leaped out the windows. There was a huge gasp from the girls as the water came out with a whoosh. The firemen put out the fire quickly. It didn't spread past the basement. I didn't care about burning down the Residence. Let it stay there forever. I destroyed the basement and the practice rooms on the ground floor. I accomplished what I wanted. I was sorry about my piano, though.

There was only smoke after the fire was put out, grainy, dense, black smoke wafting out of the broken windows. She was mingled with it, her not-quite-real self dissolved into the forever insubstantial, struggling to retrieve her solid state.

I wanted to save Lucy's soul. But I also wanted to punish Ernessa. To drive her into a horrible nonexistence, like an amphibian caught between land and water.

I walked a ways down the drive to get away from those girls. Behind the windows of the Passageway, a shadow passed along the corridor. I glimpsed it in each pane of glass, like a movie in slow motion, and as it moved, the shape clarified itself. When it had become a body, she stopped by the last window and pressed her face to the glass. No one else saw her looking out at us.

She came out the door of the Science Building, walking in that strange way of hers that doesn't seem to disturb the ground. She stood back from the other girls, as she always does, farther down the driveway. It was just before noon. The sun was bright and high in the sky. May 7, Brangwyn, bright sun. Another eventless day in eternity. Behind each girl, like a dark fingerprint on the asphalt, was a little shadow. Their souls. Something that can be fixed with a hammer and nail and snatched away if you're not careful. Only Ernessa did not have a shadow. She stood in a circle of yellow light, as if the sun were a lightbulb dangling directly above her and she could reach up and click it off at any time.

If I hadn't fought back, maybe Ernessa wouldn't have had to kill Lucy. There was enough blood in Lucy's body to nourish both of them. To keep them both here. Lucy could have lingered in that weakened state, waxing and waning like the moon. She could have remained pure.

No, Ernessa needed that orgasm with eyes wide open.

Every day she would have looked at Lucy and thought: Do it. Don't do it. Do it. The way I take that thin piece of steel out of my desk, hold it in the palm of my hand, and study it as if I'm seeing and feeling it for the first time. Don't do it. Do it. This morning I put it between the pages of my journal.

I looked out the window of Miss Norris's apartment, and I could see, four floors below me, that the pavement was still wet and dark pools of water had collected in the depressions. The firemen had roped off an area littered with broken glass and charred pieces of wood. Ernessa walked down the main steps from the Residence to the drive, climbed into the green car waiting for her, and drove off. She wasn't carrying anything. No one stopped her from leaving. They are only thinking about me.

I have less to write about than I thought I would. That's just as well. There are no pages left. I'm writing these words on the back end paper, a blank white page, without lines to keep my sentences in order. I can hear the sound of footsteps outside Miss Norris's door. I know that sound so well—the hollow tapping of a grownup's heels as she walks down the empty corridor. That's all I've heard for the last three years. Mrs. Halton is in the middle of a knot of gray-haired ladies. There are voices too. Miss Norris just came out of the other room.

They are at the door. I have to put my pen and my journal away.

AFTERWORD

I'm not sure what Dr. Wolff expects from this afterword, and I'm not even sure it was a good idea. It's a bit like offering a reformed alcoholic a drink to test her willpower. Anyway, I can only talk about myself now. I couldn't begin to sort out what I wrote thirty years ago. The whole experience of rereading this journal, which I did in one sitting, has been like gazing at a star so distant that by the time its light reaches us, it has long since ceased to exist.

I got married. I didn't get divorced, as most of the people I know did. I watched my two daughters grow up like specimens in a lab. I kept hoping that by watching them, I would be able to understand something about my own childhood. But we seem to belong to different species. Sometimes I've caught them preening in front of the mirror or agonizing over a piece of clothing, and I've thought, ah, finally the narcissism is beginning to surface. I was always wrong. It was just a momentary slip on their part. At Brangwyn, it was different. Nothing existed outside ourselves and school. For us the world of politics, social revolution, the war in Vietnam never happened. Even when it came to ideas and books, we were only interested in what reflected us. It would be easy to put all the blame on the hermetic atmosphere of school or on the fact that most of us had unhappy childhoods, but that can't explain everything.

I look at my daughters and marvel at their self-assurance, their sensibleness, their serenity. And yet, they've missed out on something in all their happiness. They don't know they've missed it, but they have. They've always been at home in the world. They don't know the pain and surprise of coming into it.

I still receive the school bulletin, even though I left in disgrace at the end of my junior year. I'm still invited to class reunions every five years. I'd be much too embarrassed to go. Charley (I should call her Charlotte, but I can't bring myself to, since Charlotte is a woman who attends AA meetings and lost ten pounds to get ready for the reunion) tried to talk me into the last reunion. She's become the class secretary even though she was kicked out. I thought about it. I was curious to see the school and all the girls. Actually, I was more curious what it would feel like to see them. My class was the last class of boarders that graduated. I know that most of the Residence has been converted into classrooms. It must have become a pretty boring place with only day students.

I knew all along I would never go, even though I let Charley try to talk me into it. She tried to convince me that no one cared about what happened when we were sixteen. We were all neurotic. I just went a little farther than anyone else. Besides, she said, when I spent my senior year in a mental hospital, everyone turned me into a tragic figure and wanted to be like me. They forgot they had looked away whenever I sat down at the table with them. They forgot they blamed me for everything that happened.

In the end, I was glad that I didn't go. Charley reported it all back to me, even though I never asked.

At the reunion, the boarders stayed together in a motel near school and stayed up all night talking. I wouldn't have had a thing to say to them, but Charley said they asked about me. One thing made an impression on me, though. A group of them went up to the fourth floor of the Residence to look at their old rooms, which aren't used anymore. The bathrooms were still intact, including the claw-foot bathtubs with separate taps for hot and cold. "It's so primitive," said Charley. "They'd be sued for that today. We always scalded ourselves."

But I wasn't listening to Charley anymore. I was thinking about stretching out in one of those big tubs in the deep, scalding water with the steam rising to the ceiling. I was thinking about hair streaming out in the water like golden seaweed. The drowning Ophelia, with hard pink breasts. She closed her eyes and let her head slip underwater. The bubbles of her breath rose to the surface and remained for an instant before bursting. I wasn't at all embarrassed. We were both so happy.

When I received the next copy of *The Brangwyn Echoes,* I flipped to the back of the magazine where they always have the photographs of the class reunions. The photograph was exactly what I expected: They were born with strands of pearls around their necks and cheerful smiles in place to meet the relentless passage of time. I didn't really expect to recognize any of the faces.

In a way, I'm glad she died and I didn't have to see her face next to theirs.

When I look closely in the mirror, my face is unfamiliar. I'm not used to the lines around my eyes and my mouth, as if I'd brushed the threads of a spider's web that will trap me in the end. But that's what recovery was all about, about agreeing to grow older, become a woman, have children, dye my hair, have hot flashes and night sweats. Let my childhood go. Let my father go. Not blame him for his despair.

Even if I wanted to, I couldn't go back to that year. This journal can't resurrect it. There's a mist hanging over it. I can blow the mist away with the softest sigh, but then it drifts back a moment later to shroud everything.

It was hard to give up the person who wrote so compulsively in her crimson notebook, to watch her be sucked into the black hole of the past. That girl was self-absorbed, but she was also excruciatingly alive, as if she had been born without a skin. Everyone secretly wanted her pain. It consumed her, until there was nothing else. I had affection for her, and I have much less for the person who has replaced her. She had a father, and I don't have one.

But I had to do it in order to exist. Just as my mother had to marry another man. I never held it against her.

And then one day, I was older than my father was when he died. I never thought that could happen. I suddenly felt so old. I knew he wasn't waiting for me. He was gone forever.

Did he go where those girls went, into that endless succession of days?

Sometimes the image of the two of them rises before me, unbidden, like a dream. They float somewhere, neither happy nor dead, young, untethered, free. Their arms are spread wide, their hair and clothing billow behind them. They are in a place without gravity, without sensations. Nothing tugs at them.

It's true that I never wanted to grow up. But how important was it really—to have decided to be human?